Kushner, Inc.

Also by Vicky Ward

The Liar's Ball: The Extraordinary Saga of How One Building Broke the World's Toughest Tycoons

The Devil's Casino: Friendship, Betrayal, and the High Stakes Games Played Inside Lehman Brothers

Kushner, Inc.

**GREED.
AMBITION.
CORRUPTION.**

The Extraordinary Story of
Jared Kushner and Ivanka Trump

Vicky Ward

ST. MARTIN'S PRESS ⚘ NEW YORK

www.stmartins.com

Designed by Steven Seighman

The Library of Congress Cataloging-in-Publication Data is available on request.

ISBN 978-1-250-18594-5 (hardcover)
ISBN 978-1-250-18595-2 (ebook)

Our books may be purchased in bulk for promotional, educational, or business use. Please contact your local bookseller or the Macmillan Corporate and Premium Sales Department at 1-800-221-7945, extension 5442, or by email at MacmillanSpecialMarkets@macmillan.com.

First Edition: March 2019

10 9 8 7 6 5 4 3 2 1

For my newly adopted country, the United States of America

Contents

Kushner, Inc.

America's Prince and Princess

January 20, 2017

On almost any other Friday night, Ivanka Trump and Jared Kushner would have been at home with their three children, celebrating Shabbat. But this Friday night was different: the couple had received a rabbinical dispensation to attend the inaugural balls in Washington, D.C.

This night was also different for them because Donald Trump—Ivanka's father and Jared's father-in-law—was celebrating being sworn in as President of the United States. And the whole world knew that his daughter and son-in-law were his most trusted advisers, ambassadors, and coconspirators. They were an attractive couple—extremely wealthy and, now, extraordinarily powerful.

Ivanka looked like Cinderella, her blond hair in a loose updo that drew attention to her diamond drop earrings and the low neckline of a crystal-encrusted champagne evening gown by designer Carolina Herrera. After only a few minutes of watching Donald Trump and his wife, Melania, shuffle awkwardly about the podium at the Walter E. Washington Convention Center for their first dance as president and First Lady, Ivanka and her husband swept onto the stage, deftly deflecting attention from Donald Trump's clumsy moves, as she had so often done over the past twenty years. The crowd roared in approval, and the couple waved to their rapturous admirers. They were now America's prince and princess.

———————

A mile or so away, Jared's father, Charlie Kushner, and his mother, Seryl Kushner, were celebrating Shabbat with the rest of the Kushner family in D.C.'s Trump International Hotel. As the sun set, the family and some of their friends—forty or so people—had gathered in a meeting room on the hotel's lower level to pray. At the dinner that followed, Charlie turned nasty toward Jared's brother, Josh Kushner, a tall, dark-haired thirty-three-year-old.

"Josh, we expect you to do the right thing," Charlie told his youngest son, according to one source. "The person you are with is not the right person."

Josh absorbed his father's abuse in silence. Everyone there knew that Charlie was talking about Josh's long relationship with Victoria's Secret model Karlie Kloss. According to multiple sources, Charlie and Seryl believed Kloss was an unsuitable match for their son, and not only because she wasn't Jewish. (Jared had supported his parents on this point.) If any of Charlie's friends dared suggest that this seemed harsh, and even hypocritical, given how the couple had eventually welcomed Ivanka, a convert, into their family, Charlie and Seryl strongly disagreed. Ivanka, they explained, was different. She was a Trump. She was also, like Jared, real estate royalty. And she'd attended an Ivy League school, the University of Pennsylvania. Kloss grew up in Webster Groves, Missouri, a suburb of St. Louis, and hadn't even been to college when she and Josh began dating.

That evening, Charlie kept needling Josh about his girlfriend, even after family friends joined the group. Josh's close friend, oil heir Michael "Mikey" Hess, stood up and performed the opening number from *Hamilton*, a rap song: *"How does a bastard, orphan son of a whore and a Scotsman dropped in the middle of a forgotten spot in the Caribbean by Providence impoverished in squalor grow up to be a hero and a scholar?"* Rupert Murdoch's ex-wife, Wendi Deng Murdoch, dressed in a yellow and white floral dress, read a passage from a Jewish prayer book.

After dinner, many of the attendees went upstairs to join investment banker Aryeh Bourkoff at his table in the main atrium, where other prominent guests, such as Greg Maffei, president and CEO of Liberty Media, and Beau Ferrari, then an executive vice president at Univision, also stopped by.

As the clock ticked toward midnight, hotel guests returned from the many inaugural balls and waited for champagne corks to pop and balloons to drop from the ceiling in the hotel's atrium. Among them were Baltimore real estate heir Reed Cordish and his wife, Maggie, both friends of Jared and Ivanka, and both hired to work in Trump's administration. And in came Trump's pick for treasury secretary, Steven Mnuchin, and his fiancée, Louise Linton, along with Mnuchin's brother, Alan, and his wife, Alessandra.

Everyone seemed elated, especially Charlie. The Kushners, it seemed, would finally get the recognition Charlie felt they had long deserved. Maybe, thanks to the ascension of Jared and Ivanka into the White House, Charlie would even get a presidential pardon and exorcise the demons from his past. It was truly an auspicious night for the Kushners. "The family was kissing," recalled one person who was there that night. "Everyone was happy." Anything seemed possible for the Kushners on this evening, perhaps even forgiveness for the family's many sins.

CHAPTER ONE

Rules Are Dangerous

"A lot of these children who are brought up with a survivor mode, where the parents had survived, they don't trust a lot of people."

—ALAN HAMMER, FAMILY FRIEND AND FORMER COLLEAGUE
OF CHARLIE KUSHNER

In 1949, Jared Kushner's grandparents, Joseph and Rae Kushner, arrived by ship in New York City, along with their infant daughter, Linda. After fleeing Poland and spending three years in a refugee camp in Italy, the Kushners were finally about to begin their new lives in America. Yet the scars the couple bore from World War II were visible in every aspect of their lives—and would also be seen in the lives of their children and grandchildren. "Everything we did was against the relief of the Holocaust," one family member explained. "Surviving, growing, getting rich, power, politics . . . this was all to spite the Nazis, to spite what they did to us."

What the Nazis did to Rae and Joseph Kushner is a familiar but harrowing story, one Rae, a striking, dark-haired woman with brown eyes, recounted matter-of-factly in 1982 in a long interview with sociologist Sidney Langer at the Holocaust Resource Center at Kean University. Rae, who died in 2004, was born in 1923 in the small Polish town of Novogrudok. Her father was a successful furrier, but in the 1930s, her relatively comfortable existence was shattered by the escalation of anti-Semitism in Poland. About half of her town was Jewish, and with the ascent of the Nazis in

Germany, some of them, including her family, wanted to escape to British-controlled Palestine. But because of byzantine laws, it was difficult for them to leave Europe, and by the time German and Soviet troops invaded Poland in 1939, at the start of World War II, the Kushners were trapped. "The doors of the world were closed to us," Rae said.

In 1941, after the German army pushed Soviet troops out of Poland, the Nazis forced Rae and her family into a walled-off ghetto, where roughly thirty thousand Jews were required to wear a yellow Star of David. She soon realized the Nazis were systematically destroying the Jews. "The doctors, lawyers, and teachers were murdered in the beginning. The Germans were afraid that the intellectuals would organize a rebellion." The next victims were the elderly and sick and even the children, as the Nazis only wanted Jews who could work. In 1943, Rae's mother and one of her sisters were shot dead. "We couldn't hide anyone. There was no time," Rae said. "The Germans threw the bodies into a grave that was a half mile from the ghetto. We saw it with our own eyes."

Rae, along with her father, brother, and another sister, teamed up with other Jews and began to dig a tunnel out of the ghetto, hoping to reach a nearby forest. The chances of escape were minuscule, but they reasoned it was far better to die together, trying. "We had heard there were Jews in the woods who were not starving," Rae recalled. "We could not imagine how you could live through the winter in the woods with the snow and the cold and the wet weather, but we decided that anything was better than staying here and waiting for a bullet."

But they did make it. Most of them. As they emerged from the tunnel, Rae's brother was separated from the family. His glasses had broken and he apparently got lost in the chaos as they all fled into the woods. Rae never saw him again, but she, her sister, and her father found the group of Jews they'd heard about, maybe a thousand of them, hiding in makeshift bunkers dug into the ground. Among them was Joseph Berkowitz, a young man near Rae's age whom she had known before the war, when he lived in a small village near hers. The two became a couple.

After hiding for nine months, the forest dwellers were all able to go home when the Soviet military reoccupied Poland. They returned to a ghost town. "You cannot imagine what it felt like to go over to the grave where my mother was buried, to the other graves where four thousand innocent men and children were buried," Rae said. "I fainted twice."

In May 1945, Germany surrendered to the Soviets and the Allied forces, but the Kushners' struggles were far from over. Unable to buy or sell goods under Soviet law, they pretended to be Greek and migrated on foot, aiming for a displaced persons camp in Italy where they'd heard Jews could apply for visas. They walked all night and slept all day as they trekked through Czechoslovakia, Austria, and then to Budapest, where Rae and Joe got married. (Joe took Rae's last name, because he came from a poor family, and her name was more respected.) The couple spent three years in the Italian camp, where Rae gave birth to Linda, before they finally got visas to the U.S.

Joe and Rae rented a room in Brooklyn, New York, where they had three more children, Murray, Esther, and Charles. Joe honed his carpentry skills and began, with an assortment of Jewish partners, to construct apartment buildings in New Jersey. The young family moved to Elizabeth, New Jersey. Joe grew so prolific that the Kushners became one of a handful of immigrant Jewish families referred to as the "Holocaust builders" of the New Jersey suburbs. These survivors transformed agricultural land into thriving suburban communities and were also known for their generous donations to Jewish causes.

Yet even as the Kushners grew prosperous—in the 1970s, they hired a housemaid—their home was not filled with much laughter. "Our children lived a little bit of our lives," Rae said. "I don't know if it is so healthy for them, because our kids are more serious than American children. It is unbelievable we had the strength to survive such a fire. Nobody believed that we would ever get married, have children, and grandchildren. When a European has a simcha [a wedding], we all rejoice. We live our lost youth through our children. We had no youth, our early years were spent hiding. Our middle years were spent rebuilding."

———

Joe was a strict, sometimes brutal father. One oft-told story is that he took the son of a pipe layer who'd come asking about payment for his father out to a construction site in the middle of a rainstorm. While standing in the downpour, the young man made some comment about this being the most miserable experience of his life, which set Joe off. "Let me tell you what a miserable night really is," he said, and launched into harrowing stories of his wartime nightmare. Joe could be even harder on his children. When young Charlie bought a guitar, Joe reportedly smashed it, saying there was no time for such a trivial activity as playing music.

His professional reputation was mixed. A 1980 series in *The Times* of Trenton noted that some of the Kushner-owned construction projects "brought criticism and lawsuits over allegedly faulty construction or inadequate upkeep of apartments." Some of the buildings in one development were lopsided. In another, the grading was off, so backyards flooded when it rained.

Joe was a traditional but not fully observant Jew, and his children—Linda, Murray, Esther, and Charlie—were allowed to watch TV after Shabbat dinner. But if their friends showed up dressed in jeans, he would react harshly. "He'd just kick you the fuck out of his house," recalled someone who knew Joe well. Family was Joe's priority. His most rewarding achievement, he said, was building each of his adult children's houses. They were mansions in their day, designed by a well-known New Jersey architect, and were close to each other—and close to him. The girls were minutes apart in West Orange, while the boys were in Livingston. As they grew wealthier and their family expanded, Joe and Rae loved taking the family away for Passovers and commandeering the largest table in the hotel restaurant.

The flip side of that tight familial bond was a deep mistrust of outsiders, not only non-Jews, but also assimilated or secular Jews. Joe and Rae's wartime experience created a sense of exceptionalism that was both good and bad, according to one Kushner, who talked to me on the strict promise of anonymity for fear of reprisal from a family known to be as punitive as it is private. The family mantra is "Think like an immigrant, act like an immigrant," this person said. "But what does that mean?"

"The Kushners' experience was unusual in the sense that . . . they were fighters," explained Jewish scholar and historian Michael Berenbaum, who knew Rae. Their "experience was not a passive victimization, but an active attack on the enemy, and thwarting the enemy. . . . You didn't survive being a [fighter] without being tough as nails." A person in that situation grew up being taught that rules are for other people. "You don't wait for the Nazis to come liquidate you. You build a fucking tunnel and get out of the ghetto. . . . You don't wait for the bastards at Harvard to let you in. You make it yourself into Harvard," the family member said. According to Berenbaum, the Kushners would have not been alone among Holocaust survivors in feeling this way. For those people, he explained, "rules are dangerous."

The Kushners displayed the same mind-set at home. Joe encouraged a rivalry between Charlie and his brother, Murray. He wanted them to excel, and being hard on them was the only way he knew to bring this about. For a long while, it seemed that Murray, the eldest and most intellectual of the children, according to family lore, was ahead in that race. Murray got into the University of Pennsylvania and then attended law school there, while Charlie went to NYU and then earned his law degree at Hofstra. (The girls' education was considered less critical by their parents; what mattered was that they married well.)

Despite the high regard Joe held for academic achievement, he was increasingly drawn to his outgoing, charismatic younger son, who so blatantly, feverishly wanted to outstrip his older brother and be his father's favorite, and, one day, assume his position as head of the family. A tragic event helped him achieve that goal, in a roundabout way. In 1980, Murray's wife, Ruth, died of breast cancer. The couple had two small children, and Susan Hammer, a housewife who carpooled with the Kushners to and from their children's school in Livingston, tearfully described to her husband, Alan, the sadness of the family's situation. "Charlie had really no appreciation for what Murray was going through in his life," Alan Hammer said.

Murray then met Lee Serwitz, who was also recently widowed, and they married in the early 1980s. She already had a son and a daughter who had been born two weeks after her father died. But unlike Murray's first wife, Lee was not particularly religious. She was a secular Jew from a working-class family, and the Kushners looked down on her even as they taught her how to observe Shabbat. That disdain would contribute to Charlie's rise in the family hierarchy.

In his romantic life, Charlie went in the opposite direction. Seryl Stadtmauer was a beautiful brunette from an Orthodox family in the Far Rockaway neighborhood of Queens, New York. She and Charlie had met in their teens. When they married, Charlie became more observant to appease both his wife and his skeptical father-in-law. "It'll be a lot easier for me to change than to ask you to change," he told Seryl, so he stopped watching TV on Shabbat and practiced a moderate form of Orthodoxy. (Charlie's family still keeps a kosher home, and when they go out to dinner, they might order fish, but never shellfish.)

Seryl remained the more religious of the two, and it became evident she found her sister-in-law's relaxed attitude toward her faith vexing. Lee had no idea how to keep a kosher household, for example, so Seryl, who lived closer to her than any of the others in the family, would pop over to educate her. Despite this, or maybe because of it, the two women never got on. "Seryl was just really fucking mean," one person who is close to Lee said. At first, Lee tried to brush her ignorance off as a joke. She would tell her friends that when Seryl said to her, *"Shavua tov"*—Hebrew for "have a good week"—Lee responded, as if Seryl had sneezed, "Bless you." But the underlying friction was anything but funny. In fact, it would be the wedge that would help split the brothers.

Joe had made his antipathy to Murray's remarriage very plain by standing with his arms folded throughout the wedding ceremony. He stopped working with Murray shortly before sending him to West Orange with a business associate, Eugene Schenkman, to build suburban apartments.

With Murray pushed aside, Charlie created an infrastructure for his father's budding development business, which until that point had been a one-man shop. Joe had had many partners, and his efforts to drum up business had been done from pay phones and out of the back of his Cadillac. Charlie had been introduced to a successful local processed-food importer named George Gellert, who wanted to invest in real estate. Gellert said he would take a piece of nearly all of Charlie's real estate projects.

In 1985, Charlie found office space, put a name on the door, Kushner

Companies, and created a management firm for the disparate structures built and owned by his father. As Charlie acquired more and more office space—and took on more and more debt—he moved from a little basement office into two floors in Florham Park, New Jersey, described by someone who visited as "the Shangri-La of power offices." The windows were huge and the surfaces on the executive floor were either gleaming wood or marble. Senior executives had their names stenciled on parking spots outside. Joe never got to see the new headquarters; he died at sixty-two, just months after he and Charlie started the company.

Charlie was now the head of the family. Throughout the 1980s, his household was the hub of all weekend activity for the local New Jersey Jewish community, partly because there were now so many Kushners. Each of Joe and Rae's children had had four children, except for Esther, who had three, so there was always something to celebrate: a birthday, a bar mitzvah, a graduation, an engagement, a wedding, a newborn . . . "When I first met Charlie . . . every weekend, it was somebody's wedding or bar mitzvah or something," said their friend Alan Hammer. "We were out all the time." After Charlie bought the Puck Building, a landmark in Manhattan's SoHo neighborhood, in 1980, he turned the ground floor into an event space, the preferred venue for his friends' children's bar mitzvahs and other family parties. His voice was soft and nasal, and his charisma drew in all his siblings and nieces and nephews. "He was the cool one," one family member recalled. "He was very lovable and very charismatic. We all wanted to hang out at his house on weekends."

The town of Livingston had not yet become a Jewish enclave when Charlie and Seryl moved there in the early 1980s, in part because there was no interstate to the town until 1973. But as he got richer, Charlie almost single-handedly transformed the town. He turned an industrial building into the Joseph Kushner Hebrew Academy and Rae Kushner Yeshiva High School. He built the local mikvah—Jewish ritual baths—and named it after Seryl's grandmother Chana. (It is still run by one of his daughters.) "He created the Orthodox community in Livingston, in my opinion," said Hammer, who added that back then, "[Charlie] wasn't that flawed. He was doing everything right. He really was a model citizen."

In 1985, Charlie hired Seryl's brother, Richard Stadtmauer, who would become his right hand at Kushner Companies. Richard was even more religious than his sister. Every afternoon in the office, either Richard or Charlie would gather up a minyan, a quorum of ten men who would pray aloud.

Hiring relatives and friends—members of the Livingston shul (synagogue) and the Hebrew Academy—became a typical Charlie practice, one that occasionally backfired. He hired his brother-in-law William (Billy) Schulder—Esther's husband—only to discover him having sex on the conference room table with the office bookkeeper and chief financial officer, Marci Plotkin. (Plotkin said this was "an outright lie.") Charlie fired Schulder and Plotkin, a ferociously hard worker, but kept her close (and quiet) by getting her a job at Schonbraun, Safris, McCann, Bekritsky & Co., the accounting firm Kushner Companies used. Of course, the knowledge of what had happened gave him leverage over both of them. Viewed one way, hiring your friends and family is an act of generosity. But it also meant Charlie held "ownership" over all his extended relatives and neighbors, which meant he could treat them however he pleased. And he did.

In his business life, he relied heavily on a different sort of leverage—borrowed money—and he got lucky in that the market swung mostly upward then. By the 1990s, there was not much he could not afford. "Charlie probably acquired more apartment properties in New Jersey than anyone ever had and anybody ever will," said Hammer. "That's not to say he owned more apartments than anybody ever had or will, but he acquired more. . . . He has no risk aversion." Other developers get rich by sitting on properties; it's a safer way to make money, but it was not fast enough for Charlie.

Though Charlie lived for over twenty years in the house his father built for him, he liked to show his wealth. Unlike his siblings, who lived low-key lives, he had a chauffeur; all four of his children—Jared, Dara, Nicole, and Josh—had tutors; and the family had a beautiful beach house in Elberon, New Jersey, where they would host a huge annual summer party. Jared, Charlie's eldest son, was perceived as a likable, well-mannered kid, not outstandingly bright, but not stupid, and serious, unlike his brother Josh, who had a lightness about him. Perhaps because he was the youngest of the fifteen Kushner grandchildren, all the cousins doted on Josh. Nicole was the hardest worker, Dara the most religious. Yet Jared was unquestionably his father's favorite, and also the one who would be groomed to fulfill his father's dynastic ambitions. What those ambitions were, exactly, was not entirely clear to the extended Kushner clan. They just knew that Charlie was insatiable, and that money and its trappings were not enough. "I want to be the most powerful Jew in America," Charlie once told a business associate.

Given those aspirations, it seems inevitable that Charlie got involved in politics, since real estate is so dependent on federal and municipal tax breaks, but there was also his personal ambition to consider. "At the time, everyone thought he wanted to be a senator," said one of his relatives. But for a long time, according to Hammer, Charlie simply made political donations, mostly to Democrats: New Jersey senator Robert Torricelli, New York senator Chuck Schumer, and later, New York senator Hillary Clinton.

Charlie's most significant foray into politics came in the mid-nineties, after he met a candidate for New Jersey governor, Jim McGreevey, with whom he developed an intense friendship, spending days at a time with McGreevey at the Jersey Shore. The entrance of McGreevey into his life would bring out a side of Charlie that was much less appealing than the honey-voiced man who hosted his neighbors' bar mitzvahs in one of his fancy buildings and was the joyful center of every celebration. As ambition unhinged him, a darker side of Charlie emerged. Behind his back, people would start to call him Jekyll and Hyde.

CHAPTER TWO

The Tuesday Beatings

"It was almost like Grisham's book The Firm *when I first got there. It all seemed great, and within three months, I remember coming home and saying to my wife, 'I got into something that I can't deal with and I've got to get out.'"*

—FORMER KUSHNER COMPANIES EMPLOYEE

As Jared Kushner grew into his teens, attending the Frisch School, a co-ed, Modern Orthodox yeshiva in Paramus, New Jersey, where he was an average student—ranked in the third track of five in his grade—his father aggressively built an empire for his firstborn to inherit. It was a pedestrian colossus: tens of thousands of so-called "garden" apartments, multifamily buildings surrounded by landscaping, mostly in New Jersey, but the income from them was enough to turn Charlie Kushner into someone whose money and approval were sought by local politicians. He was now a New Jersey power broker.

The logic behind Charlie's largesse was fairly simple, according to a Kushner family member. "[Charlie] had a messianic complex. It was his father who delivered us from Poland, and [Charlie] was going to deliver us to Manhattan. He's going to get us out of New Jersey and onto the *Forbes* 500 list. But to do that . . . you've gotta buy [Governor] Jim McGreevey." (In November 2001, McGreevey had won the gubernatorial election, with a friendly push from Charlie and his pals.)

Charlie was now an autocrat whose reign sometimes felt like a noose to the relatives, friends, employees, and even fellow synagogue members who came to be in his debt. His role as family patriarch meant his relatives were not to question his aggressive methods of social advancement. He was nicknamed "the Dapper Don" or "Don Corleone," partly because of his natty suits and perfectly coiffed hair, but the nickname was also appropriate, some felt, given Charlie's *Godfather*-like approach to running both his business and his personal life. Business was life. Life was business. Take Marci Plotkin, for example, the accountant Charlie had fired for having an affair with his brother-in-law. Even though she was now at the accounting firm of SSMB, Kushner Companies still paid her annual bonuses of between fifteen and twenty-five thousand dollars, and reimbursed Plotkin for the cost of her son's private school tuition, which was disguised to the IRS as a legal expense. Charlie wasn't just being nice; he needed her cooperation. Beginning in the mid 1990s, at Charlie's direction, according to legal records, the company began to commit financial fraud to fund his growing social, political, and financial ambitions.

As is common in real estate firms, each of the entities Charlie owned was its own LLC. And each LLC was owned by a partnership, a combination of Charlie and backers. All of the LLCs passed down by Joe Kushner were, per the instructions of his will, equally divided among Charlie and his three siblings, and their respective children's trusts. But Charlie set up a management company, Westminster Management, and made himself the manager of all the buildings. Initially, his siblings thought this was a good thing.

Charlie viewed his increasingly public profile as "public service." But his lust for the limelight brought some large bills. He invited politicians to speak (often for a large fee) in an assortment of venues, ranging from his office to his home, off-site conferences, and his synagogue. (He even invited the entire New Jersey political leadership to attend a Kushner baby's bris.) A speech by Israeli Prime Minister Benjamin Netanyahu, for example, cost as much as one hundred thousand dollars, and Charlie paid him to speak in New Jersey four times.

Rather than pay out of his own pocket for his many political and charitable contributions, Charlie—or senior executives in the firm, at Charlie's direction—took LLC money, without preapproval from the partners in the LLC, to cover these costs. None of the Kushner Companies partners were informed of how their money was being spent. Not Charlie's business partners, his friends, or even his siblings, children, nieces, and nephews. Nor did they know that neither the internal nor external ledgers presented the true numbers for each of the LLCs. If Charlie was short of cash on one project, he borrowed from the bank account of another. That wasn't the only fudging that went on. According to court documents, there was euphemistic language used at the weekly Tuesday meetings, also called "cash meetings," held at Charlie's home early in the morning. The phrase "losing a bill"—as in, "How do we lose this bill?"—meant finding a way to turn an expense from one project into a capital deduction from elsewhere.

Personal expenses were also "lost" and submitted as capital business expenses from whichever LLC Richard Stadtmauer and an executive vice president, Scott Zecher, picked. Those ranged from Charlie's home improvements to vacations, New Jersey Nets tickets, Super Bowl packages, even the alcohol Charlie and Seryl Kushner bought for holiday celebrations. A contribution from Charlie to Harvard University to smooth the way for Jared's admission was funded by the company, not Charlie. The check was signed by Zecher. And that was no accident. Charlie never signed anything. His corner office in Florham Park was enormous but spartan. It was forty feet long and had a private shower and sitting area. He also had a vast outdoor terrace on which he built a sukkah (a temporary outdoor hut) under the roof of which he and his family would celebrate the Jewish holiday of Sukkot. His desk, however, had nothing on it. No pens. No paper. No computer.

Most critical of all to the apparent health of the company's balance sheet was what was called a "Richard special," named after Richard Stadtmauer, Charlie's brother-in-law and vice chairman of Kushner Companies, which was essentially bank fraud. If Charlie wanted to make an acquisition or do a refinancing that required a line of credit, Stadtmauer, a chartered accountant (and Mensa member), would direct a subordinate to alter the figures so that the banks would be tricked into believing Kushner Companies' finances met the preconditions of their covenants. As a result, the firm would receive lines of credit and tax deductions it should not have been entitled to. (Plotkin's role as the external accountant was to accept, unquestioningly, the income statements from each property and prepare the tax returns, which she sent to Stadtmauer to sign.)

Most of the senior members of Kushner Companies knew what was going on. According to court records from the mid-1990s, some of Charlie's property managers started to use letter codes to flag misapplied expenses in order to have some idea of how the buildings they managed were really performing, because otherwise it was hard to know. The managers typically had to deliver property performance reports on Thursdays. Stadtmauer was quite unhappy when he discovered this coding subterfuge, according to court records, and ordered the managers to stop doing it.

Stadtmauer and Charlie's mantra was that there must be no paper trails, no record of what they were doing. Stadtmauer frequently reminded Zecher to be careful what he put in emails. One time, according to court records, an interim CFO, Alan Lefkowitz, sent an email asking if he should pay for the construction of a local mikvah with funds from one of the partnerships. Charlie went berserk. He printed out the email and handwrote on it, "This guy is a definite moron. We must deal with the situation." (Lefkowitz would soon be barred from the Tuesday meetings; he later resigned because he wasn't willing to go along with the firm's creative accounting.)

Lefkowitz was not the only person to find the culture of the firm unpleasant, according to another former employee. "Charlie ran the place like a dictator," this person said. He also noted that the brutal office conditions were at odds with the image of a pious, Orthodox Jewish firm presented to outsiders. (One person remembered the scurrying that was done, to appear to be a religious firm should a rabbi or someone Orthodox stop by, was almost comical. "All of a sudden, the religious books would come onto the table, [Charlie] would put on a yarmulke, and they would wait there and make it look as if they are religious Jews.")

Despite his professed liberal political views, Charlie was apparently not a big believer in diversity. Everyone at the firm was Jewish, except for some of the administrative staff, several of whom were attractive white women, hired, so it was thought by at least one senior executive, for their looks. According to another former senior executive, in 2000 there was only one black person, a woman, who worked as a secretary at the firm.

Charlie became an increasingly brutal CEO. The Tuesday meetings became known as the "Tuesday beatings." No one was supposed to go to the restroom during one, even though the meetings could run as long as three hours. And anything could set Charlie off. One time he was livid that someone was using a Montblanc pen—made in Germany—and accused that individual of bringing "Nazi paraphernalia into his home." Yet when his children interrupted the meeting to rush in to kiss or hug him, he was momentarily transformed into a doting parent. "It was almost like . . . *The Godfather*," one source said.

Stadtmauer got beat up by Charlie more than anyone else. In one of those Tuesday meetings, Charlie accused Stadtmauer of being anti-Semitic because he drove a Lincoln Continental. (Henry Ford, whose Ford Motor Company introduced the car in 1939, was a notorious anti-Semite.) "Charlie owned Richard," said someone who worked with both men. "Richard had his position, and his money, because of Charlie. Charlie could beat the shit out of him, and it wouldn't matter." (Charlie had made Stadtmauer very rich—he was worth many tens of millions of dollars by 2000.)

Stadtmauer would take out his hurt on everyone else. Multiple sources said his temper was even worse than Charlie's. "Richard was an abused child who abused his children," said Alan Hammer, speaking metaphorically. Brian Bentzlin, a former Kushner Companies CFO, likened both men to tyrants. "You had to do pretty much as you were told," he said in court testimony. "[Stadtmauer] and [Charlie] often would throw tirades at any number of the meetings on a regular, routine basis."

It was in this environment that Jared Kushner learned about the company he would later run. Jared was the firm's most sheltered trainee. On his summer vacations, he'd go to work at Kushner Companies construction sites, maybe painting a few walls, more often sitting and listening to music—or that was how it was relayed to the other employees. No one dared tell him this probably would not give him a deep understanding of the construction process. But Charlie doggedly groomed his eldest son for greatness, seeing himself, according to multiple sources, as a Jewish version of

Joseph Kennedy, with Jared as his John F. Kennedy. He brought Jared with him to meetings with politicians and hosted Netanyahu overnight at the family home, where Jared got to talk to him. (The Israeli politician stayed in Jared's bedroom, while Jared slept in the basement.) Charlie was determined, just as his own father had been about him and Murray, that Jared would be a huge success. Around the time Jared was applying to colleges, Charlie pledged $2.5 million to Harvard and made additional promises to Princeton and Cornell. He also got New Jersey Senator Frank Lautenberg, who was an investor in at least one of his projects and to whom Kushner Companies had donated more than two hundred thousand dollars, to make a call to Senator Ted Kennedy, who, in turn, phoned Harvard's dean of admissions. When Jared was accepted at Harvard, his high school teachers were aghast, alternating, according to a student, between disbelief and disgust. A classmate of Jared's, who had been in the class's first track and who had been rejected by Harvard, cried when she heard he got in. It was unheard of for anyone in the third track at Frisch Academy to be admitted to any Ivy League school, let alone Harvard. "His GPA did not warrant it, his SAT scores did not warrant it," one school official told the author Daniel Golden.

While Charlie took great interest in Jared's unsentimental education, he was less concerned with his daughters' academic results. One family member says his aloof attitude toward Jared's sisters, Nicole and Dara, was "tragic," especially given how hard Nicole worked in high school and at university. "No one told her that it doesn't matter what she does," a source close to the family told me; she wasn't the Chosen One. In his early years, Josh got even less attention than Nicole, which was, some say, a blessing. "He escaped his father's focus," said a relative.

And that focus could be a yoke. When Jared went to Harvard, his parents found it unsettling to have him so far away. "They wanted to make sure he wasn't getting involved in drugs, they wanted to make sure that he wasn't going to start dating non-Jews," a family friend remembered. They occasionally asked Kevin Swill, then the president of Westminster Capital Associates, the financing arm of Kushner Companies, to visit Jared, to take him out to dinner and to report back. Charlie even bought apartment buildings near Harvard—ostensibly for Jared to run. A Kushner relative, Mel Scheinerman, actually ran them—which meant it was also his turn to play babysitter. Fortunately for Scheinerman, Jared soon decided to come home most weekends and his parents relaxed.

While Charlie was allegedly busy siphoning off his siblings' money, Murray Kushner grew increasingly suspicious that Charlie was defrauding him. It did not help that Lee's relationship with Seryl was deteriorating further. In 1999, Murray had pulled out of a deal to acquire Berkshire Realty, a real-estate-investment trust with nearly twenty-four thousand apartments, and Charlie was pissed. The tension came to a head in Florida in the spring of 2000. The families were gathered uncomfortably for Passover at the Fontainebleau hotel in Miami Beach. Charlie told Murray and Lee that he, Charlie, was the one who had gotten his nieces and nephews into the University of Pennsylvania; he was now the head of the family and Murray was a drag on the business and on him personally. He told Murray he did not think they should do business together, to which Murray responded, "If we can't be partners, we can't be brothers." That set Charlie off on a tirade about how ungrateful his siblings were.

Murray was so upset he refused to go to the next year's Passover celebration, and stopped visiting the office in Florham Park.

Billy and Esther Schulder did attend that family Passover in 2001, even though Charlie had fired Billy and reportedly castigated him and Esther, alluding to Billy's affair—something she would find hard to forgive. Again, Charlie raged that he was carrying so many undeserving relatives. When Esther told him to cool it, that her son Jacob was suffering from cancer, Charlie mocked her. "Cancer, schmancer," he said. And with that moment of cruelty, he sparked a hatred that would nearly burn his empire down.

In 2001, Murray sued Charlie, seeking a review of business records. Behind the scenes, he was helped by Esther, who was friendly with Bob Yontef, an accounting manager who had joined Kushner Companies in 1999, reporting to Zecher and CFO Brian Bentzlin. Yontef told Esther that he'd seen much in the office that troubled him. She introduced him to Murray, and Yontef agreed to provide evidence of the financial shenanigans and give it to Murray to use in his suit.

All Murray wanted, he told a confidant, was to get his money back—for himself and his siblings. As Theodore Moskowitz, an attorney who wound up representing Yontef when he sued Charlie for allegedly firing him because of his age and for providing Murray with evidence, put it: "Murray was not looking for vengeance." He reckoned he was owed about fifteen million dollars, but he would later be awarded much more than that in arbitration, according to sources. Murray did not want to go up against Charlie, he told an associate. The person he really blamed for the firm's financial fraud was Stadtmauer. "Murray hated Stadtmauer," said a confidant of Murray's. "He felt that Stadtmauer was bad for the family, bad for business."

This internecine war would have remained private were it not for unforeseen extraneous events that all happened around the same time. The first of these was Jim McGreevey's election to the governorship of New Jersey in November 2001. McGreevey, the former mayor of Woodbridge Township, was rumored to be corruptible and in Charlie's pocket, since Charlie had been his top campaign donor, contributing $1.5 million. The two men had traveled together in 2000 to Israel, where McGreevey met a young Israeli political aide named Golan Cipel. A short time later, Cipel and McGreevey became clandestine lovers. Charlie sponsored Cipel's visa to the U.S. and housed him in an apartment on New York City's Upper West Side. (The couple often visited the Jersey Shore and sometimes stayed at Charlie's beach house.) As soon as McGreevey was elected governor, he appointed Cipel as his homeland security adviser, and it wasn't long before chatter about their relationship began.

Charlie expected payback for his campaign donation, and McGreevey did not disappoint. In 2002, he offered Charlie the chairmanship of the Port Authority of New York & New Jersey, which would have put Charlie in charge of the board that oversees all the bridges and tunnels between the two states, as well as several seaports and airports. It would have given him control of billions of dollars of real estate.

Charlie was so impressed by his lofty perch in the world that Kushner Companies hired a young writer named Ken Kurson, known for coauthoring Rudy Giuliani's self-idolizing memoir, to chronicle the extraordinary life of Charles Kushner. Kurson wrote the book, but it remains unpublished, presumably because the ending was not exactly the one Charlie was hoping for.

Charlie Kushner never got to properly accept the Port Authority job. In February 2003, the U.S. attorney's office in Newark opened an investigation into claims Charlie had illegally used company money to make political donations. The state senate also wanted Charlie to answer questions about his campaign contributions. Word of his dispute with Murray was also getting out. In late 2002 and early 2003, Yontef, who had been fired in November 2002, raised allegations regarding Charlie's questionable political contributions. Whereas Murray's lawsuit against Charlie had been under seal, Yontef's allegations were public, because they were attached to an age discrimination suit. Charlie was livid over the publicity that ensued, and blamed Esther and Murray as Yontef's puppeteers. "Murray directed the conspiracy to fulfill his depraved need to destroy his younger brother's public image," Charlie's attorneys alleged in legal papers. Charlie believed his siblings had broken the unbreakable Kushner code: family first, and last. They had just made a private squabble the government's business. "You don't bring the outsiders in," said a family member, explaining Charlie's anger at his siblings. Because of all the ugly press and pressing legal matters, Charlie was forced to back out of the Port Authority job, which only increased his fury.

Now that the allegations were public, the FBI began to look into Kushner Companies. Heading the local U.S. attorney's office was Chris Christie, a Republican who aspired to political office, and Charlie's tight bond with McGreevey made him a particularly attractive target. The feds started to pressure Kushner Companies senior executives, and also started leaning on Plotkin. It seemed as if they interviewed anyone who'd ever heard of "losing a bill" or a "Richard special."

After six months of this, Charlie snapped. He decided to coerce Esther into dropping her support of Murray and instead side with him. His plan was brutal, bizarre, and criminal. He offered a cop, Jimmy O'Toole, who was dating Plotkin and was about to retire, twenty-five thousand dollars to set up Billy with a prostitute and film the encounter.

O'Toole was said to be reluctant at first, but eventually, in early December 2003, he reportedly had his brother, a private investigator named Tommy, set up a video camera in a digital alarm clock in a room at the Red Bull Inn, a motel on New Jersey's Route 22. A short time later, a blond prostitute introduced herself to Billy while he was lunching in a diner in Bridgewater. She said she had car trouble and was hoping he would help her. Billy gave her a lift to the motel and took her number. The following day, he returned to the Red Bull Inn and was filmed getting a blowjob from her.

Charlie and Stadtmauer laughed while they watched the clandestine video of that sex act in a conference room at the Florham Park offices, and Charlie asked for copies.

A few days later, O'Toole reportedly went to Charlie's home in Livingston, where, in front of Seryl, Charlie told him to set up Yontef the same way.

O'Toole tried, and a second prostitute attempted to seduce Yontef, but he refused her advances.

Meanwhile, the feds kept asking questions and started hearing wild stories about Charlie's private life, which Yontef's lawyer, Theodore Moskowitz, was told about. Investigators—and a number of Charlie's social circle—started to hear that Charlie liked to go to New York City at night under an alias, John Hess. He was rumored to sleep with men and hire prostitutes.

In May 2004, right before her son Jacob's engagement party, Esther opened a large envelope that had been stuffed into her mailbox and found the video of Billy's rendezvous. She went to the FBI and warned Murray not to go home because she was afraid Charlie was so unhinged that he would kill him.

Two months later, on July 13, Charlie was arrested on charges of conspiring to coerce an individual to travel across state lines for prostitution, retaliating against a witness, and impeding justice.

The reaction of most Kushner family members was that Charlie had done this to himself. But Jared blamed everyone except his father, and his misplaced anger only grew stronger throughout the years. "His siblings stole every piece of paper from his office, and they took it to the government . . . ," he would say in an interview with *New York* magazine's Gabriel Sherman. "Siblings that he literally made wealthy for doing nothing. He gave them interests in the business for nothing. All he did was put the [blackmail] tape together and send it. Was it the right thing to do? At the end of the day, it was a function of saying 'You're trying to make my life miserable? Well, I'm doing the same.'"

CHAPTER THREE

Family First

*"You don't go to the FBI and bring the outsiders in.
That's pretty fucked up."*

—A KUSHNER FAMILY MEMBER

Charlie Kushner's friends figured he would fight the charges. And right up until the moment of his arrest, almost everyone on the other side of the familial battle was terrified of what he might pull off—legally or otherwise. Lee Kushner was so terrified, she thought her house would be burned down. "Who knew what he was capable of?" a person close to Lee said. Theodore Moskowitz, Bob Yontef's lawyer, told his client to be careful, and even Moskowitz thought he was not safe. Someone, he suspected Charlie, was trying to "make difficulties" for him at his New Jersey law firm, perhaps trying to get him demoted, or worse. "They were a very difficult group of people," said Moskowitz, "and they understood the power of money, and they used it as a weapon for a very long time."

It's a view held by many close to the case that Charlie would have used that money and beaten all the other charges were it not for setting up Billy Schulder with a prostitute. "I think [the sting] put him in prison," said Alan Hammer. "He gave up the moral high ground. [He] couldn't stand before a jury and tell them what a good person he is after that."

But there may have been another reason Charlie did not fight the charges. Within weeks of his arrest on July 13, a one-page document from Chris

Christie's office sputtered out of Charlie's fax machine. Because of Charlie's strong aversion to office clutter, the fax machine was outside his sumptuous personal space, in a public area where his assistant, Valerie Grundig—and anyone passing by—could easily read whatever had been sent. While there is no reason to believe he saw the fax, Josh Kushner was in the office then, on summer break before he started college at Harvard. (In one of life's great ironies, Jared was interning for Manhattan District Attorney Robert Morgenthau.)

The facsimile made for astonishing reading, according to one person who saw it. It contained a reference to Charlie's alleged alias, John Hess, and to claims that Charlie was bisexual. (Benjamin Brafman, Charlie's criminal attorney at the time, said he had seen everything Christie's office sent about the case and had no recollection of the fax. He also disputed the allegations. "We carefully investigated these matters fifteen years ago and found zero credible evidence to support them," Brafman said.) Such allegations would not be devastating for many people, but for Charlie, at the apex of a closed society predicated on the importance of family and of regenerating the blood line, it would have been a disaster. "The social stigma would be enormous," said Michael Berenbaum, the Jewish studies scholar, who did not know Charlie and had never heard these allegations. "Culturally, that would be something that at that point in time, in that generation, would be very difficult to accept . . . and with lots of consequences."

Very soon after that fax arrived, senior staff at Florham Park saw Seryl crying in a hallway and in a small conference room on the executive floor. Barbara Gellert, the wife of Charlie's great friend and partner, George, came in to try to comfort her. "For the next five days, all we saw was Seryl crying. We knew something was terribly wrong," recalled a former senior executive.

Between the criminal charges and now these allegations, some friends no doubt encouraged Seryl to leave Charlie, but she was going to stay true to her religion, which decrees that marriage is until death. She was going to be a true Kushner: She was going to put family first. "Whatever the rumors are, and I've only heard a little, they have a great marriage . . . they are truly best friends," said Hammer.

Charlie also put family first. Well, part of his family. He was not going to be publicly humiliated, and he wasn't going to let his wife be mocked. And so the Kushners huddled, cried, and then strategized. Charlie and Seryl appeared to hide little from their children, which appalled one of the Kushner lawyers so much that, atypically, he talked about it. According to one source, Jared sat in on a meeting in which prosecutors spelled out precisely the range of allegations that would come out if the case went to trial. The prosecutors told Charlie and Seryl they would pursue a so-called "speaking indictment," which meant they could bring up all the evidence they had on him in open court, even details seemingly unnecessary to argue the charges. (Brafman denied any knowledge of such a meeting.)

The family must have realized Charlie's public career was over. They had to think quickly and find a way to make the best of a horrible situation.

A day or so after that fax came in from Christie's office, Charlie, dressed in a golf shirt and jeans, gathered his top advisers in his office. The group, according to someone there, included Seryl, Richard Stadtmauer, head of land development Jeffrey Freireich, chief operating officer Stuart Epstein, and Kevin Swill, president of a Kushner Companies subsidiary. Charlie had tried to make a deal in which he alone took the fall, according to Hammer, but Christie would not accept it. Charlie told the people in that room that Christie insisted he would have to tell the government everything he knew and plead guilty to aiding in the preparation of false tax returns—meaning that, in due course, the government could indict other Kushner Companies executives for the same crime.

Seeing no way out, Charlie rolled. In front of the group, he called New Jersey Governor Jim McGreevey. "Jim, I've got to give you up," he said, according to someone who was present. "You're going to be outed any day now. Chris Christie wants you. He's using me to get to you, and he knows everything." (Brafman denied Kushner was asked to cooperate in an investigation of McGreevey.) It was unclear what exactly Charlie meant by "everything," but in the coming weeks, the strangely synchronized downfall of these two New Jersey machers would become an object of fascination and whispered speculation in New Jersey political circles. A lot of that gossip was about Golan Cipel, the young Israeli with whom the ostensibly straight, married governor had carried on an affair and whom he had put on the government payroll. (At the time, Cipel hadn't even passed a background check.) Now Cipel was allegedly trying to extort McGreevey, by threatening to file a sexual harassment suit against him. *The New York Times* reported that McGreevey's advisers speculated that Charlie, who'd quarreled with McGreevey on a conference call because the governor refused to contribute a state subsidy to Charlie's bid to purchase the New Jersey Nets, was using Cipel to punish McGreevey.

Ultimately, Cipel's efforts were irrelevant. On August 12, 2004, less than a month after getting that call from Charlie, McGreevey announced his resignation with an emotional speech in Trenton, New Jersey, saying, "My truth is that I am a gay American." (The resignation overshadowed McGreevey's admission just a month earlier that he was an unnamed official at the heart of a federal indictment for a pay-to-play scheme. McGreevey claimed not to have been involved in that, and was never charged.)

Six days later, and just over a month after he'd been arrested, Charlie pleaded guilty to eighteen counts of aiding in the preparation of false tax returns, retaliating against a cooperating witness (Esther), and making false statements to the Federal Election Commission.

Brafman later denied to *New York* magazine that Charlie had had any role in McGreevey's undoing: "I want to be very clear about this. . . . Charles Kushner had absolutely nothing to do with the recent controversy surrounding the governor and Golan Cipel. I was with Charles Kushner when he learned through the media that the governor was going to resign. He was stunned and visibly upset for his friend."

Charlie was sentenced to twenty-four months in prison and was sent to a federal facility in Montgomery, Alabama. Every weekend, he was visited by Jared and Seryl—and many of his friends, including Hammer. He was now a felon, but he still had fiercely loyal friends who never forgot the good side of him. "He can be a very difficult man. But he can be a very good man," said Hammer. "Truly charitable and kind." The stories about his private life ceased—and have never resumed.

Family mythology has it that once Charlie was locked up, Jared, then only in his mid-twenties, took over Kushner Companies while finishing his law and business degrees at NYU. But that is not true. Jared was nowhere near ready to assume such a huge responsibility. Once Charlie decided to plea, he asked Hammer to run the business while he was gone. Hammer accepted immediately, and would later tell me that from the middle of 2005 until 2007, everything was kosher at Kushner Companies. "When I was there, we made no political contributions," he said. "I told everybody they can make whatever charitable contributions they wanted, but we weren't doing anything here. We're running a business. The first day or second day, I said, 'We're not doing anything wrong. If anybody suggests we should, you talk to me.'"

Hammer also took Richard Stadtmauer aside and told him: "There's no raising your voice, no yelling at people." And, like that, the company culture changed—at least for the two years that Charlie was not in the office.

While Hammer ran the company, Seryl came into the office every day. Hammer made sure she knew every detail of what was happening. Stadtmauer threw himself into helping Hammer. "He worked like a dog," said Hammer. Stadtmauer and his sister stayed very close while Charlie was gone—despite Stadtmauer's growing legal problems. In 2006, he was indicted for conspiring to defraud the government; Plotkin and two other former senior Kushner Companies executives, Ira Bloom and Scott Zecher, were also charged in the scheme. Unlike his coconspirators, Stadtmauer could not bring himself to plead guilty. He really believed God would look after him. "I believe that Richard would sooner get convicted and go to prison than tell his family, or his rabbis, or his children that he believed he did something wrong," said Hammer. "I think it's clear, in Richard's mind, that he didn't do anything. He was just doing his job."

While in prison, Charlie had plenty of time to think over all that had happened to him. He realized, too late, that Murray had probably wanted Stadtmauer's head and not his. That if only he had fired Stadtmauer, or if he had insisted Stadtmauer be nicer to Murray, the whole sordid mess could have been averted. He now wanted nothing to do with Stadtmauer, whom he never forgave, or so it appeared to colleagues.

Despite the embarrassment over Charlie's conviction, Seryl made sure that nothing in the family routine changed. "There's not a funeral they miss. . . . Seryl never misses a phone call for a birthday. . . . They have no shame," observed a relative. Seryl was showing her children that she could compartmentalize—and so could they.

Charlie started a tefillin program inside prison for all the Orthodox Jewish men. (According to tradition, this meant that once a day, except on Saturdays, they'd pull out the black boxes containing scrolls of parchment with verses from the Torah.) Charlie went through a substance-abuse program so he could leave prison early and complete his sentence at a halfway house in Newark. According to a source, during his stay there, Charlie was permitted to work from a nearby office, where Cory Booker, who became Newark mayor around that time and is now a U.S. senator, would meet with him on the stairway. (Charlie had steered fifty thousand dollars to Booker's first, failed run for Newark mayor in 2002. Booker's opponent, four-term mayor Sharpe James, said Booker was "collaborating with Jews to take over Newark.")

After finishing up at the halfway house, Charlie returned to his Florham Park office, and he got to take his revenge on Stadtmauer: he refused to testify at his brother-in-law's 2008 trial, and the defense rested without calling anyone to the stand. Stadtmauer had hoped Charlie would take the blame for any improprieties at the company. Instead, Stadtmauer was convicted of tax fraud and sentenced to just over three years in federal prison. He got out in January 2012.

Charlie and Stadtmauer, two convicted felons, still appear to hate each other, but nonetheless invite each other to their children's weddings and other important celebrations. (Stadtmauer and his wife turned down an invitation to Jared and Ivanka Trump's 2009 wedding because Stadtmauer was in the thick of his legal difficulties.) Now, when the Kushners show up at the Stadtmauers' for family celebrations, they are seated at tables on the outskirts of the room, but regardless, they go. "Seryl would not miss her nephew's wedding," explained a family friend. Apparently, Charlie will even shake Stadtmauer's hand whenever they are in the same room, and vice versa. But that's the extent of it. "They don't speak. There's no reason for them to," says one person who knows both men. "They really, really hate each other."

Jared Kushner, reedy, dimpled, and ruddy cheeked, was the highly sympathetic public face for Kushner Companies while Charlie strategized from prison on how to rebuild the firm. Accompanied by his mother, Jared took at least one meeting with Goldman Sachs related to a real estate deal both companies were involved in. People liked him. Unlike his father, he appeared to be calm, reasonable. And he was fastidiously polite. All the Kushner children are. It was an integral part of their upbringing. Whenever one of the four Kushner kids entered a room to greet either of their parents, they'd hug and kiss them, even during business meetings. To outsiders, this was mesmerizing. "Whatever the Kushners have done with their children, I don't think there's any faking it," one senior real estate broker said. Hammer joked: "I don't understand. I certainly think I behave better than Charlie. I can't get the respect of my children. I can't get them to come to the pool on Sunday."

It soon became widely repeated that Charlie wanted to implement a grand rehabilitation plan suggested to him by the guru of New York real estate public relations, Howard Rubenstein. It was audacious, but brilliant. First, buy a trophy asset in Manhattan and shift his center of operations from New Jersey to New York City. Second, buy a newspaper or publication, ostensibly owned by Jared. Third, have Jared date someone prominent.

So, with Rubenstein's help, Jared went shopping for a media property. The main aim was to have a voice, a way to flex power. The pair settled on *The New York Observer*, which had downsized its print edition and was losing roughly two million dollars every year. "They bought the *Observer* because [Charlie] didn't like the articles about him in the Newark *Star-Ledger*," said Hammer. The Kushners thought it wouldn't hurt to have their own outlet.

Meanwhile, with Charlie's approval, Hammer began to sell off some of the firm's portfolio in order to be able to acquire the trophy tower that would be the Kushners' symbol of a new life.

Hammer also started to hire people Charlie wanted at Kushner Companies. In 2008, Jonathan Goettlich, the son of someone Charlie met in prison, joined the company as an intern. Three years later, that former inmate was hired: Richard Goettlich, who would brag to his new colleagues that in 1998 he'd pleaded guilty to the biggest Ponzi scheme in New Jersey history. He'd been sentenced to ten years in prison. He got out in 2008 and became Charlie's leasing consultant in 2011.

In 2007, Charlie made another senior hire, bringing in McGreevey's new romantic partner, a mild-mannered, likable Australian named Mark O'Donnell, who had no background in real estate. Kushner Companies employees were puzzled as to what O'Donnell, whose expertise was in running wealthy families' investments, was doing there. One former employee assumed it was a sign that Charlie may have felt guilty about what he'd done to McGreevey and had reached out. McGreevey was not in a position to earn much then, and this was a way of helping him financially.

It was a gesture that reminded people of Charlie's good side, one that engendered loyalty. Jared liked to remind people of that aspect of his father, too. A story, perhaps apocryphal, that made the rounds in the New York real estate world was that during one meeting in New York, Jared walked in and, upon learning that Charlie had hurt his foot, took off his father's sock and kissed it.

CHAPTER FOUR

She's Got the Biggest Set of Balls in the Room

*"Perception is more important than reality. If someone perceives
something to be true, it is more important than if it is in fact true.
This doesn't mean you should be duplicitous or deceitful, but don't go out
of your way to correct a false assumption if it plays to your advantage."*

—IVANKA TRUMP, *THE TRUMP CARD: PLAYING TO WIN
IN WORK AND LIFE*

Charlie Kushner once said the reason Ivanka Trump so badly wanted to
become a Kushner was that she'd never had a close-knit family; it appeared
that she never felt her parents desperately desired her presence at the dinner
table, or for that matter, ever wanted her with them. A friend at the Chapin
School, the exclusive all-girls' private school in Manhattan that Ivanka attended until she was fifteen, once brought her home for the weekend. When
she complained to Ivanka that her mother was being overly critical, Ivanka
said wistfully: "I wish my mother showed that much interest in me."

Another friend, a real estate heir from New York who is several years
older, said, "The dysfunction and loneliness of Ivanka's family, the absence
of her parents from her life, put her in a situation where she was vulnerable."

Like Jared Kushner, Ivanka grew up in awe of a domineering father—but
for wholly different reasons. Whereas Jared was the favorite and heir apparent, Ivanka had to fight for her father's attention and her ultimate role

as the chief heir in his real estate empire. And fight she did. When Donald Trump divorced her mother, Ivana, in the early 1990s, Ivanka asked her mom, "Does it mean I'm not going to be Ivanka Trump anymore?" From then on, Ivanka decided that she would go out of her way to see more of her father, not less. She made a point of dropping in on him on her way to school each day, and she'd call him during the day from a janitor's closet—and to her delight, he'd always take her call. (Trump's relationship with the two sons he had with Ivana, Don Jr. and Eric, was not nearly so close for years.) "She was always Daddy's little girl," said Nikki Haskell, a family friend. Whether out of insecurity or love—or a combination of both—Ivanka never stopped trying to please him. Her recollection of him as an accessible father is at odds with the general view, which is, in Haskell's words: "Donald was there when he was there."

In a 2013 interview, Ivanka told me she has a rosier view of her childhood. "He may be different to some dads in terms of how he interacted with us. Often, it was in the capacity of an educator and teaching us the things he was passionate about, which we, in turn, became passionate about—namely real estate—but many other things along the way. But he was a terrific father who was nothing if not accessible to us throughout our childhood and obviously today. Maybe more so today than ever." (This was more than two years before he announced he was running for president.)

The divorce and the obsessive media coverage of it (including salacious boasts by Trump in the *New York Post* about how good he was in bed; locker-room braggadocio apparently seconded by Marla Maples, the woman for whom he dumped Ivana) turned the Trump kids into a tribe. Ivanka wrote in her 2009 book *The Trump Card* that the situation "brought me and my brothers much closer together. . . . We'd been forced into us-versus-the-world mode."

And from that moment on, "the world" would rarely get the real story on what was going on with Ivanka. Instead, it would get a veneer, a mythology spun and ferociously controlled by Ivanka, and abetted by those around her. There was never any mention, until very recently, for example, that she was reportedly asked not to return to Chapin because she had been skipping classes, supposedly to work on her modeling portfolio at her father's Florida resort, Mar-a-Lago, though she was barely a teenager.

For high school, she was enrolled at Choate Rosemary Hall, a bucolic boarding school in Connecticut. Ivanka arrived to tour the school alone, in a stretch white limousine. Her tour guide, who preferred to remain anonymous, was struck by the sadness of the scene. "I felt really bad. . . . The white limo just sat there and waited. . . . She was very nice. She was very shy, she was very quiet. But the part that sticks in my mind was the fact that no one was there with her. It was a big deal. It was weird."

When her parents showed up for the occasional parents' day or at a school gathering, they stood out, according to a classmate. Ivana once came dressed in a figure-hugging leather bodysuit, which did not play well with the school's old-money students and parents. Ivanka was clearly new money.

Regardless, any kind of money bought influence, if there was enough of it. At Choate, Ivanka went to a party at a teacher's house that was rumored to be shut down because of drugs and alcohol. Other students who attended the party were expelled or suspended, while Ivanka largely escaped punishment. The story passed around by her classmates was that her father had called the school and gotten her out of any punishment. "It was unfair," said one former classmate.

While she was at Choate, Ivanka's modeling career took off, which meant she spent less time on campus than many of her peers. It was around this time that her classmates detected pronounced changes in her physical appearance. She would not have been the only person in high school to get her nose fixed, but she would have been one of a tiny number whose chest size seemed to change suddenly, and significantly. (She would later say she was a "curvy" person and told *GQ* that rumors she had gotten breast implants were "absurd"; she had no issue with anyone who got plastic surgery, but thought it was a "silly" topic to discuss.)

The pressure for her to change her natural appearance, to attain a perfect "look" at such a young age, was enormous. Her father once told *The New York Times* that he was wary about her modeling career because of the lifestyle that went with it. (He would know about this better than most, since he owned a modeling agency and a beauty pageant company.) And yet he was happy to exploit her looks and burgeoning sexuality. At fifteen, she gave a horrendously nervous interview on live TV while co-hosting her father's Miss Teen USA pageant. But she'd recover and mature, and there were many more TV and media appearances in which she shared a platform with her father. Ivanka's glossy looks and poise eventually became an important extension of his brand.

As Ivanka matured, physically and emotionally, her father talked openly about how impressed he was with her appearance—a habit he has maintained to this day. "Isn't she hot?" he will ask whomever he is meeting with when she walks in, apparently not noticing the uncomfortable expressions around him. "It's disgusting," one observer told me. He calls her "babe" or "baby."

The tastelessness of his remarks reached a nadir in March 2006, a couple of years after Ivanka graduated from the University of Pennsylvania. She was twenty-four. On the television program *The View,* Donald Trump said, "If Ivanka weren't my daughter, perhaps I'd be dating her." Ivanka laughed that off, at least in public, but the press reaction, she felt, was a "nightmare." Months later, she described the incident to a writer for *Marie Claire:* "I mean, *I've* even heard him say that before. . . . He loves seeing people's reaction, when they're flabbergasted. Plus, he was obviously making fun of the fact that he has a tendency to date younger women."

This incident showed that she was already skilled at deflection, especially when discussing her father. In 2003, the documentary *Born Rich,* about a group of mostly twenty-something heirs, gained national attention, in part because it was directed, not always kindly, by one of their own, Johnson & Johnson heir Jamie Johnson. Among the rich kids featured in the film, Ivanka arguably came off looking the best. In it, she said she was "absolutely proud to be a Trump."

She joined the Trump Organization in 2005. Like her father, she excelled at both self-promotion and media manipulation, and her vocabulary was more extensive than his, her demeanor more controlled. By 2007, she started posing erotically, and not always in a very classy way, in a blatant sell of the Trump brand. That year alone there were profiles (complete with cheesecakey photos) in *GQ, Esquire, Harper's Bazaar, Vogue,* and *The New York Times.* She seemed to be an intoxicating mix of sex and smarts. By day, she climbed construction sites and negotiated with foreign men twice her age; by night, she put on her stilettos to slay the demimonde. She also appeared in nearly ninety episodes of Trump's reality television show, NBC's *The Apprentice,* more than any of the other Trump siblings. (Tiffany Trump, the daughter he had with Marla Maples, never appeared on the show.)

Her shtick was always the sexy, bright, hardworking daughter who travels the world expanding her father's business. But court records, reports, and interviews with those who worked alongside Ivanka tell a very different story: one of mayhem and hubris, as she engineered a series of dubious business deals, many of them with people accused of crime and corruption. The Trump Organization always seemed chaotic, according to Haskell, because "Donald likes that organized confusion." Just like Charlie Kushner back then, Trump never used email. They seemed to share an aversion to paper trails. Court records show that all decision-making rested with Trump and happened in an ad hoc, often haphazard way. On-the-spot decisions were part of the Trump brand—and its value, increasingly, was as a brand and not as a conventional real estate development business. After Trump's casinos and Plaza Hotel wound up in bankruptcy proceedings in the 1990s, the number of blue-chip lenders who would do business with the firm dwindled. By the time the children joined the business, it had morphed from a development firm into more of a licensing shop, dependent on global partners. Louise Sunshine, a former Trump Organization executive vice president, thought the change was disastrous. "Once we went into the franchise business, his children did not protect him," she said. "They sold franchises to bad people"—presumably in an effort to please him.

Law enforcement has had an eye on Trump and the Trump Organization since the 1970s. And throughout the 1980s, his alleged ties to organized crime cropped up again and again, including in 1982, when he was said to have purchased land for his first Atlantic City casino from a Philadelphia mobster at an inflated price. Trump reportedly built two structures—including his flagship Trump Tower—with concrete, again bought at inflated prices, from mob-connected firms, instead of steel girders common at the time. For construction on Trump Tower, he reportedly hired undocumented workers and allegedly avoided union pressure thanks to the mob, and when he didn't feel like paying workers or contractors, he stiffed them, according to dozens of lawsuits. In the 2000s, he turned his fortunes around by selling himself as a brand, as a wildly successful businessman, a myth propagated by his TV show. According to lawsuits, Trump began grifting suckers through the now infamous Trump University, and also through seminars that licensed his name (he settled with the State of New York and the allegedly ripped-off students for twenty-five million dollars). He slapped his name on ties, vodka, steaks, and wine.

The path to success for his children in this organization was to bring him a new project, which they could retain ownership of. They did not write memos or budgets or project costs. In fact, they did not even keep files. The children would simply meet with a prospective partner and then stroll into their father's office, tell him about the deal, and he'd make a decision. Whoever brought the project in would oversee it to completion (or, as would often be the case, to its demise). The two Trump Organization executives who did have considerable experience in real estate—CFO Allen Weisselberg and then–chief legal officer Jason Greenblatt—often had to report to the children, rather than to Trump.

Ivanka's part-time, on-the-job tutor then was Felix Sater, a Russian-born businessman who had grown up in the Coney Island section of Brooklyn. Erudite, funny, and smart, he was the son of a small-time gangster and would later serve as an informant for the U.S. government. At eighteen, Sater had gone to work as an assistant on the trading floor at Bear Stearns. By nineteen, he was a senior vice president and on track to make it to the C-suite on Wall Street. Mothers in Brighton Beach, the Russian enclave of Brooklyn, next to Coney Island, would tell their kids, "Grow up to be like Felix." But Sater's ambitions got blown up in a flash of anger. He got into a drunken bar brawl over a woman one night in 1991 and hit a commodities broker in the cheek with the broken stem of a margarita glass. Sater lost his broker's license and spent fifteen months in prison. Unable to land the sort of legitimate job that interested him, he became involved in a forty-million-dollar stock scam. Meanwhile, the Defense Intelligence Agency and Central Intelligence Agency recruited him as an asset. In 1998, the stock scam caught up with him, which meant that he added a third government agency to his list of handlers: the FBI. He pleaded guilty in the racketeering case but avoided prison time, presumably because he continued to work for the FBI for years. The 1998 court records were sealed because it was imperative that his work for the government remain a secret. During her confirmation process in 2015, incoming U.S. Attorney General Loretta Lynch would declare that Sater's case had been sealed because he had spent a decade "providing information crucial to national security and the conviction of over twenty individuals, including those responsible for committing massive financial fraud and members of La Cosa Nostra." Sater claimed that he had also provided intelligence on Osama bin Laden.

Trump met Sater around 2000, while Sater was secretly working for the FBI. He had joined a development firm, Bayrock Group. Sater appeared to be a rainmaker with contacts everywhere, so, according to Sater, Trump wanted a first look at his deals, and wanted him close. Sater and his Bayrock colleagues took office space in Trump Tower, two floors down from Trump. He was already in the building when Ivanka joined the Trump Organization. Sater found her to be bright, although somewhat volatile if she did not get her way. "There was a lot of yelling back and forth," he recalled. "She was a born promoter. . . . Her appearance and her tenacity made Donald look at her and say, 'Wow. . . . She knows how to get shit for free and get her name on stuff.'"

Trump asked Sater repeatedly what he thought of his kids and which one of them should run his company. "I thought she was the one who can run it the best. She's got the biggest set of balls in the room." In 2006, it would be Sater who took Ivanka on a scouting trip to Moscow, and it would be Sater who, while they were on a private tour of the Kremlin, pleaded with a member of Vladimir Putin's security detail to allow her to sit, briefly, in the Russian president's chair.

Ivanka's early projects included developments in Chicago, Panama, Dubai, Toronto, and New York City's SoHo district. Panama was the site of the first international Trump-branded hotel, and Ivanka reportedly took the lead on the project. She told *The San Diego Union-Tribune* that she negotiated the terms just a week after joining the Trump Organization. "We lock ourselves in this room and it's me sitting there, knowing squat . . . and across from me there are around ten men." This seems to have been a typical Trumpian exaggeration. The deal reportedly took five months to iron out. But her hyperbole would be the least of the project's problems.

Ivanka seemed oblivious about the Trump Organization's seedy overseas partners. One of her chief points of contact for the Panama project was a Brazilian, Alexandre Ventura Nogueira, who had been the subject of a money-laundering inquiry by Spanish authorities in 2005 and would be arrested on fraud charges in Panama in 2009. (He fled the country in 2012.) In a November 2017 interview with *Reuters*, he had a lot to say about the support he received from Ivanka, who, he claimed, helped him become a major broker and top salesperson for the project. In turn, he allegedly cheated people over apartments in the Panama project by pocketing their deposits, or by selling the same unit to multiple buyers. Nogueira has also admitted to laundering money. He denied doing so knowingly on the Trump project, but told *Reuters* that no one—including the Trump Organization—ever asked him where the money was coming from. For the Panama project, Ivanka also presented sales figures that were patently false. She told a reporter that 90 percent of the units had been snatched up and that they were sold at astronomical prices for the area. This was not the case.

The Panama hotel is one of several shady Trump licensing deals scattered around the globe that Ivanka helped oversee. Thanks to her current prominence as both presidential adviser and First Daughter (a title she reportedly likes), the allegations of criminality surrounding projects the Trump Organization has worked on has largely emerged over just the past two years. In Azerbaijan, it's been reported, she oversaw a project for which the Trump Organization partnered with Elton Mammadov, whose brother, a government minister and oligarch, was once described in a U.S. diplomatic cable as "notoriously corrupt." The Mammadov family has ties to Iran's Revolutionary Guard. As a result, it's possible that the Trump Organization violated the Foreign Corrupt Practices Act, which forbids American companies from bribing foreign officials or benefiting from bribery carried out by a business partner—even unknowingly. A violation of the FCPA requires only that the American company could have reasonably discovered a partner's bad behavior, preventing businesses from simply turning a blind eye. By the time the Trump Organization entered into its project with

Mammadov, his family's reputation—and Azerbaijan's—for graft was widely reported.

Under Ivanka's supervision, the Trump Organization partnered with a long list of what Sunshine, the company's executive vice president from 1972 to 1986, would call "bad people." The firm was limited as to who it could partner with, said a former senior associate, because the amount Trump demanded as a management fee was far, far greater than the amount, say, a Four Seasons or other similar hotel chain would demand. "The only people that would give [that kind of fee] to them are hustlers who in turn resell that to others," said this person.

The Trumps' overseas licensing deals attracted hustlers of every persuasion. The company's original partner for a project Ivanka would later supervise in Toronto, for instance, would be extradited to the U.S., after fleeing the country following a guilty plea for bankruptcy fraud and embezzlement. The development would be taken over by a Russian-Canadian businessman who, it was reported, appeared to be using the building for a money-laundering scheme. By March 2018, the FBI was looking into the deal she helped put together with a Malaysian backer in Vancouver. No reason was given for this. But in the former Soviet republic of Georgia, Ivanka participated in the interior design on a project for which, according to *The New Yorker*, the Trump Organization received its licensing fee from a developer funded by a bank mixed up in a money-laundering scandal. Accepting money that stems from illegal activity would seem to have put the Trump Organization at risk of violating money-laundering laws. But it appears the company did not ask questions before taking the money. And in October 2016, a Brazilian federal prosecutor announced an investigation into the financing of a Trump-branded hotel in Rio de Janeiro. (The Trump Organization withdrew from the deal around two months later.) The project was largely financed by public pension funds whose participation, the prosecutor alleged, Trump's partners may have secured through bribes. Ivanka helped negotiate the deal.

Ivanka's questionable business decisions go beyond her involvement in properties with shady partners and financing. In 2009, the Trumps were sued for allegedly taking advantage of prospective buyers by exaggerating their involvement in a failed condo project in Mexico. Ivanka had said in a video on the project's website that the Trumps were developing the property; in fact, they had merely lent their name to it. (The suit was settled in 2013.)

In June 2008, Ivanka and Don Jr. brashly announced false sales figures for Trump SoHo; buyers later sued the Trumps and the project's developers, one of which was Bayrock, for fraud. In a rare concession for a man who lives to drag things out with lawyers and threats, Trump settled with the buyers in 2011, refunding 90 percent of their deposits, but admitted no wrongdoing. Separate from that civil suit, the Manhattan district attorney's office launched an investigation into whether the Trump children broke any laws by making false claims about the project. That case seemed to be heading toward an indictment until Manhattan District Attorney Cyrus Vance Jr. overruled his prosecutors, which happened after a visit from Trump's lawyer Marc Kasowitz. Just prior to their meeting, Vance returned a twenty-five-thousand-dollar donation Kasowitz had given to his campaign, which Vance has described as standard practice when a donor is involved with a case. Less than six months after Vance dropped the case, Kasowitz came back with an even larger donation to Vance's campaign. He raised more than fifty thousand dollars for the DA.

As Ivanka's role in the Trump Organization grew, she became more assertive and began to wield the power she'd carefully cultivated while working under her father. In 2007, Sater's lurid past was exposed in *The New York Times*. Initially, Ivanka and Don Jr. were extremely supportive; they asked what they could do to help. Sater thanked them but said their help would not be necessary: he decided to work in London, where he would attract less scrutiny.

Upon Sater's return to the U.S. in 2010, Trump made him a senior adviser and placed him two doors down from his own office on the twenty-sixth floor of Trump Tower. This change, according to a person who visited the Trump offices at the time, did not make Ivanka happy. (Her office was on the twenty-fifth floor, along with those of Don Jr. and Eric.) As a joint venture partner, Sater had been valuable to Ivanka, but as a senior adviser with unfettered access to her father, he was a threat, or that's how he felt she perceived him. Trump had started to ask Sater questions about Ivanka's deals and, according to Sater, she bristled at this.

In the fall of 2010 Trump told Sater that Ivanka had told him he had to go. Trump was extremely reluctant to push him out. A source with knowledge of the father-daughter conversation remembered him saying, "Are you fucking kidding me? Felix is a moneymaker."

Ivanka's reply was apparently along the lines of what she'd written in her 2009 book, *The Trump Card*: "Perception is more important than reality." She'd be willing to partner with Sater, but she didn't want him two doors down from her father.

Trump reluctantly did what his daughter wanted, and Sater left the company. It was a seminal moment that demonstrated Ivanka had real influence over her father, the limit of which had not yet been found.

CHAPTER FIVE

The Tower of Debt

"Charlie was always a big fish in the little pond of New Jersey. He was always going to outgrow New Jersey. Charlie's not the kind of personality who was going to stay in the garden apartment business."

—SENATOR ROBERT TORRICELLI

After Charlie Kushner returned home from prison in August 2006, he reclaimed his company and pursued the firm's most ambitious project yet: a New York trophy tower that would create a new, prestige brand for the Kushner name. And Jared quickly came up with an attractive target: he knew Rob Speyer, the heir apparent and soon-to-be president and co-CEO of Tishman Speyer, which was considering selling 666 Fifth Avenue. The building had long been considered one of New York's trophy office towers, in part because of its location, close to both Central Park and Grand Central Terminal. Under Tishman Speyer's watch, Citibank was one of the tower's biggest tenants, and its logo had replaced the "666" sign at the top of the building. Its top-floor restaurant, Top of the Sixes, had been a popular hangout for the financial elite. The sculptor Isamu Noguchi had created the famous waterfall and ceiling in the lobby.

At Charlie's urging, Jared phoned Speyer to ask about 666 Fifth, but Alan Hammer, ever cautious, was not convinced. "When you buy a trophy property in New York, they don't make any money. The people who sell trophy properties are smart, and they do not sell a building that enables you to make money. You have to add value. You have to make it better."

But Charlie saw potential in the deal. Because of the booming market, the initial investment would be relatively small. "Debt was Charlie's friend," Hammer explained. "It has always been Charlie's friend. It enabled him to buy what he bought. He competed for properties and he paid more than other people for great properties because the other people didn't have the nerve to pay the price and take the debt."

When Charlie sold his apartment portfolio, some of it through Hammer while he was in prison, he used a classic legal real estate tax dodge. On paper, he'd made around two billion dollars from the sales, but most of that—$1.8 billion, according to a source—was debt. To put off paying taxes on his capital gains, which would be roughly two hundred million dollars, he did what are called 1031 exchanges. By law, he could defer paying taxes on the sale if he reinvested the income into other commercial real estate projects. And he planned to do just that with 666 Fifth.

Charlie gathered his staff in Florham Park the day after Thanksgiving, 2006, to put together the financing for 666 Fifth. He reportedly told his accountants, "I buy it, you make it work." Documents show that the colossal amount he'd pay for the building—at $1.8 billion, then the most ever paid for an office building in the United States—was more than 97 percent debt. The Kushners (and their partners, the Gellerts) put down fifty million dollars, and the banks Barclays and UBS provided the rest in a loan.

The terms of the loan severely restricted both the percentage of equity Charlie could own and his management role. It wasn't just his prison sentence that troubled lenders. In February 2005, the Federal Reserve Board and the Federal Deposit Insurance Corporation had announced joint enforcement actions against Charlie and the NorCrown Trust, a bank holding company based in Livingston, New Jersey, for which he served as a trustee. Regulators prohibited Charlie "from participating in the conduct of the affairs of any financial institution or holding company."

"Lenders [tend] not to like to lend to convicted felons," explained one person involved with the loan for 666 Fifth. "Particularly ones who are messing with savings and loans and things like that. The loan documents stipulated that the property must at all times be managed by a qualified manager, of which the Kushners cannot meet the criteria." Further, it was specified, Charlie could not direct the operations of this building until the loan was paid off.

But Charlie got around all this, or at least that is the belief of many people who negotiated with Kushner Companies over the next few years. "No one ever thought for a minute, even though Jared was the face of all this, that it wasn't Charlie pulling the strings. . . . Jared was too young," said one of the lenders. "[Jared] didn't have the experience to be playing these games that Charlie was playing. Charlie had thirty years of doing this. . . . The documents say one thing; doesn't mean the people actually do it."

The loan documents said the Gellerts "must at all times control and own at least 38 percent interest in the borrower." (Charlie and Seryl Kushner had 19 percent and the remaining 41 percent was divided equally among their four children.) This structure meant George Gellert was on the hook if Charlie breached the terms of the 666 Fifth covenant. But Gellert, a convivial, charming man sixteen years older than Charlie, was apparently willing to take the risk. He told friends that Charlie had made him wealthy, and the real estate business was a great deal more exciting than his business importing cheese.

Plus, the two men had a real bond and talked all the time. "Every morning, when [Charlie] wakes up, his first phone call is to George. Every night, before either one of them goes to bed, they call each other. It's the weirdest relationship you could ever imagine," observed a former senior Kushner Companies executive.

Jared, as the "face" of the project, got to announce the close of the 666 Fifth deal on his twenty-sixth birthday, January 10, 2007. He told *The Real Deal* later that year, "The building shows very, very well, it's got some unbelievable space; the views from up top are breathtaking." As for the exorbitant price, he boasted, "We thought it was a number that would get the seller's attention."

It was also a number that would come to haunt the Kushners. The next year, 2008, Lehman Brothers collapsed and the financial crisis hit. Although the Kushners had posted an interest reserve of $114.4 million (from which they would later draw to cover the cost of tenant improvements), it wasn't nearly enough. Lenders' records show that as early as 2008 they had to spend a further $200 million to pay down part of the loan. The Kushners had to scramble. Or rather, Charlie had to. Jared, according to someone who worked at Kushner Companies for those first two years, was hardly ever in the office.

In the summer of 2008, it was announced that the Carlyle Group and Crown Acquisitions had bought a 49 percent interest in the retail portion of 666 Fifth for $525 million. It sounded impressive, but it would not be enough to save the Kushners. In August, it was reported that a major tenant, the law firm Orrick, Herrington & Sutcliffe, was considering moving out, figuring it could get cheaper space at the market rate of ninety dollars per square foot rather than the $110 Kushner Companies was seeking.

That the Kushners did not lower their rents and keep the law firm in the building would outrage at least one of their lenders. And the number of lenders expanded beyond just Barclays and UBS, as the emerging crisis forced UBS to sell the debt it had not yet securitized off its books—at a discount of roughly seventy cents on the dollar. Around $285 million was sold in thirds. The buyers were AREA Property Partners, run by Bill Mack, a New York developer who is also the chairman of the Guggenheim Foundation; Paramount Group, a real estate investment trust; and Starwood Capital Group, run by the famously tough negotiator Barry Sternlicht. The Kushners knew Mack and Sternlicht socially and hoped that "friends" would be softer on them than strangers.

As part of his desperate search for capital, Charlie, whose strong pro-Israel views were well known, was prepared, for the first time, to take Arab money. If he could get it. In late 2007 or early 2008, Jared, Kevin Swill, Mark O'Donnell, and an outside attorney, Jonathan Bernstein, flew to London to meet with the Abu Dhabi Investment Authority (ADIA), a sovereign wealth fund represented by Raja Ammoun, Nabil Joumma, and Hamad Salem Kardous Al Ameri. Over tea in the lobby of the five-star Dorchester hotel, the ADIA businessmen listened to the pitch, which was, according to someone in the meeting, "desperate." The Kushners' plight was obvious: they were stuck with a loan they were not in a position to pay off, thanks to the financial crisis and declining rents. Jared did the talking, which was possibly a mistake. "Think about how young he was," remembered one person at the meeting. "Think about him just starting out in the business, not knowing the ropes. Not understanding how international people work. Not understanding the culture."

The talks lasted ninety minutes but went nowhere.

In his glass-walled office on 666 Fifth's executive fifteenth floor, which had a view of Fifth Avenue but was otherwise far less impressive than his office in Florham Park, Charlie took endless meetings with bankers, with private equity funds, and with foreign sovereign wealth funds, because he knew he had just one year to refinance. Jared appeared for most of the important meetings, and Seryl was a constant comfort; she used the office that had been assigned to Marci Plotkin, who was now mostly gone, like so many other familiar Kushner Companies faces. (She did not go quietly. Plotkin pleaded guilty in February 2008 for her part in the Kushner Companies' fraud and temporarily gave up her license to practice public accounting. She was sentenced to eight months of house arrest and three years of probation.) Scott Zecher, who had turned state's evidence against Charlie, had also left. Jeff Goldstein, the controller, was phased out, since there was less for him to do after the sale of the garden apartments. Jeff Freireich, the vice chairman and director in charge of land development and acquisition activities, had stayed in New Jersey and left the firm in September 2007, because the Kushners were no longer really doing any construction.

Richard Stadtmauer had kept working in the New Jersey offices while he prepared for his trial. Despite his belief that God would look after him, he hired a prominent lawyer and prepared for the worst. He asked Charlie to liquidate all of his financial positions so he could take care of his family if he went to prison. That meant Charlie was forced to pay his brother-in-law around $120 million, something that apparently irked him deeply.

Now, of the old-guard senior executives, only Swill remained, and Charlie wanted him gone, too. Swill was extremely close to Stadtmauer. One problem, as Charlie saw it, was that Swill's job was to arrange financing for acquisitions and refinancings, and this job was moot once the company acquired 666 Fifth. "There was no role for him in New York," said Hammer, who was friendly with Swill.

On his way out, Swill argued with Charlie about money. Per his contract and a formula that had worked on approximately one hundred previous transactions, Swill was entitled to commission for the loans he brought to Kushner Companies, according to a complaint he filed in court. After the deal for 666 Fifth closed, Swill was expecting his usual payout, which would have earned him $5.2 million, according to Swill's complaint. Charlie refused to pay that much. He offered Swill five hundred thousand dollars, according to the complaint, and, in a profanity-laced tirade, threatened that if Swill asked for more, he would "regret it."

Charlie eventually agreed to pay him $750,000, according to the lawsuit. Meanwhile, the eighteen-million-dollar fee Westminster Capital received for the purchase, according to the filing, was disbursed the following ways: five million dollars went to the children's trust funds; $1.1 million to a personal mortgage (allegedly on an apartment in NoHo for Jared); two million dollars on bonuses; two hundred thousand dollars on Mikvah Chana in Livingston (a Jewish ritual bath where his elder daughter, Dara, has served as vice president); and so on. Swill alleged in the filing that three to four hundred thousand dollars of that money was put in a separate bank account for O'Donnell, ex-governor Jim McGreevey's partner, to whom Charlie still turned for advice on structuring his family trusts and finances.

In July 2008, a portion of 666 Fifth was refinanced, and so Swill argued he was now entitled to a larger share, since Barclays lent an additional $325 million to Kushner Companies. He also argued he had not yet been paid for the financing of a Chicago office tower Kushner Companies bought in 2007. Rather than pay him, Swill claimed, Charlie and Jared fired him.

Swill sued. Charlie countersued, claiming a breach of an NDA. (All employees had been made to sign NDAs in 2005, in the wake of Charlie's legal problems.) But Swill had leverage because he knew so much about the Kushners. In an early hearing, in front of Stadtmauer, who was called as a witness, Swill's attorneys started to ask questions that touched on the events of the summer of 2004 and the buried secrets of the talks between Charlie, Chris Christie's prosecutors, and McGreevey. The last thing Charlie would have wanted was any reference to those private conversations appearing in open court, especially after he had just a few years before pleaded guilty and gone to prison to avoid a trial. The matter quickly went to a private arbitration, where the two sides reached a settlement that remains sealed.

Not that Charlie wanted to completely suppress his time behind bars: in the summer of 2008, he caught up with some of the people he'd met in prison and he remained close to them. In addition to Richie Goettlich, he brought in Avram "Avi" Lebor, a very close, old friend of Ben Brafman's, who had been Charlie's criminal defense attorney. Lebor was from an Orthodox family; his father had fled the Nazi invasion of Poland. He had gone to prison for wire fraud. Charlie clearly preferred hanging with people whose experiences he could relate to. The "felons," as they were nicknamed within the firm, had plenty of stories to tell their new colleagues about life inside prison. Charlie, Goettlich claimed, had told fellow inmates his darkest secrets while in Alabama. The "felons" were said to be the source of a rumor that spread around the company that Seryl had been the one to sign off on the hooker sting. Charlie had tossed out the idea of a hit man, but Seryl, so the gossip went, preferred a prostitute. There was nothing to indicate this was true (Brafman called it "absolutely false")—and many of the people who knew Goettlich thought he was a bullshitter—but the apocryphal story had a strong impact at the Kushner Companies office, according to one former staffer. Employees were frightened. They knew they were still working for a Jekyll and Hyde.

Goettlich got more out of his relationship with Charlie than a job; on January 4, 2015, he married Plotkin. Despite everything that had happened to Charlie, Kushner Companies remained as insular, as incestuous, and as firmly in Charlie's debt as ever.

CHAPTER SIX

The Conversion

"It is shocking that they let Jared marry a convert. If she hadn't been rich and famous, that wouldn't have been allowed."

—KUSHNER FAMILY MEMBER

While Charlie Kushner was frantically chasing refinancing for 666 Fifth, and often losing his temper in the process, he usually kept Jared out of the office, encouraging him to spend time at *The New York Observer*. This kept father and son separate in the minds of most New York City influencers, which was critical if the Kushner name was to be rehabilitated. Buying the *Observer* was a big part of that. "It put Jared on the map socially. It put him on the map, maybe, intellectually. It put him out there," said Alan Hammer. The New York demimonde knew dimly of Charlie and his scandal, but it did not really care. It did care, though, about the new young newspaper proprietor in its midst.

It was Jared who handed the ten-million-dollar check to the paper's previous owner, the investment banker-turned-publisher Arthur Carter, in the summer of 2006. He was just twenty-five and finishing a combined MBA and law degree at New York University. He spent 2007, his first full year as publisher, in the *Observer* offices in Manhattan's Flatiron district, according to Bob Sommer, former president of the Observer Media Group. The *Observer* was his baby.

The social benefit of becoming the owner of such a venerated paper was almost instantaneous. The *Observer* may have been a money-losing, salmon-colored broadsheet, but it was read each week by the city's political, cultural, and business elite. Its gossipy media pages, culture critics, and distinguished columnists were essential reading for that crowd. It was also a haven for young talent, providing training to many of today's high-profile journalists, including *Vanity Fair*'s Gabriel Sherman, NBC and MSNBC's Steve Kornacki, and *The New York Times*'s Choire Sicha and Alex Kuczynski. Candace Bushnell's book *Sex and the City* began as a column in the *Observer*. Jared was now meeting people who would never have welcomed him when he was just another real estate heir. He befriended media moguls like Rupert Murdoch and the then-chairman of advertising giant WPP, Sir Martin Sorrell. Michael Ovitz, the former Hollywood mega-agent, became a mentor. New York politicians also had a reason to court him. He hung out with financial stars like Blackstone's Jonathan Gray; Jeff Blau, the CEO of Related Companies; and the tech entrepreneur Kevin Ryan. Because he beefed up the *Observer*'s commercial real estate coverage, creating the Power 100—an annual industry ranking—and ultimately a separate real estate paper, he became a figure with clout in that world. The annual Power 100 party became viewed as something like "the Oscars of real estate," according to a leading broker.

Jared used his new status to cultivate a social group whose other members were considerably older than he was. "He's not hanging with James Murdoch or Lachlan Murdoch. It's Rupert that he's hanging with," said a Kushner associate who knows him well, referring to Rupert's two sons.

But at a networking lunch thrown by a diamond heir, Moshe Lax, at the Prime Grill restaurant in midtown Manhattan, Jared was introduced to Ivanka Trump, who, at twenty-five, was just ten months younger than he was. Part three of Howard Rubenstein's plan had been "Jared should date a high-profile woman." And there she was. As Kenneth Pasternak, a friend and Kushner family business partner, would observe, "You couldn't write that script."

Jared and Ivanka quickly became an intriguing gossip column item. They seemed perfectly matched: two good-looking real estate heirs who were, unusually for that industry, fêted by members of New York's media whirl.

They both *seemed* gracious and mature, polished foils to the scrappy crassness of their fathers.

But after a year of dating, they split in April 2008, in part because Jared's parents were horrified by the match. Seryl and Charlie were dismayed at the idea of their son marrying outside the faith. The idea was particularly offensive to Seryl, who had raised the children. They were her world, and her world was the closed conservative Jewish culture she had grown up in. Charlie and Seryl refused to even meet Ivanka, although Hammer repeatedly talked to Charlie about it. "You're the closest people to your children of anybody that I know," he told his friend. "So, what are you going to do, Charlie? Are you going to go sit shiva for your favorite child?"

Jared and Ivanka were apart for around three months. They were reunited that summer, on a boating holiday orchestrated by Rupert Murdoch's then-wife, Wendi Deng Murdoch. Neither had any idea the other would be there. Soon after, Ivanka agreed to convert to Judaism.

The family agreed to this compromise, but it would happen on Charlie's terms, under the instruction of Rabbi Haskel Lookstein, then the rabbi of Congregation Kehilath Jeshurun on New York's Upper East Side. Lookstein had gravitas as a member of the Rabbinical Council of America, which has tremendous influence over whether a conversion is legitimate. He was also a modernizer who had worked to help unhappily married Orthodox women obtain a religious divorce recognized by the community. This was often difficult, and sometimes impossible, because men are traditionally granted all the power in this decision.

According to friends, Charlie was going along with his favorite son's plans because he had no other option, and he remained skeptical of his future daughter-in-law. Family friend Bob Sommer recalled that Charlie wanted to test Ivanka's devotion to his son and her future life, so he made her conversion as challenging as possible. "This wasn't like, 'Talk to a rabbi, read a couple of paragraphs,'" Sommer said. "It was hard, and it was on Charlie's terms."

By the time the wedding took place, on October 25, 2009, Charlie and Seryl were effusive about their new daughter-in-law. According to Sommer, Ivanka had not just passed the tests—she had far surpassed Charlie's expectations. She had also charmed Charlie, who would proudly explain to a friend that she really *wanted* to be a Kushner. They were the close family she had never had.

So, at Trump National Golf Club, in Bedminster, New Jersey, in front of an eclectic mix of high-powered media figures, Hollywood celebrities, New York socialites, politicians, and a vast tranche of real estate people, Charlie raved about what a fantastic addition to his family Ivanka would make. Multiple sources said Charlie's speech at the wedding dinner was memorably, startlingly emotional.

Then Donald Trump got up to speak. He "didn't seem as emotionally involved," said one guest, being charitable. Another described his toast as "lame and embarrassing. . . . He gets up and says, 'Ivanka's great, and Jared's great, and they're great together, so let me give a toast,'" said this person. "I'm like, is that all you've got?"

Trump was said to be discombobulated by the enormity of what his daughter had done. Trump, a Presbyterian, who strikes no one as particularly religious, was baffled by his daughter's conversion. When his future political aide Sam Nunberg later mentioned that he was a member of the synagogue where Ivanka had converted, Trump was displeased. "Why should my daughter convert to marry anyone?" he asked. He also told an associate that he thought Charlie was "stupid" to have been caught by the feds. "He really looked down on that," said this person. (Ivanka's wedding party was also a "shock" to her father, according to a friend of Trump's. Women were given shawls when they arrived, and Ivanka's dress covered her shoulders in keeping with conservative Jewish tradition. The sexes were asked to dance separately several times that night.)

Trump liked Jared, but among friends would openly say things like, "Why couldn't she have married Tom Brady? Have you seen how far he throws a football?" In front of Trump Organization colleagues, he joked to Robert Kraft, who owns the New England Patriots (and therefore pays Brady's enormous salary): "Jared is half the size of Tom Brady's forearm."

Jared seemed to also have some doubts about his new father-in-law. He would occasionally poke fun at Trump's more extreme behavior. A real estate executive who dealt with Jared recalled, "Jared would talk about his father-in-law like he's one-of-a-kind. You know, roll his eyes."

But Jared discovered that there was much to learn from Donald Trump. A former Kushner Companies employee remembered that Jared used to talk admiringly about how Trump rounded up the numbers in his marketing material—and said the Kushners should do the same. "If you have one hundred million feet, you tell them two hundred million feet, because no one will ever check," remembered this person. The Kushners recently said their "reach consists of up to 20,000 multifamily apartments"—but as *Bloomberg* points out, that number includes properties in which Kushner Companies have only a marginal share.

The newlyweds worked hard to perfect the image, increasingly displayed on Ivanka's Instagram account, of a young family mastering the work-life balance. It was an image that matched Ivanka's brand as a successful working woman, one who had started her own fine jewelry line in 2007 (it folded in 2017) and would launch a fashion brand in 2012 (it folded in 2018). Jared told a colleague he was proud of how hard his wife worked, especially during her pregnancies. The couple had three children in fairly quick succession—Arabella in 2011, Joseph in 2013, and Theodore in 2016—and Jared's view of parental leave seemed to evolve. Initially, he told that same colleague he was amazed that, within days of giving birth to Arabella, Ivanka was down in Miami, closing a deal on the Doral Golf Resort and Spa for the Trump Organization. "She feels she has to prove herself to her father," he said, clearly both surprised and impressed. But after Joseph was born, Jared was more blasé—and clueless. According to that same colleague, he opined at an *Observer* event that he could not understand why people took so much time off around pregnancies. "After all, there are so many people helping."

The couple first lived in Jared's duplex on Astor Place, then moved to a Trump building on Park Avenue and Fifty-ninth Street. They liked to entertain, and still do. Friends like Michael Ovitz and Jimmy Choo cofounder Tamara Mellon, to whom Ovitz would later get engaged, would be invited for Shabbat dinner, where they were impressed that Ivanka cooked the meal herself. Mostly, in the early days of their marriage, their social group consisted of fellow silver-spooners (Rob Speyer, Jamie Johnson, David Lauren), or the older moguls they aspired to be like. It was a very insular and often smug world. At one Astor Place dinner party, Richard Mack found himself sitting next to Blake Lively. Mack is serious-minded; he had absolutely no idea who the *Gossip Girl* actress was. But he did remember that at one point in the conversation, Ivanka was adamant that "libertarian" and "liberal" were the same thing, and would not be dissuaded. When Mack suggested they look it up, she said, "I'll take that under advisement."

It was felt both at the offices of the *Observer* and at 666 Fifth Avenue that the couple was well-mannered and more self-controlled than either of their volatile fathers, but beneath the polish was a toxic mix of arrogance and ignorance. Elizabeth Spiers, a former *Observer* editor, noticed during a visit to Jared and Ivanka's apartment that there was not a book in sight and that the pair had zero intellectual curiosity. (Others dispute that "no books" claim: they recall "a few art books"—or "decorator-curated books.")

Jared once complained to Spiers about an *Observer* story concerning the move of author Martin Amis from London to Brooklyn, then an emerging hub for creative types. Even though the story garnered a huge following online, Jared had a problem with it. "Nobody knows who this Martin Amis guy is," he told Spiers. "Nobody reads novels." To which Spiers replied, "No, *you* don't read novels."

Spiers and Jared clashed over a long list of editorial issues that she felt exposed Jared's shortcomings as both a publisher and a person. She had been hired in 2011 because she came from the world of digital media. Jared thought that she might be the person to transform the *Observer* staff's analog way of thinking and possibly even make the paper profitable. The two hashed out a business plan, and under Spiers's direction, the paper did turn a profit. In return, she expected a promised investment of resources into the newsroom—which never came.

Where to begin describing the frustrations Spiers felt with her new boss? First, there was the way Jared viewed journalists. Unlike his mentor, Rupert Murdoch, Jared seemed not to understand them. And he certainly did not respect them. "He'd be condescending to them and he didn't understand why anybody would go into journalism," said Spiers. "He was like, 'Why are these idiots taking these low-paying jobs when they could work in commercial real estate and make a ton of money?' He did not understand public service at all."

Second, apart from being pro-Israel, Jared had no ideology that his editors could discern, and little editorial vision. "When I first took the job, he wrote this kind of manifesto about what the *Observer* should be about. It was, like, four pages long, and two of them were about Israel. I thought that was bizarre," Spiers said. "*The New York Observer* had traditionally been about New York."

Third, he had no interest in good writing. It seemed to Spiers that what he wanted—or rather, what he and Charlie wanted—was a vehicle through which the Kushners could flex their power. This meant running hit pieces on people who'd upset them and glowing articles on those they wanted to win over.

When new allegations surfaced in 2011 about the News Corp phone hacking scandal, which had first been reported in the mid-2000s (it involved journalists hacking into phones of subjects of news stories), Spiers said Jared made sure the paper's editorial page defended Murdoch, the News Corp executive chairman whom Jared has said he considers his "idol." But when it came to the paper's news coverage of the scandal, which was far less fawning than the editorials, Jared "was pissed," said Spiers, who had not given him a heads-up, figuring he'd have killed the articles.

She made weekly visits to the 666 Fifth offices, largely to keep Jared out of the newsroom's bullpen, where he was not welcome. Charlie refused to shake her hand when she first met him. "He referred to her as a 'bitch' behind her back," remembered a Kushner family friend.

Jared's temper occasionally bubbled over when on the phone with Spiers, but mostly he avoided confrontation. Instead they'd argue with curt emails. Or he'd just lie—which Spiers viewed as typical of the industry he was in. "You have a lot of people with mediocre skill sets and intellects who advance in that industry, just because it is so small and incestuous. And they believe everybody else outside of that industry also behaves that way."

Spiers quit in 2012 because she believed Jared was not committed to properly funding the paper. Her decision came after she and a colleague went over budgets with Jared at his apartment. Because it was a Friday, they had to work on printouts from Microsoft Excel, rather than on a computer, because observant Jews are prohibited from operating electrical devices on Shabbat. (Spiers felt Jared was flexible when it came to "what he does and doesn't do on Fridays"—a criticism that would be raised again and again in the Jewish press after he and Ivanka went to Washington. "He'll be really observant, but then, of course, if it gets in the way of social climbing, he discards it," Spiers said.)

She felt that the *Observer* was not really that important to him as a business. (He would later tell me that there were "not enough zeros" for it to hold his attention.) That Friday, as they looked at the Excel spreadsheets, she recalled, they had a twenty-minute debate over whether she could give a reporter a two-thousand-dollar raise. The conversation went nowhere. "Finally, I was just like, 'Take it out of my salary,'" Spiers said.

She suggested at one point that she and a colleague find a way to buy the paper from Jared, but despite his disinterest in the business, he was "offended" by this proposal. What mattered were appearances. Selling the *Observer* would be embarrassing, he told a Kushner Companies employee.

It wasn't just his journalists who found Jared difficult to work with. When he did show up at 666 Fifth, some colleagues there found him unbearable. Unlike his father, with whom he now co-chaired the weekly Tuesday meetings, he wasn't that interested in real estate. Also unlike his father, he didn't bother with details. When people asked him for cold numbers of what, for example, their leasing figures were, he referred them to someone else. He was an imperious delegator. He told the head of leasing on a project in DUMBO, Brooklyn: "If I had your job, I'd be so much better at it."

The Tuesday meetings again became the "Tuesday beatings," as Jared and Charlie frequently blamed anyone not considered "family" for decisions *they* had made. "It literally can never be the fault of anybody whose last name is Kushner, no matter how stupid the decision was . . . because frankly, all of the decisions [were] theirs . . . and this is why the Tuesday morning meetings were terrible," remembered a former employee, whose view was endorsed by two others. "It was just a fight to throw colleagues under the bus."

According to multiple sources, Jared was doggedly unrealistic about some projects, such as the asking price for luxury penthouses developed at the top of the Puck Building in 2011. Two of the properties were still listed as available seven years later. The asking price for the penthouses was well above the market price for that location, but Jared would not budge. Someone close to the project said he seemed to have a "reality distortion field," a *Star Trek* term that people also applied to Apple cofounder Steve Jobs to describe how he would use charisma and persistence to ignore the truth and convince people, including himself, to believe what he needed them to believe at that moment.

This attitude was partly ascribed within the firm to Jared's cloistered life. "He had zero awareness that he was born on third base," said one former colleague. The firm had around six hundred employees, and some would share unflattering stories about him: it was whispered that Jared's summer internship at Goldman Sachs had been deeply unimpressive and that he had not put in the hours. "I think he thinks it's all sort of this weird game and [he doesn't] understand that at the end of the day, people's jobs are an important part of their lives," said one former Kushner Companies employee.

On Jared's office walls at 666 Fifth, along with a photograph of John F. Kennedy, was a frame containing the first page of the Charles Dickens novel *A Tale of Two Cities*, which famously begins, "It was the best of times, it was the worst of times." Jared once told a reporter he bought it because he so loved the phrase. But when a different visitor asked what he thought of the novel, a classic set during the French Revolution, Jared was dismissive. "I haven't read it."

That superficiality extended to his approach to the real estate business. He would relationship-build while everyone else dug in to facts and contracts. He had a lot of meals with high-profile people. His friends included NBA Commissioner Adam Silver and former New York City Schools Chancellor Joel Klein. Colleagues thought, as they watched the clock tick on and his desk sat empty, that his networking might be very helpful to his brand—but it did zero for Kushner Companies' bottom line. Yet he spent an inordinate amount of time helping, as he saw it, the real estate concerns of his powerful new friends. Another way to label this activity, according to an industry associate, was "interference."

In 2016, I reported for *Esquire* that Jared did a voluntary analysis in 2015 for Sir Martin Sorrell, founder of WPP, the advertising and PR giant. Jared concluded that WPP wasn't using its office space effectively. When an office lease for J. Walter Thompson, a WPP company, was coming due, Jared thought he had the right new location for the firm and initiated conversations on its behalf. But without his knowledge, the real estate team at WPP had already renewed JWT's lease at 237 Park Avenue. Jared was livid, viewing the move as rude and boneheaded. He told WPP's head of real estate, "You're the stupidest person I've ever met in this business."

Jared's naivete about the world extended to how he and his family were covered in the press. PR people were excoriated for articles that were not sufficiently hagiographic—or that referenced Charlie's ugly past. The company burned through six publicity firms in about six years, because Jared and his father demanded the impossible of their publicists. They wanted the media to take dictation, and they went berserk if they didn't get what they wanted. Plus, as it looked like a default was imminent on 666 Fifth and as lenders angrily closed in, the Kushners' corporate posture would become increasingly defensive. Recalled one insider, "Every day felt like a fire fight. It was more and more crisis PR."

CHAPTER SEVEN

"They Are Like Robots"

*"Jared is as sinister as Donald Trump is. . . . He's not a pussycat,
although he appears very pasty, well dressed, well put together, and
always saying the right thing, doing the right thing. He'd be tough, too."*
—A BUSINESS ASSOCIATE OF JARED KUSHNER

In early 2010, LNR Partners, a special servicer that manages troubled commercial real estate loans, stepped in on behalf of the lenders on 666 Fifth Avenue to figure out what could be salvaged from this financial disaster. Loans go to a special servicer only if they are in default or imminent danger of default. The lenders for 666 Fifth feared the Kushners were about to run through their reserve fund, and it was time to see whether there was some way, any way, to protect their money. LNR had a reputation for being tough on borrowers. By the summer of 2010, it was part-owned by Vornado Realty Trust, a public company that, at the time, had more than twenty billion dollars in assets. The company specialized in owning and running office and retail buildings. Almost from the moment Kushner Companies had acquired 666 Fifth, Vornado's wily chairman, Steve Roth, had been "hanging around the hoop," according to one observer. Roth wanted in, but on terms that made sense for his shareholders. LNR's role in the seemingly inevitable restructuring gave him the perfect opportunity.

Leading LNR's restructuring team was Justin Kennedy, the son of then–U.S. Supreme Court Associate Justice Anthony Kennedy, and Toby Cobb, the son of a former U.S. ambassador to Iceland. Kennedy approached the restructuring with the same general philosophy he espoused on other deals. "We do not want to do a foreclosure," he said to Jared. "We're here to make a deal, but it'll be a good deal for us. So, if you want to fight, just throw us the keys right now, because we're going to win."

There was a real risk the Kushners would be foreclosed on. It took two years of intense negotiations to avoid that, during which Charlie Kushner had to remain on the sidelines—per the terms of the loan. (He got around this by having Jared put him on speakerphone but tell the room it was his lawyer on the line.) It was left to Jared—with Charlie acting as puppeteer—to cut the best deal he could. During a vacation in Aspen, Ivanka and Jared bumped into Kennedy, and Ivanka made a point of charming him; she invited him to sit with them and told him how she'd always liked his wife. Would they like to come and stay at Mar-a-Lago? She told Kennedy, "You know Jared—he just wants to do the right thing."

But getting the Kushners to do the right thing was often tricky. As a first step, in early 2011, after many months of negotiations with LNR, Kushner Companies began selling off the rest of the retail space at the bottom of the building. The retail would eventually go for $1.057 billion. Charlie was furious about giving up any of 666 Fifth. "Over my dead body," he said to one person.

"Charlie's not a seller . . . Jared was working all sides and I think got in the middle of so many different situations, [and] not everything came out perfectly," explained someone who participated in the negotiations.

For the most part, Jared was quiet in the talks. "At the end of the day, I don't think he was the original thinker here," said one person at the table. But in early 2011, Jared went over the heads of the people Kushner Companies was tussling with in the day-to-day negotiations and called Bill Mack's son, Richard Mack. He asked him to take a write-down of his loan. He thought that if Mack agreed, other lenders might follow suit. But Mack dismissed the proposal out of hand. He told Jared that he had a fiduciary responsibility to his investors and he also felt the Kushners had mismanaged the building. He was polite, but Jared went berserk and began shouting at him, "I've been working my ass off!" The yelling, Mack felt, was wholly inappropriate. The bottom line was that Jared owed his lenders money. "I don't know who the hell you think you're talking to," Mack told him, and hung up.

In 2011, Jared got some help on 666 Fifth from his father-in-law. Donald Trump put him in touch with Tom Barrack, a Lebanese American financier whose investment firm, Colony Capital, raises significant amounts of money from the Middle East. Barrack had just set up a debt fund, so the timing was good. Without approaching any of the other lenders, which would have been normal procedure in such circumstances, Colony went right to Paramount Group and bought half of its debt. One lender remembered that Todd Sammann, Barrack's point man in the negotiations, was softer on Jared than the other lenders were.

Around June, Kushner Companies negotiated to sell the air rights for the nearby Baccarat Hotel and Residences, which Barry Sternlicht's Starwood was developing. Roth's charismatic right hand, Vornado CEO Mike Fascitelli, was friends with Sternlicht, and he helped Jared talk to Sternlicht and Barrack. "Jared did an amazing job with older [and important] people, sucking up and making them feel [good]," he has said. "Myself, Tom, Barry."

But other Vornado executives—ones who were less powerful—found Jared condescending and disrespectful. David Greenbaum, the president of the New York division, and Wendy Silverstein, then an executive vice president, got into shouting matches with him over deal points and management issues. At one point, according to a colleague familiar with the exchange, Greenbaum, who had dealt with Ivanka on a dispute her father had with Vornado, said in an internal meeting: "It would be so much better if we could deal with Ivanka." Someone who worked for Starwood was stunned to be threatened by Jared, who had allegedly said, "I will kill you." He probably did not mean it, but Sternlicht was appalled when he heard about it.

Despite Jared's histrionics, the adults in the negotiations made progress. In December 2011, Vornado announced it had bought 49.5 percent of the thirty-nine office floors at 666 Fifth. And then, in 2012, it bought Kushner Companies, the Carlyle Group, and Crown Acquisitions out of their jointly owned, very valuable retail section at the base of 666 Fifth. The office section of 666 Fifth now was valued at $820 million—well short of the $1.8 billion the Kushners paid. But, at least, by the end of 2012 the pressure on the Kushners was eased—or, more accurately, postponed. The $1.2 billion mortgage from when the Kushners purchased the building was deferred until February 2019.

The new problem for Charlie was that he was now chained to Roth, and the two men hated each other. They had partnered on the Monmouth Mall in New Jersey in 2002—and there had been friction. It was "Whose dick is bigger?" said someone who knows both of them well. It must have also galled Charlie that the Vornado folks were perceived to be the "adults" in the room at 666 Fifth. Now, according to the partnership agreement, Vornado and the Kushners each had a veto right on every management decision at the building for the next fifteen years. Roth's plan seemed obvious: wait for the Kushners to implode and take full ownership of the tower. It didn't help relations between the two sides that Fascitelli left Vornado in 2013. Jared and Charlie found Fascitelli much easier to deal with than Roth.

In September 2015, the New York Post revealed Kushner Companies' audacious plan: extend the tower to nearly triple its height and fill it with a retail mall, a hotel, and residences. The company had sought out several leading architects and chosen renderings by the Pritzker Prize–winning British architect Zaha Hadid. Roth initially encouraged the idea, according to someone involved in the planning, but came to consider it wildly impractical. (There are no schools nearby, making condos less attractive to families.) Roth openly opined, "It would be worth a lot more if it was just dirt." The partners were at a stalemate, and the building slowly emptied as tenants moved out and were not replaced.

Meanwhile, Jared started occupying himself with new projects, ones for which he could claim ownership. There was a mix of commercial and residential projects in Brooklyn and elsewhere that garnered buzz. Josh Kushner, now a venture capitalist, had told his older brother that young tech start-ups wanted cheap, cool, communal spaces in hip neighborhoods, so Jared looked to develop projects in booming areas like Brooklyn's DUMBO neighborhood. "Jared, I think, gets a lot of his self-confidence from the fact that he feels like, at a very young age, he learned under fire, and did all these workouts and restructurings, and then came out of that with this great ambition and started buying the shit out of everything, and the timing was good," said a friend and business associate.

Mack, the lender with whom Jared clashed, viewed his spending spree less kindly. "There's a level of entitlement that Charlie possessed and passed on to Jared, which is that the rules don't apply," he told a colleague. "They think they can push people around. They failed to learn the lessons from [their restructuring]. What they learned was, 'Yeah, that wasn't so bad.'"

Soon after the restructuring talks, Kushner attempted to use the *Observer* as a bully pulpit—which was what both father and son told a friend they thought it should be. Kushner asked Elizabeth Spiers, the *Observer* editor, to look into a damning story about Richard Mack. Spiers gave the assignment to Dan Geiger, a beat reporter at the *Commercial Observer*. Kushner called Geiger and complained that Mack was a "bad fiduciary" who carelessly risked his investors' money on suspect deals. Geiger called everyone he could think of and found nothing to support Kushner's claims. He sent Kushner a memo outlining exactly whom he had phoned and what the upshot was. A week or two later, Kushner called Geiger, and, as if he had never received the memo, told him: "There's a guy named Richard Mack, and we've got to get this guy." Geiger was bewildered—and uneasy. He went to Spiers, who, he said, recognized Kushner's obsession as a "powder keg." Kushner insisted that it was a reporting problem. To humor him, Spiers assigned a second reporter, who also got nowhere. And then, at Kushner's insistence, she turned to a third reporter: me. I didn't even work for the *Observer*, and I had no interest in looking into it, having never heard of Mack. I said no. The story never ran, but from around that time, Mack fell off the *Commercial Observer*'s Power 100 list. He told his employees not to worry.

Spiers's default position was to protect her reporters from Kushner's interference. She noticed he tried to kill stories out of blatant self-interest. What she did not know was that he had asked a software developer, Austin Smith, to go behind her back and delete published items Kushner found offensive. Kushner instructed Smith to delete four articles from the website. Three involved the New York City landlord Vantage Properties and its founder, Neil Rubler; the fourth was about a real estate purchase by Jared's friend—and future NBA commissioner—Adam Silver.

Spiers gave notice in the summer of 2012. The paper's executive editor, Aaron Gell, briefly succeeded her. Charlie Kushner's biographer, Ken Kurson, was installed as editor in early 2013. Inside 666 Fifth, both Jared and Charlie talked openly about their relief at his appointment. "Finally, we get to write what we want," Charlie said. When people got in the way of the Kushners' plans, Jared was overheard saying to a colleague: "Tell them that if they don't do what we want, we'll write a negative article about them in the *Observer*." Multiple people overheard Charlie and Jared boasting about possible hit pieces on the Wilf family and Michael Stern, both rival developers.

After 2012, the relationship between father and son evolved ever so slightly. While no one close to them doubted that all decisions ultimately lay with Charlie (Jared continued to put him, and others, on speakerphone without announcing it), they had a bad cop, good cop routine they used to their advantage. Jared would tell potential partners it would be in their interest to go along with a deal the way he wanted it, because otherwise, "My father is crazy and will blow it up." He was the cool, calm one, the voice of reason his father listened to. Or so it seemed.

Jared's carefully cultivated image as the soft-spoken, well-mannered young man who'd thwarted his father's recklessness was a useful marketing tool. "People who didn't want to be seen with Charlie were happy to be seen with Jared. The Jared that he and Ivanka and Charlie created was a star. People want to be with the stars," observed Alan Hammer. Andrew Silow-Carroll, the editor of *The Jewish Telegraphic Agency*, a news outlet that had initially been caught between the two sides of the Charlie/Murray Kushner war, felt that the perception of the family changed dramatically in the New Jersey Jewish community. "For a long time, Jared did a lot to restore the family name," Silow-Carroll said. "He was a financial success. He helped grow the business. He stayed out of scandal. He married a lovely young woman who converted to Judaism, so I have the feeling in the community people felt Jared went a long way to rehabilitating the family reputation."

Many people who came in and out of Kushner Companies' offices at 666 Fifth could not help but remark on the tightness and apparent piety of the Kushner family. At *Observer* events, all of them would show up— Charlie, Seryl, Jared, Nicole, Dara, and Josh. They kissed each other warmly every time they saw each other, as if they hadn't been together in years. One person said their closeness spooked him. "They still vacation together. They eat together, they all office together. They're all in meetings together. . . . They are like robots, these kids," said this same person. "They're well-dressed. A hair's not out of place. You never see Jared sniffling. Never sick. Never see him down. It's strange."

Josh, however, never quite fit into the homogenous world of his family. Out of respect for his mother, the youngest Kushner tried to remain an observant Jew—but he did not find it easy. He once broke his wrist playing basketball on Shabbat and was reprimanded by his parents: "This is what you get." A former colleague observed that Josh would "sneak" onto his electronic devices to answer emails on Friday night and Saturday. He dealt with the embarrassment of his father's imprisonment in a direct and easy manner. He once told a colleague casually: "If you read about it, I'm happy to give you more context."

Josh is perceived to be more easygoing than his brother, not so pent-up or angry about the past. "People like dealing with him," one of his mentors told me. Someone who has dealt with both brothers explained the difference between them: "Jared could be a little bit of a bully. . . . Josh is generally more open-minded to other points of view, particularly when you make a good argument for it, whereas I think Jared can be very, very narrow-minded."

Jared's mind-set was made quite apparent when, in 2012, Josh started dating the Victoria's Secret model Karlie Kloss. When the *Observer* editor Aaron Gell mentioned it to Jared and offered his congratulations, "Jared said something like, 'Don't worry. The family is going to take care of that. We're not very happy about him dating a shiksa. We're hoping he'll move on.' He also said, 'She's not that smart,' which I don't think is true."

Few who know him doubt Josh's intelligence. While still an undergraduate at Harvard, he cofounded Vostu, a briefly profitable social gaming company. Then, while studying at Harvard Business School, he founded an early-stage venture capital firm, Thrive Capital. Joel Cutler, a mentor and fellow venture capitalist based in the Boston area, introduced him to Andrew Golden, who runs PRINCO, the Princeton Endowment fund. PRINCO invested in Thrive, and it expanded from there. Josh hired three partners, Chris Paik, Jared Weinstein, and Will Gaybrick; each had skill sets that complemented the others'. The money snowballed. Yale, Duke, Harvard, the Ford Foundation, and the Wellcome Trust all invested in the company. And Thrive got lucky. In April 2012, it joined a few other firms in a fifty-million-dollar funding round for Instagram. A few days later, Facebook purchased Instagram for one billion dollars, which doubled the value of Thrive's investment. The company's other investments include Warby Parker, Artsy, Spotify, Zola, Kickstarter, GitHub, and ClassPass.

As of October 2018, Thrive had $2.3 billion under management. "This is big-boy-type stuff," said Jon Winkelried, one of Josh's mentors and co-chief executive of TPG, one of the world's largest private equity firms. The speed of Josh's success was much discussed among Charlie's friends. "I had heard when Josh started that he was going to make more money than everybody," said Hammer.

For a time, Charlie kept an office open for Josh at 666 Fifth. The elder Kushner would sometimes eye it forlornly, but it remained empty as Josh excelled. It must have comforted Charlie a bit that ultimately Thrive took offices in the Puck Building, so Josh was at least in a Kushner building. George Gellert eventually took over the empty office at 666 Fifth that had been kept open for Josh.

Jared was intrigued by his brother's success. The companies Josh invested in were helmed by some of the most creative minds in the tech industry: Daniel Ek of Spotify, Kevin Systrom of Instagram, and Neil Blumenthal and Dave Gilboa of Warby Parker. In Thrive's early days, Jared would show up once or twice a month at the Puck Building and sometimes sit in on the firm's Monday meetings—which began to grate on some of the partners. They did not like him "swanning in and swanning out," a former colleague told me. His visits gradually became less frequent.

In 2012, Josh approached Mario Schlosser, a fast-talking German-born engineer who was a Vostu cofounder. Schlosser, who had been spending most of his time in Brazil, needed to move back to the U.S. full-time (his wife, a researcher at Columbia University, was pregnant with their first child). Josh said he wanted to start a health insurance company and wanted Schlosser to build it with him. The German was surprised, but Josh explained that he had gone to the hospital for a sprained ankle and found the bill from his insurance company incomprehensible. He wanted to make health care consumer-friendly. Schlosser signed on. Before long, they had landed on the concept: an insurance provider for the internet age that would be designed for the day when individuals, not employers, were responsible for purchasing plans. It would be called Oscar Health, after Josh's great-grandfather.

The timing was impeccable. Schlosser would later say that the team was able to make the company work because of the Affordable Care Act, since the health care landscape had been monopolized by large insurers. Soon after the Supreme Court upheld the central provisions of the Affordable Care Act, in the summer of 2012, Schlosser and Josh were ready to pitch their idea to investors. Brian Singerman, a partner in the San Francisco-based venture capital firm Founders Fund, got interested in the company after Michael Ovitz sent him an email saying, "Trust me on this one." Oscar launched in late 2013.

The following year, Josh, Jared, and Ryan Williams, a young associate from Blackstone, cofounded Cadre, a real-estate-investment technology platform. By 2016, Mike Fascitelli was on its investment committee (his son works there), and one of their investors was Fascitelli's former employer Goldman Sachs.

Jared and Josh talked every day back then. While Thrive soared, someone who had worked in accounting at Kushner Companies started to ask questions about an entity that had appeared in the financials: BFPS. BFPS, this person was told, stands for Brothers First, Partners Second. It may be a vehicle for an arrangement Jared had talked about. The way he described the arrangement, in detail, to a former business associate, was that each brother gives 50 percent of his profits to the other, so as to avoid disagreements. If such an arrangement existed, it is possible that it changed when Jared went into the White House. However, a BFPS Ventures is listed on Jared's financial disclosure forms. (A spokesman for Josh said there is no such arrangement and this is "completely and utterly untrue.") Charlie once told a confidant that it would make life easier for him if his sons "had a sharing arrangement." He thought it would prevent friction between the brothers. No one foresaw that it might become the antithesis of that: a critical vehicle for potential ethics violations.

CHAPTER EIGHT

A Most Convenient Candidate

"Take everything you've learned and throw it out the window."
—JARED KUSHNER TO JASON MILLER UPON MILLER'S
JOINING THE TRUMP CAMPAIGN

Ivanka Trump was critical in promoting her husband as the smoother, softer counterpart to his father's volatility. The couple seemed like mirror images of each other. They could both work a room, ask after people's children, talk without notes, occasionally fake a sense of humor. People in real estate who didn't know her well thought she was "impressive." Very smart, very polished. And unlike her husband, she seemed to have a ready command of figures and a detailed, working knowledge of all the properties she was involved in.

She also seemed to be more on top of the personal stuff. One person who knew the couple felt she was in charge of their marriage. "He doesn't have a thought she didn't give him," this person joked. Ivanka was always giving Jared input, including on public relations. At least one publicist said that Ivanka would weigh in on the smallest of details, things that would not occur to most people. For example, Ivanka told the publicist, Jared should not turn down interviews with the words "Jared Kushner declined to comment," instead choosing some more elegant way of saying the same thing. "I just felt like I was being handled in such an icky way," said the publicist.

The couple's professional circles overlapped, obviously. Ivanka had been critical in smoothing over tricky talks in the late 2000s when Vornado became entangled in a legal tiff with Donald Trump. It was an ironic twist, given that Steve Roth would regularly invite Trump to play golf during the suit. Early on in the litigation, Trump phoned Mike Fascitelli, saying, "I love you, I like Steve, and I have to sue you." The backstory: a Chinese group bought Trump out of a parcel of land on Manhattan's West Side in 1994 and agreed to share some of the future profits with him. When the group sold the land in 2005, Trump sued the Chinese, claiming they sold it too cheaply. Complicating matters was that the Chinese used the proceeds of that sale to purchase two buildings: one in Manhattan and one in San Francisco. During the litigation, the Chinese partners sold their stakes in those buildings to Vornado, which is why Trump felt he also had to sue the firm. Roth and Trump—and Trump and Fascitelli—continued to socialize while the lawyers tried to settle. Trump teased Roth at one point on the phone, "I don't need you, Steve. I'm a TV star," referring to his starring role in NBC's *The Apprentice.* "They were friends and contentious at the same time," recalled a former Vornado executive. Ivanka was the one who had to represent her father's position in the negotiations. "Ivanka was wonderfully diplomatic through the entire process," the former executive said.

But there was another side Ivanka hid from public view. No one on the outside knew, for example, that in discussions with the West Coast–based real estate firm CIM Group, which wanted to kill the licensing deal with the Trump Organization at the Trump SoHo after taking control of the property in 2014, she would lose the softness in her voice and talk coldly and menacingly, according to someone who was told about the conversations. "Ivanka could be very tough and she can come after you," said someone who has seen her in meetings.

Ivanka seemed to control the marital relationship, but she also played the role of devoted, traditional Orthodox wife. For Kushner's thirty-fifth birthday, she put together a dinner at the top of the Gramercy Park Hotel for dozens of guests, including Hugh Jackman, Joel Klein, Kevin Ryan, Mike Fascitelli, and Michael Ovitz. One guest joked that the median age was seventy: "It wasn't a fun party." Ivanka also spent many weekends in New Jersey with Charlie and Seryl Kushner, though not as many as the couple spent in Bedminster at the Trump National Golf Club.

In June 2015, Ivanka's father announced he was running for president. The Trump campaign afforded the couple networking opportunities that Jared and his father were swift to take advantage of. They'd been courting Sheikh Hamad bin Jassim bin Jaber Al Thani (HBJ), the former prime minister of Qatar, worth a reported $1.2 billion. They finally secured his interest once Trump's presidential run gained momentum. HBJ is known to be a shrewd investor but is up for the occasional vanity project. His circle of advisers knows he will sometimes buy a very prestigious building, even if the economics don't make much sense. His ultimate dream is to buy the George V hotel in Paris, said someone who knows him well. Jared's plan for a luxury mall with condos at 666 Fifth Avenue excited HBJ. "Jared had convinced them that this was going to be the first luxury shopping mall on Fifth Avenue," said someone in the talks. "The hotel was gonna be *this*, and the retail *that*, and the condos were gonna sell at seven thousand or eight thousand dollars a foot, or whatever the hell it was. The stuff was all stratospheric. . . ."

HBJ initially said he would put in five hundred million dollars—with the proviso that someone matched that. (The sheikh thought the perfect fit would be François Pinault, the French luxury goods mogul, who was approached. Pinault's competitor Bernard Arnault also reportedly listened to a pitch from the Kushners.) A term sheet was drawn up that stipulated the Kushners would have to find somebody at the same level as HBJ. "No one wants to look like a schmuck for doing something outsized without having a legitimizing, validating, triangulating sort of participant, right?" said one of HBJ's advisers.

HBJ's enthusiasm for the project started to wane when, in the fall of 2016, he heard the Kushners were thinking of bringing in a Chinese firm, Anbang, as a partner. He lessened his offer to $250 million. The Qataris had hoped for a Western partner to go in with them on 666 Fifth, said someone familiar with HBJ's thinking. "They wanted a white man to do [it]," said this person. Moreover, Anbang, a giant insurance company that had recently bought the Waldorf Astoria, had a suspect reputation. It was unclear who owned the company, and it had grown from a minor player to China's eighth-largest insurance company over the course of a single year.

HBJ grew more leery of doing a deal with the Kushners the tighter the presidential election got. "If [Trump] wins, you don't want to be anywhere near this thing," his adviser warned him. The optics would be horrible if HBJ got near a situation with a whiff of corruption, and so it made sense to avoid pursuing a deal with a company that could have ties to a U.S. president.

From the beginning of the Trump campaign, Charlie brushed aside the possibility of a Trump victory with a standard joke. "I've already told Donald I will not be running as his VP," was his line at meetings. But he and Seryl donated one hundred thousand dollars to a super PAC supporting Trump. In the summer of 2015, he and Seryl hosted an event for Trump at their house on the Jersey Shore, which was viewed by Kushner friends as mere lip service. Said one family friend, "What's a hundred thousand dollars? What's whatever he paid for the party? . . . Nothing. What's the benefit of Donald owing him a favor? It's like Avi Lebor once said: 'Never miss a shiva call, because that's when you get the most business done.'" Charlie's true political loyalty, a former colleague felt, was to Bill and Hillary Clinton. Charlie would say, wistfully, "Hillary used to call me." He would note fondly that, unlike Senator Chuck Schumer, Clinton had not returned or given away his donations when he was indicted.

In the early days of the Trump campaign, Kushner was mostly somewhere else, but as Candidate Trump gained traction, all of a sudden, he was by his father-in-law's side at rallies, on the plane, and at Trump Tower meetings. He'd later say that a rally in November 2015 in Springfield, Illinois, was a turning point for him. There, he was introduced to a crowd whose point of view he'd never heard or considered, and he was struck by it. "You don't understand what America is or what American people think," he later told a friend, apparently omitting any reflection on the cloistered world he had inhabited for so long.

Trump turned to him for help with his March 2016 speech to the American Israel Public Affairs Committee. (Kushner got help from Israeli Ambassador to the U.S. Ron Dermer and *Observer* editor Ken Kurson, who did not disclose his involvement. When Kurson's role in the speech emerged two weeks later, the *Observer*'s senior politics editor was forced to issue a statement saying that Kurson would no longer advise the campaign.) In April, Rupert Murdoch's *New York Post* endorsed Trump for the New York Republican primary, which friends believed Kushner helped bring about. Though he is widely considered a conservative, Murdoch had to be persuaded to take Trump seriously.

Kushner and Ivanka's friends and business associates were initially understanding of their loyalty to Trump during the campaign. Prominent broker Mary Ann Tighe relayed Ivanka's thoughts, as told to Tighe by Kushner, to *The Real Deal*: "[My father's] whole life has been a dream come true. If this is his dream, we have to back him and believe in his dream." But as Trump's rhetoric grew more and more divisive, and he kept pushing the notion that a wall should be built at the U.S.-Mexico border to keep Americans safe, the New York real estate community, which is largely Jewish, was aghast. One guest at Kushner's thirty-fifth-birthday party told me, "We're Jews. . . . It's just as easy to say the Muslims can't come to the United States because they're gonna blow you up and the Mexicans are gonna rape you [as it is to say] the Jews are gonna steal all your money. And so, we're not on the side of this sort of craziness, because we're always the one being blamed for everything." Trump, who has called a former female colleague "a fat elephant" and has allegedly used the N-word, has also been accused of condoning anti-Semitism. Multiple members of Trump's social circle noted his reluctant acceptance of Ivanka's conversion.

No one thought Kushner or Ivanka believed in Trump's populist platform. "The two of them see this as a networking opportunity," said a close associate.

Because Kushner and Ivanka only fully immersed themselves in Trump's campaign once he became the presumptive Republican nominee in May 2016, they had to push to assert themselves with the campaign staff. Thanks to Ivanka's persistent lobbying, Kushner quickly got control of the campaign's budget, but he did not have as much authority as he would have liked. The main obstacle was Trump's campaign chief, Corey Lewandowski, a forty-two-year-old political operative with Machiavellian instincts and, as one RNC operative described it, a "huge chip on his shoulder." A failed political candidate from Lowell, Massachusetts, who had once been arrested for carrying a gun into a building on Capitol Hill tucked in his laundry bag, Lewandowski almost certainly would not have been any of the other Republican candidates' first choice for campaign chief. But Trump adored him. "He's like the son he never had," said someone on the Trump campaign. "Corey is amoral. He's the closest thing Trump can get to Roy Cohn [Trump's ruthless mentor], without the law school degree. He's cunning. He's crafty. He comes up with the kind of cunning shit that Trump loves. And he's cheap."

Even when, in March 2016, Lewandowski was seen on videotape manhandling *Breitbart* reporter Michelle Fields at a campaign event in Florida, Trump stood by him. (He was charged with battery, but the charge was later dropped.) Trump's three eldest children—and Kushner—hated Lewandowski, who, they believed, was encroaching on their territory. Lewandowski would tell people that Trump called him "my Corey" or "my kid" in private.

Enter Tom Barrack, who was becoming a mentor of Kushner's—and not without self-interest. (Barrack's investment firm, Colony Capital, was known to have been struggling ever since oil prices fell in 2014. But his numerous contacts in the Middle East would happily find ways to reward him if he got them access to the U.S. president.) Barrack suggested to Kushner and Ivanka that the campaign supplement Lewandowski with an old political hand, Paul Manafort, who had the expertise to get them through a presidential convention. Barrack and Manafort had known each other for over three decades and were very close, according to a former Manafort colleague who knows both men well.

Everyone with D.C. political experience knew Manafort was sleazy, and he'd been out of U.S. politics for ten years because of his ties to foreign powers—he'd taken money from Ukrainian oligarchs, Russians, and, well, anyone who would pay him. He was not particular if that money "went through twenty-five foreign bank accounts" and, to boot, he violated the

Foreign Agents Registration Act (FARA), which requires people who lobby for foreign interests to register with the federal government. "He's never understood in his entire life that the implications of his relationships are enough to sink him," said the former colleague. Manafort's weakness had always been the champagne lifestyle—six-figure shopping sprees and an estate in the Hamptons. But Kushner and Ivanka had no political experience with which to judge Manafort's résumé. They wanted an experienced political manager to get Trump through the convention and to muzzle Lewandowski.

On May 19, Manafort was promoted to campaign chairman and chief strategist. Trump quickly regretted the appointment. Or so it seemed. He lit into Manafort one Friday evening upon discovering that Manafort had proposed that he and not Trump should go on the Sunday morning TV shows. In front of Lewandowski, Trump shouted at Manafort, insulting his appearance, including his coiffed hair and tailored suits. "He ripped his skull right off," remembered Lewandowski. Hours later, Kushner phoned Lewandowski and accused him of stirring up Trump's animosity. "You're not a team player," Kushner yelled. "This is not helpful . . . Paul wants to do the TV shows." From then on, Lewandowski sensed he was on borrowed time. Soon after this, Ivanka received evidence from former Trump campaign aide Sam Nunberg, who had gotten it from a reporter, that Lewandowski was trying to leak negative press on Kushner. Nunberg assumed she took it to her father.

In late May, a New York friend of Ivanka's, Janet Boris, brokered a meeting between Kushner and Ivanka and Rebekah Mercer. Rebekah's father, Robert Mercer, is a brilliant computer scientist who had cohelmed Renaissance Technologies, the ultrasuccessful, ultrasecretive hedge fund. He was also a stakeholder in Cambridge Analytica, a data analytics group in London whose proprietary psychographic modeling had been deployed by its parent company, Strategic Communications Laboratories (SCL), in elections in Argentina, Kenya, Ghana, and Indonesia—and was later used during the Brexit vote. (The Pentagon used SCL to conduct propaganda analysis in

Afghanistan.) The Mercers had become a powerful force among conservatives, not just because they were huge donors but also because they were the majority stakeholders in *Breitbart*, the right-leaning populist website run by Steve Bannon. Robert Mercer did not like Trump. He thought he was a "clown." But after Senator Ted Cruz dropped out of the Republican primary, Bannon told Mercer that Trump could win and could be the "agent of change" Bannon had been seeking for years to lead a populist revolution. Mercer instructed Bannon to help Trump. "I don't care, whatever the money is, whatever he needs, [give it to him]," Mercer said. "But I don't need to meet him."

Instead, Rebekah and Bannon went to Trump Tower to meet with Kushner and Ivanka. Lewandowski and Manafort were in the room, and pollster Kellyanne Conway, then serving as a Trump campaign adviser, came in late. When the young couple walked in, Bannon noted that Ivanka had a commanding, towering presence. She exuded power.

But when they all got down to business, Bannon quickly went from being impressed to being concerned. Mercer was a source of much-needed financing, and Kushner and Ivanka were both ignorant and disorganized. Worse, they were not inquisitive—they did not ask Rebekah one question. Bannon, who has spent a large chunk of his career raising money for media groups and a think tank he founded, was amazed. "They had no idea how to fund-raise," he would tell people, wondering idly what it was they were good at.

Bannon sensed that Lewandowski was distracted in the meeting and seemed to be stalling; Bannon later learned that Lewandowski knew the Trump children and Manafort wanted him gone and was trying to survive by continually presenting Trump with more potential donors, including the casino tycoon Sheldon Adelson, in the hope that this would make him indispensable. So, while Lewandowski wanted the Mercers' money, he also wanted a courting period. Rebekah told Kushner and Ivanka that she and her father wanted to run Trump's super PAC. But when Rebekah asked about where the campaign was financially, Kushner and Ivanka seemed, Bannon thought, to have no idea.

The meeting was salvaged by the unexpected appearance of Trump, who dazzled Rebekah. At one point, she jumped up, whipped out her phone, and asked people in the corridor outside to take a photo of her with Trump. Bannon later teased her that her behavior was "an embarrassment." Despite the teasing, Bannon was also impressed. If Trump had that effect on a New York City billionaire, imagine how well he would play in Kansas and Pennsylvania. He was excited.

The meeting ended inconclusively. "[Kushner and Ivanka] have no earthly idea how to close," Bannon thought to himself as he walked out and rode down the elevator with Kushner. Rebekah was prepared to unleash her family's resources, and yet she had received little attention from a campaign that was barely surviving. It was perplexing.

Afterward, Bannon and Kushner made small talk in the Trump lobby. Kushner said to him, "I've been meaning to talk to you about *Breitbart*." Bannon said he'd be delighted to chat, and for the next ten minutes they shot the breeze. Again, Bannon was left feeling depressed. He had loved *The New York Observer* in its heyday, but the more Kushner talked about the *Observer*, the more he realized Kushner knew little about media.

In June, Kushner reached out to Jason Miller, a dark-haired, soft-spoken Republican operative who had worked for the Cruz campaign. Miller and Kurson were close friends, so Miller wasn't *that* surprised to receive the call. Kushner, as was his habit, wanted someone he thought would be loyal to him. But Miller was apprehensive about signing on: "I don't want to get in the middle of Corey and Manafort," he told Kushner, referring to the well-known friction between the two political operatives. Kushner phoned him back the next day and told him: "Don't worry—that won't be a problem."

According to Lewandowski, around the time of Kushner's call to Miller, Kushner and the three eldest Trump children went to Trump and delivered an ultimatum. "It's Corey or us." According to Lewandowski, Trump phoned him three times on Father's Day, June 19, 2016. He told Lewandowski: "Corey, [Kushner and the children] hate me because they hate you." Lewandowski replied: "No, sir. They hate you all on your own, and I am just part of it." The next morning, Lewandowski took the 5 A.M. shuttle from Boston to New York and prepared as usual for the Monday "family" meeting at 9:30 A.M. But a few minutes before it started, he was asked to come into a conference room, where he was confronted by Trump Organization attorney Michael Cohen, Trump Organization Chief Operating Officer Matthew Calamari, and Don Jr. Cohen did most of the talking, with Don Jr. chiming in. Lewandowski said he was fired without any explanation. While the meeting was happening and before Lewandowski had left the building, Manafort put out a press release announcing the news.

So, on June 20, Manafort was now nominally the campaign chief, but everyone knew Kushner was the one with budgetary power. He had asked for, and received, his own pot of money—and the candidate's trust. Everyone knew Kushner was in charge.

CHAPTER NINE

Making New Friends

*"This guy, he's a silent killer . . . Trump, you get what you get.
Charlie Kushner, you get what you get. Jared, you're not
really sure what you get."*

—A KUSHNER BUSINESS ASSOCIATE

In May and June, the Trump campaign offices were visited a few times by Alexander Nix, who talked like one of the aristocrats on the TV series *Downton Abbey*. He was the CEO of Cambridge Analytica, the political data firm whose parent company SCL was based in London. Cambridge Analytica was owned by the Mercers. (Steve Bannon also had a piece.)

Nix, an Old Etonian who played polo, was a slick salesman, but his background was in financial services, not data analytics. He spoke a lot of incomprehensible jargon about "communications and behavioral research," and he was arrogant. But Jared liked him. "They struck up a bromance," according to an eyewitness.

Nix claimed Cambridge Analytica was a groundbreaking data analytics firm. Most political campaigns run highly sophisticated microtargeting efforts to locate voters; Nix promised his firm could do much more, claiming to be able to manipulate voter behavior through something called psychographic profiling. Cambridge Analytica had been enlisted by Ted Cruz's presidential campaign—the Mercers were among Cruz's chief financial supporters—and also by Dr. Ben Carson, another Republican hopeful who crashed early. Now that Cruz was out of the race, Nix was looking for a new source of income.

What Kushner did not know was that Cruz campaign senior staff had found Nix to be extraordinarily pushy and tiresome, and his predictive models to be, initially, suspiciously inaccurate. Chris Wilson, the Cruz campaign director of research, analytics, and digital strategy, thought Cambridge Analytica was a fraud. He suspected the firm did not own any proprietary data and that the company had acquired its data from Facebook. (A 2015 report in *The Guardian* noted that the SCL Group had based its data on research "spanning tens of millions of Facebook users, harvested largely without their permission.") Wilson also noticed the Cambridge Analytica models were rarely ready on time, and when they were tested in phone surveys, the models were often inaccurate.

At a Cruz campaign meeting in 2015 attended by Cruz, Nix had suggested that the National Rifle Association's database of members would be a valuable way to target donors. Wilson typed an emoji of rolling eyes next to the statement as he was taking notes, because it was such an obvious suggestion. He told people that he came away thinking, "Red flag, red flag, red flag." Regardless, the Cruz campaign wound up paying Cambridge Analytica more than three million dollars.

Nix approached Paul Manafort about working for the Trump campaign. Manafort, in turn, reached out to Brad Parscale, a web designer based in San Antonio, who had been one of Trump's first campaign hires. Parscale had worked for the Trumps for years and came cheap—he designed a presidential exploratory committee web page for fifteen hundred dollars. He was proud of his roots in rural Kansas, where his parents owned a restaurant. His influence in the campaign had grown considerably, partly because the staff was so lean. "I would show up to a meeting and somebody would go, 'This needs to get done,' and I would raise my hand, 'I'll do it,' and I ended up taking over everything," he told me. By June, he was in charge of the entire digital outreach effort—and more. Kushner trusted him, so much so that he inspired jealousy: one campaign staff member described Parscale, probably unfairly, as "Jared's lackey."

Parscale took an instant dislike to Nix, but the idea of using a strong data analytics group that wasn't closely affiliated with the RNC appealed to his—and Kushner's—outside-the-Beltway sensibility. Parscale desperately needed manpower with political expertise, and unlike many people in politics, he knew what he did not know. Nix had on his team a young data scientist named Matt Oczkowski who had worked on Scott Walker's short-lived presidential campaign.

Oczkowski visited Parscale in San Antonio and the two bonded. Nix wanted a contract for six hundred thousand dollars. Parscale persuaded Manafort and Kushner to let him hire the firm, starting it off with a contract for one hundred thousand dollars. On June 23, a contract reportedly was signed, and on July 29, according to FEC records, a payment was made by the Trump campaign to Cambridge Analytica. The campaign eventually hired six Cambridge Analytica employees. "I made the decision that we needed them, and Paul and Jared approved it," Parscale claimed. "I pushed for them because I wanted the staff. I needed the staff."

In June, Nix reached out to WikiLeaks founder Julian Assange because he had read that WikiLeaks planned to publish a trove of emails related to Hillary Clinton, the Democrats' presidential candidate. Those emails had been stolen—hacked—by Russian intelligence from the account of Clinton campaign chairman John Podesta and from the Democratic National Committee. (In July 2016, the FBI started an investigation into the thefts.) Nix, not one to be troubled by ethics, wanted to know if Assange would share the stolen material with him. More than a year later, *The Wall Street Journal* would report that Assange's answer was no.

While Parscale was trying to scale up the campaign's digital manpower, Kushner was busy with so-called "foreign outreach." The timing was opportune for Kushner Companies. The statesman Henry Kissinger introduced Kushner to Cui Tiankai, the Chinese ambassador to the U.S., a relationship that could have been helpful, as, around the same time, Anbang was entering negotiations with the Kushners over 666 Fifth Avenue.

Tom Barrack introduced Kushner to the United Arab Emirates ambassador, Yousef Al Otaiba, who had invested at least one million dollars with Barrack. "You will love him, and he agrees with our agenda," Barrack had written to Otaiba. Otaiba reported to Sheikh Mohammed bin Zayed Al Nahyan, the crown prince of Abu Dhabi, known as MBZ. A wily strategist, MBZ, fifty-seven, is the mentor of Saudi Arabia's Prince Mohammed bin Salman. The Obama administration had left both princes feeling isolated when it signed the Iran nuclear accord. MBZ had hoped Trump's foreign policy would more closely align with their goals in the Middle East, but Otaiba told Barrack he was also extremely concerned by Trump's anti-Muslim pronouncements. Barrack had tried to reassure MBZ that Trump was unlikely to take action against him or his country. He wrote to Otaiba and reminded him of Trump's business interests in the UAE. (He owns the Trump International Golf Club in Dubai.)

Kushner and Otaiba got on well, probably because Otaiba is very wealthy. (*The Wall Street Journal* reported in 2017 that Otaiba had received sixty-six million dollars misappropriated from Malaysia Development Berhad, a Malaysian state investment fund, between 2009 and 2015.) His wife, Abeer, has a fashion line. The couple is frequently photographed at parties in Washington. At one point, Otaiba emailed Barrack and asked for a "small favor"—"Any chance we can get an introduction to Melania's stylist for Abeer's fashion line?"

Federal election laws bar campaigns from knowingly soliciting contributions from "foreign nationals," a category that includes foreign citizens, corporations, and governments. These same laws bar such people and entities from contributing to a campaign anything of value—directly or indirectly, money or otherwise (with some limited exceptions). Foreign nationals are also barred from having decision-making authority in U.S. political campaigns.

But on June 21, Barrack felt confident enough in the new friendship to write to Otaiba: "I would like to align in Donald's mind the connection between the UAE and Saudi Arabia, which we have already started with Jared." Barrack wrote to Otaiba that Manafort was "totally programmed on the closeness and alignment of the UAE." On July 13, Barrack told Otaiba that the Trump campaign had removed a proposed Republican Party platform to release potentially embarrassing information about Saudi Arabia in a report on the September 11 terrorist attacks. (By the time the party finalized its platform that summer, Congress had already released the declassified pages.)

There were also complicated geopolitical motives behind Otaiba's outreach. Both the UAE and Saudi Arabia apparently had an interest in softening the U.S. opposition to Russia, since they reportedly believed Vladimir Putin was willing to help get Iran out of the war in Syria.

All these new "friends" were discovering their shared common interest at a most opportune time. Because of his campaign role, Kushner was becoming acquainted with influential Russians who wanted access to his father-in-law. As the campaign barreled toward the November presidential election, Kushner helped organize Trump's first major foreign policy speech, in April 2016, at Washington's Mayflower Hotel. There, he was introduced to Sergey Kislyak, the Russian ambassador, and three other ambassadors. There was a private reception for Trump before the speech, at which the ambassadors gave Kushner their cards and invited him to lunch.

In May, Rick Dearborn, a Trump campaign adviser, received an email from Republican operative Paul Erickson, explaining how the NRA had, for years, cultivated a back channel to Putin's Kremlin, and that Putin wanted to extend an invitation for Trump to visit Russia before the election. Less than a week later, Dearborn received—and forwarded to Kushner—another email, this time from a West Virginia man who said Alexander Torshin, the deputy governor of the Bank of Russia, wanted to meet a top campaign official at an NRA event—and mentioned an "overture to Mr. Trump from President Putin." Kushner responded to Dearborn, "Pass on this. A lot of people come claiming to carry messages. Very few we are able to verify. From now on I think we decline such meetings. . . . Be Careful."

Despite that warning, Kushner attended a meeting in Trump Tower on June 9 with Kremlin-linked lawyer Natalia Veselnitskaya, who had promised dirt on Hillary Clinton. The meeting had been organized by Donald Trump Jr., who had been approached by a British publicist, Rob Goldstone, who had mentioned that Veselnitskaya would provide the aforementioned dirt. Trump Jr. had replied, "I love it," and invited Kushner and Manafort to join them. But when they all gathered, Veselnitskaya shoveled no Clinton dirt. Instead, she wanted to talk about the Magnitsky Act, the American law passed in 2012 to sanction Russians after the Russian accountant Sergei Magnitsky died in a Moscow prison in 2009. Before his death, Magnitsky had blown the whistle on Russian government–sponsored corruption, including alleged money laundering by Prevezon Holdings—a company that also did business with a Kushner business associate, Israeli diamond tycoon Lev Leviev. But if Kushner found the topic interesting, he did not show it at the meeting with Veselnitskaya, apparently. Kushner in July 2017 released a statement saying that he felt his time was not "well-spent" at the meeting with Veselnitskaya.

Kushner's international power Rolodex was quickly expanding. He already had a friend in Benjamin Netanyahu. And now he had access to influential government officials in Russia, China, the UAE, and Qatar. All these new business contacts! Michael Fascitelli ribbed him that the only foreigners he was interested in meeting were people who could help the Kushners financially. What about the Syrians? Fascitelli joked. Kushner smiled.

Ivanka appeared thrilled by her husband's rising prominence in her father's campaign. It was a huge change from the days when Trump had made belittling jokes about him. If Don Jr. and Eric were irked by the new favorite in Trump's court, they did not show it publicly. "Jared and I are very different" was the strongest statement Don Jr. made recently, when asked about his relationship with his brother-in-law.

Meanwhile, Ivanka continued to run damage control after each of Trump's routinely offensive remarks on the campaign trail. Given his many sexist and misogynistic pronouncements—Trump had accused Fox News anchor Megyn Kelly of having "blood coming out of her wherever" after she grilled him during the first Republican debate, on August 6, 2015—Ivanka spent a great deal of her time in the public realm defending her father's record with women. On April 12, 2016, she said during a CNN town hall: "His actions speak louder than the words of many politicians who talk about gender equality, but it's not evidenced in their daily employment practices." She would later tell *CBS This Morning*: "He's not a groper. It's not who he is."

The fact that neither she nor Eric had registered as Republicans in time for the New York primary, and were therefore unable to vote for their father that spring, did not throw her. Instead, she criticized New York's "onerous rules" on voter registration.

Unlike her husband, she was not often seen on the Trump Tower campaign floor, the fourteenth floor. Instead, if people wanted to see her, they visited her up in her office, where she was mainly building her brand, which was increasingly about women's empowerment—or at least it pretended to be. She had created the hashtag #womenwhowork and was beginning a new book, *Women Who Work: Rewriting the Rules of Success*, which was due out the following spring.

She spent some of that early summer preparing for her speech at the Republican National Convention, in which she planned to position herself as her father's advocate for making childcare affordable and more accessible—not a topic he had talked about, but one that fit nicely with her branding. To prepare for her speech, she brainstormed both with Kushner and a seasoned speechwriting team. The speech, which Ivanka delivered in a petal-pink dress from her own line, also attempted to humanize her father. She spoke of his "empathy and generosity towards others, especially those who are suffering." The morning after her speech was delivered, her brand would tweet—from her personal account—"Shop Ivanka's look from her #RNC speech."

But any attempt to soften Trump's image was too little, too late. Just two weeks before the convention, Trump had tweeted an image widely viewed as anti-Semitic. It showed Hillary Clinton against a backdrop of money with the words "Most Corrupt Candidate Ever!" written over a Star of David. It was Jason Miller's first week on the job as senior communications adviser, and his reaction was, he recalled, "Holy shit!" He tried to reach Kushner, but he was offline for Shabbat. Trump was golfing, so Miller turned to Dan Scavino, who was in charge of social media. "Dude," he said, "you have to take this thing down." Scavino replied, "We never take things down." But Miller insisted and Scavino took it down. When Trump came off the golf course and found out what had happened, he phoned Miller. "This looks to me like a sheriff's star," said Trump, adding that by removing it, Miller had created a whole new news cycle about the tweet. By the time Kushner reemerged on Saturday evening, Miller thought he had lost his job. But Kushner told Trump he supported what Miller had done.

Dana Schwartz, then an *Observer* writer, criticized Kushner in his own newspaper for standing "silent and smiling in the background" while Trump made "repeated accidental winks" to white supremacists. "You went to Harvard, and hold two graduate degrees," Schwartz wrote. "Please do not condescend to me and pretend you don't understand the imagery of a six-sided star when juxtaposed with money and accusations of financial dishonesty."

Kushner wrote a response in the *Observer*. Or, rather, Kurson most likely did, according to a source who says Kushner never wrote his own articles or speeches without help, since writing was not his forte. Kushner's piece insisted that Trump was neither anti-Semitic nor a racist. He used his grandparents' harrowing experiences during the Holocaust to explain his reasoning: "I know the difference between actual, dangerous intolerance versus these labels that get tossed around in an effort to score political points."

Not all of Kushner's relatives appreciated his efforts to cover Trump's pandering to white supremacists. Two of Kushner's cousins complained on Facebook about his willingness to invoke their grandparents' suffering to defend Trump. "Thank you Jared for using something sacred and special to the descendants of Joe and Rae Kushner to validate the sloppy manner in which you've handled this campaign," wrote Jacob Schulder, whose ill health Charlie Kushner had scorned as "cancer, schmancer," and whose father had been set up by Charlie with a prostitute. "Please don't invoke our grandparents in vain just so you can sleep better at night. It is self-serving and disgusting."

In May, Trump was besieged by people urging him to focus on staffing a transition team, in case he won. He didn't want to deal with it, partly because he was concerned that it would require money he'd prefer to spend on the campaign, or even worse, that he'd have to pay for it. He also thought it was bad luck. On a Friday afternoon, he asked Kushner if he would take charge of it. Kushner said his plate was already full. According to an eyewitness, the scene unfolded as follows: "On a Friday afternoon, 4:20 P.M. to be exact, Donald Trump, then not even Nominee Trump, said, 'Don't worry, I got a guy who can help you,' and picked up the phone and dialed Chris Christie, [and] said to Kushner, 'He really knows politics, he's tough. He can help you.'"

Jared did not challenge Trump. He raised no objection to the hiring of the man who had put his father in prison. But Chris Christie's wife warned her husband that Jared would find a way to pay him back for what he'd done to his father, according to a source Christie told about the conversation. "The kid is going to get you," Mary Pat said. "You'll see."

CHAPTER TEN

Is This That Bad?

"They didn't build a ground organization. They used disinformation,
and fake-news bots, and fake news to run their campaign,
and nobody has ever done that."

—RICK DAVIS, REPUBLICAN CONSULTANT
AND ADVISER TO SEN. JOHN MCCAIN

By mid-August, the disorganized Trump campaign reached a chaotic na-
dir. It had no money, no coherent plan, and an undisciplined candidate.
INSIDE THE FAILING MISSION TO TAME DONALD TRUMP'S TONGUE was the
headline in *The New York Times* on August 13. That evening, an enraged
Rebekah Mercer, whose family had become a major financial supporter of
Trump's, planted herself in front of Trump at a fund-raiser in the East
Hampton, New York, home of Johnson & Johnson billionaire Woody
Johnson, and told him things had to change. She arrived with a printout
of that day's *Times* story, which she brandished as evidence that campaign chairman Paul Manafort had to go. And she had a solution: Trump
should put Steve Bannon in charge, and Kellyanne Conway's role should
be formalized as campaign manager.

Trump listened, and a day later, he met with Bannon over lunch and
appointed him campaign chief executive. Conway was promoted to campaign manager. Bannon headed immediately to campaign headquarters in
Trump Tower that Sunday evening, and found only one person there. That

night, Bannon told Manafort he did not intend to fire him—as long as he did not interfere. "You have no authority, ever," Bannon told him. "You just keep the office. We'll pay your expenses. Just stay out of the way."

Manafort said that was fine by him, and added: "Trump is going to fuck you, too."

Bannon shrugged. "Hey, look, I'm not here to make friends."

The next morning, August 15, *The New York Times* published an in-depth article showing that Manafort had received $12.5 million in off-the-books payments from pro-Russian Ukrainian government coffers. It was now clear to Bannon that Manafort would have to be fired. But Bannon's new role had not yet been announced. Where was the person who needed to step in and execute? Where was Jared Kushner?

Upon being told that Kushner and Ivanka Trump were vacationing on a yacht in Croatia—he didn't know it belonged to billionaire David Geffen, a big Democratic fund-raiser—Bannon exercised his new authority. He phoned Kushner and told him he had to return to New York immediately because Manafort needed to be fired. Trump "wouldn't want to do it," Bannon said. (Trump's view was that Kushner had been responsible for hiring Manafort, so he needed to fire him.) "He's got to go," Bannon told Kushner. "You're the only one able to do it." Bannon stressed the speed at which this needed to happen. "Dude, it's eighty-five days [until the election]." He warned Kushner that the media would "start coming after you guys" if he and Ivanka stayed on Geffen's yacht while the campaign they were supposedly leading collapsed. (Photographs of Ivanka posing with Wendi Deng Murdoch in Croatia were all over the internet.)

The couple arrived back in New York on August 16. The next day, Bannon was officially in. Two days after that, Manafort was officially out.

While he waited for the vacationing couple to return, Bannon decided to study the campaign's numbers. Over the phone, Kushner had introduced him to the campaign's chief operating officer, Jeff DeWit, the state treasurer of Arizona. When the two sat down together on August 15, DeWit told Bannon Kushner had hired him after he spoke at a Trump rally—and that he hadn't been in Arizona for a year. "How does that work?" Bannon asked him. "Did you take a leave of absence?" DeWit said, "No. . . . Look, if we win, you know, I'll be secretary of commerce or undersecretary of the treasury." (DeWit ended up as NASA's chief financial officer.)

Kushner had told Bannon the campaign had about twenty-five million dollars on hand, but as Bannon went through the figures with DeWit, he sensed quickly that something was wrong. DeWit, he discovered, didn't seem to know much about accounting. He had been a stockbroker. And the campaign did not have twenty-five million dollars. It was in the red, Bannon felt, because not all of the unpaid invoices and expenses had been properly documented.

When Kushner finally returned from Croatia, Bannon told him and De-Wit, "You understand you're broke right now?" Kushner disputed that, but Bannon overrode him: "Jared, we're going to need fifty million dollars coming out of the last debate [on October 19], fifty million for TV for the run of that. We can stumble through between now and then. But we're going to need fifty million."

Bannon also told Kushner and DeWit it was essential they replace the abstruse computer program on which the accounting was kept. "You've got to get a simple system. You guys have no earthly idea where we are financially." Kushner disagreed, but then Bannon sat down with him and went through the numbers. It was at that moment that Bannon discovered what Kushner's colleagues at Kushner Companies already knew: that understanding cash flow statements was not Kushner's strength. He was not an "in the weeds" person.

Bannon next got introduced to how the campaign's schedule had been set up. This is arguably the most important thing on a campaign, because it determines how every precious second is spent. That first week of Bannon's involvement was dubbed "education week." The campaign calendar had themes marked on it like "women's empowerment" and "entrepreneur week." Bannon thought they did not have time for this. "The guy is sixteen points down!" he told Kushner, who agreed. (News reports had him as seven or eight points down.) Bannon threw the schedule out.

Bannon also started adding people he knew could do what he wanted done. Even before Bannon's role in the campaign was announced, he phoned the RNC chairman, Reince Priebus, and told him he needed to get to Trump Tower right away. He asked for Priebus's deputy, Katie Walsh, to get to New York with Sean Spicer, the RNC's communications director and chief strategist. He wanted Walsh, along with RNC political director Chris Carr, to give a presentation about the RNC's data and what it showed. By September 1, Bannon had named one of his closest friends and an old ally of Trump's, the experienced Republican operative David Bossie, as deputy campaign manager. Bannon told Priebus: "Basically, it's going to be Katie and Bossie running the nuts and bolts of the whole campaign." Bill Stepien, a ground game expert recommended by Chris Christie, would work closely with them as national field director. Priebus said, "Fine."

This was what Priebus had spent the last four years planning for. After former Republican presidential candidate Mitt Romney's defeat by Barack Obama in 2012, the RNC, under Priebus, had spent more than $175 million on upgrading its data operation. Not only did it now have vast amounts of consumer data nationally, it had voter scores on local subsets within congressional districts, known as turfs. Ironically, the "turf map" matched that of the Obama field office when RNC executives happened to compare the two, which showed progress for the Republicans. The map measured how many undecideds, independents, and potential Republicans were in each of those areas and what their local concerns might be. Walsh, who is blond, petite, and short on small talk, could pick out all sorts of granular details from her turf maps, such as what kind of car each of her targeted voters drove. It was Walsh's job to ensure that the Trump campaign quickly understood the value of what the RNC now had.

Trump and Kushner were reluctant to use the RNC data, given the results of the last two presidential elections. In turn, Walsh and Priebus were skeptical of Cambridge Analytica's methods. Bannon told Walsh he had spoken with Brad Parscale and it was all sorted out. Parscale had taken on the six Cambridge Analytica staffers he needed. Parscale's staff of around a hundred was mostly down in San Antonio. But after the convention, Parscale spent most of his time in his Trump Tower office managing budgets for the TV ad buys, because Kushner—and Trump—trusted him with the money. The digital operation in Texas was spearheaded day-to-day by the RNC's director of advertising, Gary Coby, who had embedded himself in San Antonio once Trump was the nominee, and he had gradually gained acceptance by Parscale. Coby and the RNC understood the importance of digital advertising and Facebook in this campaign: 69 percent of all individual contributions to the Trump campaign and related GOP committees would come from small-dollar donors reached via Facebook, who gave two hundred dollars or less. (By contrast, small donations comprised 28 percent of Obama's individual contributions in 2012, while Hillary Clinton accumulated just 22 percent.) Reaching voters online was essential. Coby needed video footage to put on Facebook of Trump and his kids talking about the issues and asking for money. But for several months, he couldn't get an audience in Trump Tower. Finally, at the end of August, Kushner called him and told him to write some scripts and get up to New York. Coby's cheesy scripts along the lines of "If you give ten dollars, I'll make it twenty dollars" met with initial resistance from Trump. Regardless, they worked. Coby's ads raised $256 million in eighteen weeks.

Kushner's access to the candidate made him a valuable conduit for senior members of the campaign staff. When Bannon, Bossie, or Walsh needed something done, they got Kushner to agree to it and then get Trump's acquiescence. But Kushner was not focused on the minutiae. He still spent a great deal of time over at 666 Fifth Avenue. He did not even have an office with the other campaign staffers; when he came over to Trump Tower, he hopped around. Every day, Walsh would host a check-in call at 5 P.M. with Bannon, Conway, Bossie, Parscale, Stepien, RNC data adviser Bill Skelly, and sometimes pollster Tony Fabrizio. Bossie would determine which state to send Trump to, Stepien would suggest to Bossie where precisely in the state to send him, and Bannon would think about the message that Trump needed to deliver. Kushner was never on those calls.

Ivanka was mostly absent from the campaign, partly because she and Kushner had a new baby—their third child, Theodore James, born in March. She did have a campaign staffer, Kelly Love, who worked with her and her brothers, Don Jr. and Eric—both avid sportsmen—who played much stronger with the Trump base than Ivanka did. She was considered, said a source close to the campaign, a "CNN" person—in other words, a moderate. (The label was ironic, since Kushner hated CNN's coverage of Trump so much that he stopped campaign staff from appearing on the network.)

The Trump sons were much more useful than their sister on the campaign trail. "They would go to small events, not staged events. They would really campaign. They'd do all the radio to get the base out," recalled Sam Nunberg, who was in touch with the campaign and gave advice unofficially. Bannon sent Ivanka on day trips to suburbs in Philadelphia and towns in Florida that had large numbers of college-educated Republican and independent women. "She was obviously frustrated that she couldn't do more," said a source who talked with her then, adding that the couple's commitment to their faith, while admirable, also was a logistical problem. "Every Friday night, people were calling Jared as the sun was going down. . . . 'What about this, what about that?' . . . And Jared was very good about going down, not being in contact [during Shabbat], and it was frustrating for us, because if you didn't get an answer by sundown, you were basically just in a holding pattern for twenty-four hours."

Toward the end of August, Kushner asked Bannon to join him and Ivanka at the Trump National Golf Club in Bedminster on a Friday. Bannon arrived to find a bucolic scene: Ivanka and Kushner playing with the children. Kushner broke off to talk. "What do you think about us going to Mexico?" Kushner asked him. "I fucking love it," Bannon replied. "We've got to take the microphone out of the newscasters' hands. We have to put him in big settings he looks presidential in."

He asked Kushner: "Do we know anybody there? It would look bad if we just showed up."

Kushner told him he had been in secret conversations with Luis Videgaray, then Mexico's finance minister, whom he had been cultivating as an ally, about renegotiating the North American Free Trade Agreement (NAFTA). Bannon and Kushner did a conference call with Videgaray and settled on a date for a Trump visit, August 31. Their plan was that Trump would meet with Mexican President Enrique Peña Nieto and that the two would do a friendly press conference discussing the importance of the U.S.-Mexico alliance and calming tensions created by Trump's constant talk of "building a wall" and making Mexico pay for it. There would be no talk of how to pay for the wall from the podium on this trip, they vowed.

Trump liked the idea of the trip, but he was nervous. "I'm not going from the airport [in Mexico] in a car," he said, fearing for his safety. A helicopter was suggested. "Anybody can shoot a helicopter down," retorted Trump. Trump's private plane, with its big logo, was an obvious target, so that was out. They borrowed the plane of Las Vegas billionaire Phil Ruffin, which was smaller than Trump's, so Bannon offered to stay behind. The Mexican government sent the Mexican presidential helicopter for Trump to travel in from the airport so that he might feel secure.

Bannon watched the press conference with great satisfaction. Trump walked onto the platform with Peña Nieto, and Bannon loved the visual. "Trump is so much bigger than the guy," he thought. He had campaign spokeswoman Hope Hicks on the line. "This looks amazing," Bannon told her. But then ABC News White House correspondent Jonathan Karl asked Trump if Mexico had committed to paying for the wall. Trump started to answer the question.

Bannon called Hicks. "What the fuck is going on?"

Hicks was flustered. "I can't get him off," she said.

Kushner rose from his seat, apparently to head off questions. Reporters yelled at him, "Sit down!" Trump continued speaking.

Unlike his daughter and son-in-law, Trump was talented at fund-raising. The two donors essential to his campaign, along with the Mercers, were Sheldon Adelson and Home Depot cofounder Bernie Marcus. Before Trump had even announced his presidential run, Kushner had sought the support of billionaire Paul Singer, but "that was a bust," said Nunberg. The Koch brothers, two of the largest Republican donors, had stayed out of the primaries and Charles Koch had said in late July that he wouldn't support Trump come November. So, Trump knew he needed Adelson and Marcus.

Bannon watched with awe as Trump showed a humble side of himself most people never see. A late August meeting with Adelson was centered on Israel. Adelson's chief concern was that the next U.S. president move the U.S. embassy in Israel to Jerusalem. During that conversation, Kushner was not consulted. "Sheldon thought Jared and Ivanka were just kids," observed someone with knowledge of the meeting. "He was completely dismissive of them."

Israeli Prime Minister Benjamin Netanyahu was far friendlier to "the kids." The Netanyahus and the Kushners were old friends. On September 25, during the UN General Assembly, the Israeli ambassador to the U.S., Ron Dermer, and Netanyahu came to meet with Trump, Bannon, and Kushner in Trump's penthouse in Trump Tower. Trump had been reluctant to meet the Israeli premier: "He and Bibi had a history," was the impression Bannon got. "Two alpha males. Trump had thought Bibi didn't treat him with respect." But the meeting in September was considered an extraordinary success—at least by Trump. Netanyahu and Trump each sat on a chair that looked like a throne. Netanyahu spoke for two hours and gave what Bannon called "a Middle East master class. He was adamant that American foreign policy for fifty or sixty years since Gamal Abdel Nasser [the Egyptian president from 1956 to 1970 who accepted military support from the Soviet Union], the central tenet of U.S. foreign policy in the Middle East, had been to keep Russia out. And then Obama had essentially allowed Russia to come in [to Syria] and get quasi-permanent status and they weren't going to leave, and they would have to be dealt with. . . . He talked about Hezbollah. He talked about Iranian expansion in the region. He talked about Yemen. He talked about Qatar and Egypt . . . the whole region. And he and Trump really got along, big-time."

In that conversation, Trump let Kushner jump in, because U.S.-Israel relations was the one political issue anyone in the campaign ever saw Kushner get worked up about. "On the Israel stuff, Jared at least comes across like he knows what he's talking about," said someone who was at the meeting.

———

By October, the campaign had some semblance of order. According to the polling numbers, Trump had a narrow path to victory—or at least Parscale thought so, provided the predicted turnout was the typical midterm election turnout, not a general election one. But on October 7, two events of enormous political importance happened almost simultaneously. A batch of Clinton campaign chairman John Podesta's emails was released by WikiLeaks. The most damaging revelations concerned payments to the Clinton Foundation that appeared to be politically motivated. That was bad for Clinton, but the other bit of news was much worse for Trump: about half an hour before the Podesta emails leaked, *The Washington Post* published a video from 2005 of Trump bragging to television host Billy Bush that, thanks to his star power, he could grab women "by the pussy."

Trump was in the middle of prepping for the October 9 debate in St. Louis. Christie was playing the role of Clinton, Priebus was playing the role of moderator, and Bannon was coaching Trump to walk around and "stalk [Clinton]." Suddenly Hicks, "nearly in tears," gesticulated that she needed Bannon's attention. She showed him the transcript of the video that was about to come out. "Is this that bad?" Bannon asked. "Are you kidding me?" Hicks replied. And then the video was on *The Washington Post*'s website. One early question from Trump to the room was: What year was that? The team figured he was concerned as to whether or not it predated his marriage to Melania. (It was recorded several months after their wedding.)

Many members of the team headed home that night, rather than stick around as planned. They thought the campaign was dead. But Bannon insisted that Trump had to answer the video with a statement. Ivanka and Kushner, unusually, did not go home to celebrate Shabbat. Instead, Kushner, Bannon, and campaign speechwriter Stephen Miller started drafting a response. It took multiple drafts. And then, in a scene reminiscent of a *Saturday Night Live* skit, once they finished the statement, they discovered that they didn't have a teleprompter from which Trump could read it. They searched around for appropriate equipment. "It took literally hours and [Trump] lost his shit," recalled one person. Trump paced back and forth.

He went up to the penthouse, to his apartment, presumably to talk to Melania. It must not have gone well. Trump quickly came back down, obviously upset.

Sensing her father's pain, Ivanka put her hands on his arm to calm him down. "She saved the day," Bannon would later say to colleagues. Pizza was ordered, and the response video was finally shot and released around 12:30 A.M. It ended with Trump saying, "See you at the debate on Sunday."

The next day, Kushner and Ivanka climbed multiple flights of stairs in their sweats—thereby adhering to the rule that states you must not operate electrical devices, elevators included, during Shabbat—to be with the team. Trump's senior campaign officials were divided over what to do. Bannon had wanted to hold a rally. Kushner told Bannon he'd put the New York Hilton on hold, but by noon they'd have to pay for it. Bannon scoffed. "What is it, five thousand dollars?" Conway wanted Trump to do an interview with David Muir on ABC, one in which he would sit with a forgiving Melania. Former New York mayor Rudy Giuliani, a longtime friend of Trump's, and Christie pushed for *60 Minutes*. Bannon told Bossie they'd overlooked one small problem. "Has anyone checked with Melania?" Melania was clearly upset and it seemed unlikely she was going to sit for that kind of interview.

At 1 P.M., Trump's running mate, Mike Pence, who is deeply religious, released a statement, beginning: "As a husband and father, I was offended by the words and actions described by Donald Trump in the 11-year-old video released yesterday. I do not condone his remarks and cannot defend them." Over the weekend, a letter arrived for Trump from Pence, the contents of which clearly disappointed Trump. He offered to show it to several people, but nobody wanted to read it. "I think his wife wrote it," Trump told the room.

Bannon cornered Kushner and suggested a devious ploy. Bannon had reached out to the journalist Aaron Klein, who had been filming Juanita Broaddrick, Kathleen Willey, and Paula Jones—all of whom had accused

Bill Clinton of sexual assault or rape. Kathy Shelton, who said Hillary Clinton ruined her life when she defended Shelton's rapist as a young lawyer, was also part of the group. Klein's interview was supposed to run on *Breitbart* that night, but Bannon told Klein to ask the women if they would mind a change of plan. Could he fly them to St. Louis for the debate? They agreed.

Bannon told Kushner he wanted to have Trump meet the women before the debate and then bring in reporters. The media would be told they'd be allowed in to watch the end of Trump's debate prep—and then, of course, they'd be in prime position to gauge how the Clinton family reacted to the presence of those women. The element of surprise was critical. "Don't tell anybody [about the plan]," Bannon said. "Can't tell Reince, can't tell Ivanka." Priebus, he knew, would not have approved of it. Kushner nodded and said, "I love that."

Somehow, the crisis dissipated, and the campaign continued.

Trump was extremely irritated when, after the final presidential debate in October, his campaign finance chairman, Steven Mnuchin, told him he needed to loan the campaign ten million dollars and had him sign the wiring instructions on the spot. Trump read in *The Washington Post* that Parscale's company, Giles-Parscale, had been paid more than twenty million dollars. (It was the conduit through which the campaign paid for advertising, but Trump thought it was Parscale's fee.) Trump was so enraged, he paid an unexpected visit to Parscale on the fourteenth floor. "You are stealing my money! You are stealing my money!" he shouted. Parscale started stuttering, "I'm just a vendor!" The two men started walking toward the kitchenette close to Bossie's office. Bossie, sensing Parscale had been startled, rushed into the kitchenette and perhaps defused the tension by standing between them. It was campaign lore that Parscale never spent a dime without Kushner's approval. "Jared would approve it. Brad would execute it," remembered one person.

Around 11 P.M. on Election Night, it became clear that Trump could win. Ohio was called for Trump, then Florida, then North Carolina. The senior members of the team went up to the Trump penthouse. Melania had gone to her bedroom and would only reappear around 1 A.M. At 2:29 A.M., the Associated Press called Wisconsin for Trump and declared him the winner. Christie had given the White House his number and wanted to be the one to hand Trump the phone when President Obama called. In a sign of things to come for the disgraced governor of New Jersey, Trump cut him off: "Just give him my number."

Bannon and Miller started working fast on a draft of Trump's victory speech that Miller had prepared. Bannon was getting revved up to write something "fire-breathing"—something that gave a shout-out to the people he fondly called the "hobbits" and the "forgotten" men who had voted for Trump. He was clear on what was needed in the moment: "We're marching on Washington. . . . This is a rally speech." He barely noticed Ivanka coming up to him with some notes. "What do you think of this?" she asked politely.

Suddenly Trump was in his ear as well: "You know . . . I think we've got to try to bring the country together."

Bannon later realized that Ivanka and Kushner had persuaded Trump to deescalate. They wanted a speech about harmony. So, when Trump took the podium at the New York Hilton hotel in midtown Manhattan at almost 3 A.M., he began by praising Hillary Clinton and saying: "Now it's time for Americans to bind the wounds of division. . . . We will seek common ground, not hostility; partnership, not conflict."

In fact, most of Trump's inner circle had urged him to make nice, said someone who was there that night. Anthony Scaramucci, a financier and campaign member, had been on the phone warning Trump that the markets had plummeted. Trump had said, "Jared . . . make sure Steve puts some stuff in there to calm the markets."

In hindsight, Bannon would see something more profound in the alterations. Right there, within thirty minutes of winning the election, was the first sign of the personal conflict that would later wreak so much havoc in the Trump administration. The speech was a mess; contradictory and strange, wimpy and tough. "That speech is the original sin of this administration," he thought.

Bannon had believed—and still believes—that Trump is a transformational historical figure, a disrupter, an agent of change. The man might be temperamental and deeply flawed, but his ability to connect to the forgotten man, to articulate the raw anger among the working class, is extraordinary. But Kushner and Ivanka, Bannon felt, had no understanding of that. What they saw was raw power, and they wanted Trump to be liked.

But that night showed them they'd face an uphill battle to become America's first prince and princess. Kushner was shocked that Trump never mentioned him in his speech and would later tell people he felt slighted. He was going to find a way to get Trump to notice him more, to trust him more. Ivanka would help him. As Trump moved toward the White House, the couple would become known as a single, powerful entity: Javanka.

CHAPTER ELEVEN

Kushner's Disappearing Act

"Gary Cohn told Jared to take a lawyer with him to meetings. 'You're in a world right now where everything you do is discoverable from this moment on.' But Jared didn't understand what Cohn was talking about."

—TRANSITION COMMITTEE OFFICIAL

Jared Kushner and Steve Bannon reconvened early the morning after the election. There had been no time for sleep: just a quick shower and then back to work. It was time to focus on the transition. Donald Trump had around four thousand jobs to fill, from cabinet members on down. (A presidential transition team generally has as many as two hundred people vetted and lined up for appointments in its last week; the Trump team had only thirty appointees ready for vetting by the beginning of January.)

Since Trump had not wanted to focus on the transition during the campaign, Chris Christie had been left largely unmonitored at the transition offices one block away from the White House, in the same building as Hillary Clinton's transition team. Someone who visited the Trump transition office said that if you went someplace near the office to talk, "you had to post lookouts" to avoid being overheard by the opposition.

That morning, as they looked over the transition books, the documents that list the jobs to be filled and prospective candidates to fill them, Kushner said, "Christie has to go." Bannon agreed. Kushner had appeared to work well with Christie, not betraying any personal animosity toward the New Jersey governor during the campaign. Ironically, it had been Bannon who had fought with Christie—they had almost gotten into a fistfight the weekend the Billy Bush tape was released. (Christie had accused Bannon of being an "enabler" of Trump's extreme pronouncements.)

But now the three people who had run the campaign would also run the transition: Bannon, Kushner, and Reince Priebus—and Priebus had little or no say in Christie's fate. Early on November 9, Kushner and Bannon squared it all away. Christie would be replaced by VP-elect Mike Pence as "the face guy" of the transition. A small group of Trump loyalists were appointed to the transition committee, including PayPal cofounder Peter Thiel, Rebekah Mercer, Steve Mnuchin, Anthony Scaramucci, U.S. Representative Devin Nunes from California, as well as Ivanka, Don Jr., and Eric Trump. There would be meetings helmed by Pence every other week, but that was "just fluff," in Bannon's view. The three principals would oversee their different areas: Kushner would handle appointments in foreign affairs, Bannon would take cabinet staffing, national security, and intelligence, and Priebus would take White House staffing and operations.

A few hours later, Kushner came to see Bannon again. "I was talking to Ivanka. She and Don Jr. and Eric agree that [Michael] Flynn gets anything he wants. And that should be national security adviser." Bannon agreed, with the proviso that retired lieutenant general Keith Kellogg serve as the National Security Council's chief of staff and executive secretary. Bannon felt Kellogg would be a stabilizing influence. Trump had loved Flynn ever since he had started shouting "lock her up" about Clinton at the Republican National Convention. (Flynn would later apologize for the chants.)

On Thursday, November 10, Trump and Kushner visited the White House, where, in a one-on-one Oval Office meeting, President Barack Obama gave Trump two pieces of advice: One was that the biggest problem he would face as president was the nuclear threat posed by North Korea. The second was a warning against hiring Flynn: "He'll cause you nothing but problems." Trump later told Bannon, who told others: "Obama is a cool guy. I like him. He likes me. You'd like him." Bannon told people that Trump never felt as positive about Flynn again.

When Trump and Kushner got back to New York from the White House, Kushner phoned Bannon—again about Christie. "Tomorrow, there's going to be a meeting at 11 A.M. Pence and Christie are supposed to co-chair. We want you to pull Christie out when the meeting starts, bring him down to your office, and fire him."

The next morning, that 11 A.M. meeting was interrupted twice, first by Ivanka, who praised Flynn for "his amazing loyalty to my father" and then asked him what job he wanted. A person in that meeting told *The New Yorker*'s Jane Mayer: "It was like Princess Ivanka had laid the sword on Flynn's shoulders and said, 'Rise and go forth.'" Flynn was now the new national security adviser-in-waiting. Then Bannon broke in and asked to speak with Christie in his office. That meeting, visible to all because Bannon's office had glass walls, ran for three or four hours because Christie was so devastated. "I know who got me, it was the kid," he said over and over, referring to Kushner. "It's Lucy and the football," he said, referring to the recurring gag in the *Peanuts* comic strip in which Charlie Brown is fooled into trying to kick a football Lucy is holding, only for Lucy to pull it away, causing Charlie Brown to fly into the air and fall on his back. Christie felt like a fool. As his wife, Mary Pat, had told him from the start, "The kid is going to get you."

Later that evening, around 6 P.M., to Bannon's surprise, Christie reappeared in his office. He rehashed the sorry saga for one more hour. But even after that, Christie was not finished venting. Around midnight Christie texted and then phoned Bannon, waking him up. He wanted to talk it through *yet again*: "I feel like such an idiot. I should never have done this."

Priebus would say later to colleagues that he felt helpless about Christie's firing. "I wish I would've done more to protect Governor Christie, because he deserved better. [What happened] just wasn't right. He should've been taken care of, and he wasn't, and that's not right."

It was announced that weekend that Bannon would become White House chief strategist, and that Priebus would be White House chief of staff. Everyone noticed the order in which the appointments were announced and understood its significance.

Rob Porter, the former chief of staff for Senator Orrin Hatch, who had undergraduate and law degrees from Harvard and a political theory degree from Oxford as a Rhodes scholar, seemed a good fit as White House staff secretary—the coordinator who would organize policy briefings and the decision-making process for Trump—except he'd been a reluctant Trump supporter. Priebus had a more pressing concern about Porter. "Will you be loyal *to me*?" he asked Porter, who reassured him that he would. Later, Porter went to meet with Kushner, who clearly thought he had veto power, even if the others wanted Porter. Kushner asked him how he could be loyal to Trump, given that he and Hatch had initially supported one of Trump's primary opponents, Jeb Bush. Porter replied that he could be loyal to the office of the president. Don Jr. may have saved Porter at that point by walking past, seeing him with Kushner, and interrupting them to embrace Porter. The two had become friendly during the final week of the campaign in Nevada and Arizona.

Meanwhile, Kushner got busy hiring people he knew would be loyal to him and axing those he wasn't sure he could count on. For his vetting team, he made a couple of slightly odd choices: former U.S. Representative John Sweeney from New York, who had lost his reelection in 2006 amid allegations of spousal abuse. (Both Sweeney and his wife denied the allegations at the time, although months later Sweeney's wife told the *Albany Times-Union* that her statement had been "coerced.") Sweeney had also been arrested and convicted multiple times on drunk driving charges. Another was lawyer Ira Greenstein, a Kushner family friend then working for the New Jersey–based energy firm Genie Energy, which had a controversial drilling contract in Israel and is led by the Orthodox Jewish billionaire Howard Jonas.

David Bossie was surprised to see Bill Stepien arrive at Trump Tower one day dressed in a suit, rather than the khakis and button-downs he'd always worn during the campaign. (Stepien was considered fantastic at "ground game" analysis—the work of directly mobilizing voters to vote for their candidate. But he had been Christie's guy, and was gossiped about on the campaign trail because he'd been involved in Bridgegate, the scandal in which Christie allies created traffic gridlock as political retribution, and because he had had an affair with Christie's aide, Bridget Anne Kelly, against whom he later testified. She was sentenced to time in prison, but he glided on.) Suddenly, a door opened and Kushner came out to get him. "Aha," thought Bossie. Stepien's flexible loyalty would now come in handy. He was named White House political director and from then on would be considered a "Kushner guy," not a "Christie guy."

The transition team's key meetings took place on the twenty-sixth floor of Trump Tower, and Jason Miller was initially disappointed that he got left behind on the fourteenth floor. But after a few weeks, Trump reassured him: "You are one of my core guys." He was offered the job of White House communications director. The only problem was, he had personal issues, about which he went to talk to Bannon right before they exploded in public around Christmas. In October, he'd begun an affair with a campaign operative, A. J. Delgado, who was now pregnant with their child. Miller's wife was also pregnant, and he told a furious Delgado that he'd be staying with his wife. Miller thought that probably disqualified him from a White House job, but Bannon thought it could all be worked out, eventually. And when Miller phoned Priebus, he, too, gave his support. "We are 100 percent behind you." Bannon and Priebus knew Miller had been seen with Delgado at a club. They suspected Miller had had an affair, but later said they had no idea Delgado was carrying Miller's baby.

They put out the announcement that Miller would be Trump's communications director on December 22, and Delgado immediately sent a series of tweets hinting at their relationship. Miller resigned forty-eight hours later, before coverage of his affair lit up the internet.

Kushner phoned to wish Miller "Happy Christmas," and added, "You should have come to see me sooner." Miller told him, "I understand from Reince and Steve that I need to take a time-out, maybe a year or something." Kushner stopped him. "It's going to be a lot longer than that."

Part of the problem was that, as Miller explained to Kushner, it had not been easy for Miller to get a one-on-one with Kushner during the transition. He didn't even have an office in Trump Tower, although his assistant did. Avi Berkowitz, a graduate of Harvard Law School (he'd met Kushner playing basketball on a family holiday), took the space next to Gary Cohn, the former Goldman Sachs president, who was selected as director of the National Economic Council. Kushner had introduced Cohn to Trump. Cohn was a Democrat, but he was by far the most blue-chip hire the transition team made—and Kushner was proud of that.

But Cohn kept wondering openly, as did others: Where was Kushner? There was so much work to be done, so many hires to be made—but he was either at 666 Fifth Avenue, busy with Kushner Companies work, or, according to Berkowitz, attending "secret" meetings. Cohn knew that Trump was not in those meetings and he was concerned. He didn't know with whom Kushner was meeting, but he did know Kushner should not be meeting with *anyone* alone. Cohn told him in front of people that this was no longer the reckless, ruthless world of real estate. He told Kushner he should not go into any meeting without a lawyer, but Kushner just shrugged.

In the week following the election, Bannon and Flynn were contacted by Matthew Freedman, a political operative who had State Department experience and was overseeing the National Security Council transition. "The [Trump] kids [and Kushner] made a request to put in for security clearances," he told them. Bannon replied, "Security clearances? Unless they are coming with the administration, absolutely no way they'd put in for the family for security clearances. As soon as that happens, it will leak."

But Flynn had no problem with the clearances. One senior campaign official suddenly realized why Ivanka had been so eager to "reward" Flynn's loyalty. "Flynn is totally malleable," this person told me. "Jared [and Ivanka] realized it would be a client relationship." That is, Kushner and Ivanka would be Flynn's VIP clients.

As Bannon had predicted, it was immediately leaked that Kushner wanted a security clearance. (The Obama White House was still involved in the clearance process and received the request.) The transition team's response? Fire Freedman—a move that unsettled even Bannon. Trump put out a narrowly worded denial, tweeting: "I am not trying to get 'top-level security clearance' for my children. This was a typically false news story."

(A Kushner spokesman told *The New Yorker* that Kushner was unaware of any such requests made on his behalf.)

But Congressional Democrats were not satisfied. On November 16, eight days after the election, U.S. Representative Elijah Cummings from Maryland, the ranking Democrat on the Committee on Oversight and Government Reform, wrote a letter to Pence asking whether Kushner had requested a security clearance or might do so in the future. Cummings pointed out that Kushner was barred from becoming part of the administration due to anti-nepotism laws and that giving him access to material such as the President's Daily Brief would "demonstrate a breathtaking lapse in judgment and an astonishingly cavalier attitude towards our nation's most sensitive secrets."

There were lots of reasons Kushner should not have been given daily access to America's most sensitive intelligence. First, he was still conducting business on behalf of Kushner Companies, which was desperately looking for a way to pay off the $1.2 billion mortgage on 666 Fifth by February 2019—and, as would become clear to his transition team colleagues, he never properly divested from his business interests, although his lawyer Jamie Gorelick stated that his legal team had consulted with the Office of Government Ethics and was in compliance with their requirements.

Second, the guidelines for a transition are normally to coordinate with the sitting State Department. "The idea is, we're supposed to have one foreign policy at a time," said former deputy secretary of state Antony Blinken, "so if you're having conversations that undermine existing policy, that's a problem. But if you're having conversations for the sake of making contact, normally, you would do that . . . by looping the State Department in." Kushner was already freelancing on his version of "foreign relations."

On November 16, three days after the Trump family's *60 Minutes* interview—following which Ivanka's brand emailed out a "style alert" advertising the gold-and-diamond bangle she'd worn for the show, available from Ivanka Trump Fine Jewelry for $10,800—Kushner attended a dinner hosted by the chairman of the Chinese insurance giant Anbang, Wu Xiaohui, and other executives, in a private dining room at the restaurant La Chine at Manhattan's Waldorf Astoria hotel. (Anbang was the potential lifeline investor for 666 Fifth.) Weeks later, *The New York Times* reported that they dined on "Chinese delicacies and $2,100 bottles of Château Lafite Rothschild." Kushner did not tell any of his senior transition team colleagues about the dinner—not Bannon, Priebus, or Cohn.

Kushner Companies' other potential investor in 666 Fifth, Hamad bin Jassim bin Jaber Al Thani (HBJ), reportedly popped into Trump Tower during the transition. He wanted to be respectful and "gracious" to both Trump and Kushner, according to two sources, though he had decided that he would not invest in 666 Fifth.

That first week of the transition, Bannon ran into Ivanka, who breezily informed him that Japanese Prime Minister Shinzo Abe had just been on the phone and Abe was planning a visit to Trump Tower. On November 17, Abe was photographed sitting with Trump, Kushner, and Ivanka in Trump Tower. Ethical questions were raised, especially by the *Times,* because both Kushner and Ivanka were still running their businesses. (Ivanka's brand was closing in on a licensing deal with Sanei International, a major Japanese clothing company whose largest shareholder is the government-owned Development Bank of Japan.) Those concerns were dismissed in the *Times* by "an individual close to the family" who said the "meeting was very informal" and that the family still needed "to adjust to the new realities." After the media outcry, Ivanka's brand pulled out of the deal.

It seemed obvious to Ivanka's colleagues that not only was she trying to promote her business abroad, as if nothing had changed, but also that she did not care about—or had not even considered—the inherent appearance of corruption in that. The New York billionaire developer Leonard Stern, who has a decades-old dislike of Trump, stemming from a fight about an article (in a publication owned by Stern) that stated that Trump Tower resale prices were below the original offering prices, has studied Ivanka's finances. Although Stern has no firsthand knowledge of them, he does have a deep understanding of how intergenerational wealth is usually managed in real estate families. He observed that Trump, atypically, to his knowledge, has not given his adult children substantial legacy assets. Instead, it appears that Trump prefers to retain the majority of the equity. (For example, regarding the Trump International Hotel in D.C.—a project Ivanka led—it was reported that the three eldest Trump children own 22 percent between them.) Ivanka's brand was therefore much more potentially lucrative than her Trump Organization role, Stern contended, because it was solely owned by her. "She wasn't sacrificing any large investments [when she left the Trump Organization]," he said.

Kushner continued taking meetings with foreigners that would draw major scrutiny when they later came to light. On December 1, the Russian ambassador, Sergey Kislyak, met in Trump Tower with both Flynn and Kushner. According to a statement later delivered by Kushner to congressional investigators, they discussed Syria, where the regime of Bashar al-Assad is supported by both Iran and Russia, which has military bases there. Kislyak had asked for a secure way to allow his "generals" to communicate with Flynn about Syria. Kushner had suggested using the secure facilities in the Russian embassy. This notion was met with fierce condemnation from Congress when it heard about the meeting months later while probing into Russian interference in the 2016 election and possible coordination with the Trump campaign. Intelligence analysts were appalled.

Kushner probably felt emboldened to do this because of a new so-called "grand bargain" that was being negotiated between Israeli Prime Minister Benjamin Netanyahu, Abu Dhabi Crown Prince MBZ, and Saudi Arabia's heir apparent, Prince Mohammed bin Salman (MBS). Because Obama had cut each of their countries out of the Iran nuclear deal negotiations, which they had opposed, the Palestinian dispute, which had always divided the Israelis from the Arabs, was now secondary to a far more pressing concern that united them: Iran. This new alliance believed that a cooling of animosity between the U.S. and Russia was critical in pushing Iran out of Syria.

This was not a view endorsed by many Middle East experts in the U.S. Bruce Riedel, a former CIA officer and an expert on policy in the region, explained, "The Iranians regard Syria as their single most important ally in the world, and they're not going to abandon the Syrians, and they're not going to leave. Bashar Assad needs the Iranians. He needs Hezbollah [the Iran-backed militant group based in Lebanon]. He needs the various Shia militias that the Iranians recruit for him in Afghanistan and Pakistan. I think this is a fantasy foreign policy, which is something that Bibi Netanyahu has long indulged in."

Nevertheless, Michael Oren, the former Israeli ambassador to the U.S., told *The New Yorker* that Kushner, who'd later be tasked with bringing peace to the Middle East, had one big advantage: "Obama set out to bring Jews and Arabs closer together through peace. . . . He succeeded through common opposition to his Iran policy."

The Russians did not leave Kushner alone after that first meeting. Almost two weeks later, Kislyak met with Kushner's assistant, Berkowitz, and stressed the importance of a meeting between Kushner and Sergey Gorkov, the chairman of Vnesheconombank (VEB), a state-owned Russian bank. Gorkov was a close ally of Vladimir Putin. Kushner would later testify before Congress that Kislyak said Gorkov could provide crucial understanding of the thinking of the Russian premier. Kushner met with Gorkov, but would later insist that the approximately twenty-minute meeting had been largely substance-free. No policies were discussed, nor was personal business, Kushner would say. Gorkov had bought him a piece of art from Novogrudok, his grandparents' village, and a bag of dirt from there, and Kushner would later say he formally registered the gifts with the transition office. The Russians would also say later that Kushner acted as the head of his family's real estate company when he met with Gorkov. Executives from the bank were meeting "with a number of representatives of the largest banks and business establishments of the United States, including Jared Kushner, the head of Kushner Companies," the bank said in a statement only released after the meeting was revealed.

Cohn was horrified when he read about the meeting in the press. He reiterated the message he had kept trying to drum into Kushner almost every day: "You shouldn't go to any meeting without taking a lawyer with you [as a witness]. . . . Everything you do is discoverable from this moment on." But, as usual, he felt that Kushner just didn't seem to get it. Or didn't want to.

Senator John McCain had been openly concerned about the Trump campaign's methods—as well as its pledges. He felt it had suspiciously little ground game and too heavy a reliance on TV ads and fake-news bots. Rick Davis, a senior McCain adviser who knew Roger Stone, Trump's longtime political adviser, had discussed how campaigns connected to Stone were often known for dirty tricks. Soon after the election, McCain had issued a strong statement that a "reset" of Russian relations would be "unacceptable."

That irritated Kushner, who did not know McCain, so he phoned Davis. Kushner began the call calmly, mentioning that their mutual friend, Revlon chairman Ronald Perelman, had suggested he reach out. And then, in a flash, he turned hostile: "Has McCain got a strategy or is he just an egomaniac?" Davis, taken aback, said that McCain had always taken a negative view of Putin since he'd been elected to the Senate twenty years earlier. Kushner carried on with his tirade: "He needs to step back. We have a plan. He ought to give us time to implement our plan. He's being obstructionist." And then he added, "He does not want to get on Donald Trump's radar screen." Davis was shocked. He recommended that Kushner treat McCain with some respect. Six previous presidents had found it worth their while to engage with McCain one-on-one. Perhaps it would be sensible for Trump—and Kushner—to do likewise? Kushner appeared to be unimpressed and hung up.

On December 2, Kushner called Bannon, sounding worried: the president of Taiwan, Tsai Ing-wen, was on the line. How? asked Bannon, thinking this was a brilliant example of Trumpian disruption. Ever since 1979, when America recognized the government in Beijing as the ruler of China, a stance since termed "One China," no American president or president-elect is known to have spoken to the Taiwanese leader, because doing so would suggest recognition of that government. But for Bannon, who saw China as the biggest threat to American prosperity, the phone call was an unexpected gift. "It's a fuck-up," said Kushner. He explained that somehow the Taiwanese had gotten through to Trump's longtime executive assistant at the Trump Organization, Rhona Graff. "Is that going to be a problem?" Kushner asked. Bannon was thrilled. "Jared, it's going to fucking blow their heads up. We've got to do it. It's amazing." Kushner said: "If we connect now, we're connected."

After the call, Trump tweeted, "The President of Taiwan CALLED ME today to wish me congratulations on winning the Presidency. Thank you!" He later gave an interview positing that he might dump the "One China" policy.

The Chinese were predictably apoplectic. Kushner went back to Bannon: "We've got a problem." China's highest-ranking diplomat, Yang Jiechi, was already flying to New York, demanding a meeting. "We must meet with them," Kushner said. Bannon agreed. He told Kushner, "You understand how much face they've lost having to talk to us about this?"

The meeting with Yang and the Chinese ambassador, Cui Tiankai, was held not at Trump Tower but at the Kushner Companies headquarters at 666 Fifth, over a two-day period, December 9 and 10. Since December 10 was a Saturday, Kushner had to skip that session. "You're my partner. I trust you," he told Bannon. So, on Friday, the Americans were represented by Bannon, Kushner, and transition official K. T. McFarland. The second day was Bannon, Flynn, and transition team economic adviser Peter Navarro. Bannon anchored both days.

As he stepped out of the elevator and onto the fifteenth floor at 666 Fifth, Bannon was greeted by an effusive Charlie Kushner, who shook his hand with a vise grip. "My kid loves you," he said. "You're what he needs. They need assholes. You're an asshole. You've got to be tough."

Then Bannon, Jared, McFarland, the two Chinese diplomats, and a handful of others from China all filed into a conference room. Yang started off with a two-hour lecture on Chinese history. Reading from a neat stack of papers, he repeated several times, "The territorial integrity and the sovereignty of the People's Republic of China is not to ever be questioned."

Bannon was enjoying all this so much that he threw in a question about the Spratly Islands, a contested archipelago in the South China Sea where Beijing has built up a military presence. He said he'd sailed past them, "guns-up," when he was in the navy. Yang was startled—and, if this was possible, even more displeased: "You're not questioning our sovereignty of the Spratly Islands, are you?" The meeting ended without a resolution.

Trump would eventually change his mind on Taiwan after Chinese President Xi Jinping said he'd refuse Trump's invitation to Mar-a-Lago unless Trump assured him, publicly, that he was behind the "One China" policy—or that's what Bannon was told. But what was far worse, not just from Bannon's point of view but also from Cohn's, was the revelation, published on January 7 by *The New York Times,* of Jared's dinner and ongoing talks with Anbang. They realized Jared had been conducting personal business negotiations around the same time he'd been hosting the Chinese government at 666 Fifth. Cohn told Jared in front of several eyewitnesses: "You've got to be crazy." He warned him that *everything* he did from now on could look as though he was trying to enrich himself or his family. Bannon did not agree with Cohn on much, but on this issue, he told colleagues, they were completely in sync. "The most shocked I was in my entire career [with Trump] . . . was when I read that *Times* story about Anbang," he told multiple people, including Priebus, who was also taken aback.

When Rex Tillerson, who was stepping down as Exxon Mobil CEO to become secretary of state but had not yet undergone Senate confirmation, read the story, he told a colleague that he felt Jared needed coaching. He said he'd make a habit of dropping in on him, once he was running the State Department.

Kushner was increasingly caught up in his own mythology. He was the president's son-in-law, so he apparently thought he was untouchable. On November 22 *Forbes* published the online version of their new cover story: THIS GUY GOT TRUMP ELECTED. It equated what Kushner had done to running a stealth Silicon Valley start-up—and was strewn with flattering quotes from luminaries like former Google CEO Eric Schmidt. (In the piece, Kushner denied having anything to do with Christie's firing: "I was not behind pushing him out or his people.")

Bannon was surprised by the article, since he knew Kushner preferred to be behind the scenes. But Kushner, presumably thinking of how he'd been slighted by Trump on Election Night, told both Bannon and another senior transition official it was important to speak up: "You always have to remind Trump from the outside what your value is."

Ivanka also fostered political ambitions. She had told the world on *60 Minutes* that she would not be joining the administration, but that wasn't what it looked like to the transition team. In December, she enlisted Risa Heller, a Kushner Companies spokeswoman, who had a political background, to help shape her image. (Heller had worked for Senator Chuck Schumer, a Democrat.) As schematics of the new West Wing layout were worked on, there was a large office designated for Ivanka. She would hire a team of three, which was unusually large for someone with a nebulous White House role.

Ivanka had, initially, been overseeing plans for the East Wing, ordinarily the First Lady's job. Two transition officials saw the plans upon which Ivanka, or someone acting on her behalf, had stenciled in the corner office of the East Wing as "Trump Family Office." The transition officials were surprised that the First Lady did not appear to have an office. So, too, was Melania Trump, who quickly put an end to Ivanka's scheming. When she saw the plans, according to one official, "Melania put her foot down." Two sources confirmed that Ivanka was clearly told to back off. After that, there was no more talk of the "Trump Family Office."

The person appointed to run the inauguration committee was Tom Barrack, who'd been busy attempting to broker deals in the Middle East. Soon after the election, his jet touched down in Qatar, right around the time the Qatar Investment Authority was finalizing negotiations, as part of a consortium with Swiss mining firm Glencore, to purchase a nearly 20 percent stake in Rosneft, the Russian state oil company, for $12.2 billion, during a partial privatization. An Italian banking group, Intesa Sanpaolo, which, according to a source with knowledge, has ties to Barrack, would be involved in the transfer of funds. A few months later, Barrack (in the wake of a separation from his wife) would ask Trump for the ambassadorship to Brazil, according to a source. Trump turned him down, fearing he might not pass a Senate confirmation hearing. Barrack would try to wield influence in other ways, including advising Trump and Kushner on how to bring peace to the Middle East.

In mid-December, Bannon told colleagues he was surprised when Kushner asked if he and Flynn would join him at breakfast with Tony Blair. Bannon had almost no interest in meeting with the former British prime minister, who, it had been reported, had been conducting personal business with both the UAE and Qatar while serving as a Middle East envoy for a UN-affiliated diplomatic group working to bring about peace between the Israelis and Palestinians. Bannon would later complain that he thought the meeting was a waste of time; Blair essentially said that none of the players in the Middle East could be trusted, which was not revelatory. But Bannon did remember a guy in the meeting who he assumed worked for Blair and sounded like a mid-level political operative. He was surprised when Kushner told him afterward it was his "buddy" Rick Gerson, a staunchly pro-Israel hedge fund manager with financial ties to the court of MBZ, the Abu Dhabi crown prince. Gerson would travel soon after to the Seychelles, around the same time as a meeting was arranged by the Emiratis between Blackwater founder Erik Prince and the head of a Russian fund, Kirill Dmitriev, at MBZ's resort, that would come under scrutiny by congressional and Department of Justice investigators. One person who knows Gerson and his brother Mark told me that "they like hanging out with powerful people, particularly if those people are helpful to Israel."

On December 15, MBZ arrived in the U.S. without bothering to announce his visit to the Obama White House, which only became aware of it because his name was on the flight manifest. His meeting with Kushner, Bannon, and Flynn took place at the penthouse of the Four Seasons in New York to avoid the media scrum at the base of Trump Tower. According to one person briefed on the meeting, MBZ had an entourage of around thirty. This person said: "Flynn really knew his stuff, knew details about the region, and carried on a really intelligent back-and-forth with MBZ. Jared added some preliminary ideas about the Israeli-Palestine peace process."

The Emiratis talked about how Obama had hurt UAE security. Flynn talked animatedly, discussing Russia's attempted involvement in the region for decades, and terrorism. Atypically, Bannon just listened. He was mesmerized by MBZ. "He looks like Sean fucking Connery," he'd later say.

After an hour, MBZ turned to Bannon. "You haven't said anything. Why did you even show up?"

Bannon said, "Persian expansion."

The words resonated with MBZ, whose country considers Iran a primary foe. MBZ talked for another hour while Kushner stayed pretty quiet.

The one topic Kushner was talkative about was Israel. Or at least that seemed to be the perspective of Ron Dermer, the Israeli ambassador, who, having consulted with Netanyahu, reached out to Kushner in late December to ask for his assistance. The Obama administration was supporting a UN Security Council resolution condemning the construction of West Bank settlements. Kushner was upset. "[The Obama people] had their turn. They failed. Why are they trying to make our job harder on the way out?" he was reported saying in *The New Yorker*. He and Flynn got to work trying to reach out to foreign dignitaries whose phone numbers, for the most part, they did not possess. The idea was that these people would help influence the vote. Ultimately, their incompetence did not really matter; the U.S. abstained—though the resolution passed, with fourteen votes for it and none against. What was highly unusual, however, was the battle between the transition team and the sitting government. It was as if Kushner viewed Netanyahu as his boss and Obama as his enemy.

Meanwhile, the transition was moving extraordinarily slowly. Every day, from 10 A.M. to 7 P.M., candidate after candidate was presented to Trump, who complained: "I feel like an employment agency."

On December 14, Trump hosted a roundtable of technology leaders, including Apple CEO Tim Cook, Amazon CEO Jeff Bezos, Facebook COO Sheryl Sandberg, Alphabet CEO Larry Page and then–executive chairman Eric Schmidt, Microsoft CEO Satya Nadella and president and chief legal officer Brad Smith, Oracle co-CEO Safra Catz, then–Intel CEO Brian Krzanich, Cisco CEO Chuck Robbins, Tesla CEO Elon Musk, IBM CEO Ginni Rometty, and Palantir CEO Alex Karp. Bannon complained to anyone who would listen that the whole thing was not about any substantive government policy. It was a networking opportunity and a show for the cameras. It was a charade, a "circle jerk," he said. (Although he had loved it when the doors got closed and the cameras stopped flashing—and for a whole hour his favorite topic, China's supposedly unfair trade policies, was discussed.)

Even so, after that meeting, Bannon told multiple people he warned Kushner to be wary of "press events" that catered to a Democratic crowd: "These things are bad because nothing gets done. The media is eventually going to say nothing is getting done. It's just crony capitalism. They're all in here looking for a favor. They don't support Trump. In the first sign of trouble, they're going to head for the hills."

Kushner ignored him.

On December 16, Kushner went to the offices of Morgan Stanley in New York City's Times Square to speak before the Partnership for New York City, a gathering of some four hundred New York senior business and financial executives. In his address, Kushner said Trump was "easy to hate from afar," but he told the crowd not to assume he'd govern as he had campaigned. He said the administration would likely take a "rational" stance when it came to immigration, which startled some Republicans in attendance. He was very prickly on the subject of the media, which he said was deluded about the country's state of mind. Since he had viewed CNN as being against Trump, he'd given more interview access to Sinclair, a local-news conglomerate, which agreed to broadcast the Trump interviews without commentary and which, according to Kushner, had much greater reach. He believed that had helped the campaign reach wider audiences in states Trump later won. "It's math," he said. A senior investment banker who attended that meeting said Kushner came off as extraordinarily arrogant. "It came across that he really believed he could control Trump."

In early January, Trump's incoming White House counsel, Donald McGahn, came to see Priebus and Bannon. McGahn was from New Jersey and his uncle Paddy had been a prominent lawyer who had represented Trump and been on the other side of a legal dispute with him. Trump had admired him: "Paddy—he was a nasty piece of work," he'd say to senior transition staff.

McGahn liked Kushner, but sources say he'd received feedback from the Justice Department's Office of Legal Counsel suggesting that neither Kushner nor Ivanka could legally join the White House staff without a legal opinion, due to anti-nepotism laws. Further, McGahn was on the fence about them coming in; his job was to protect the president. "You know the real reason there's an anti-nepotism law?" he told Bannon. "It's not so much about corruption—though it is, partly—as it is about incompetence. You can't fire family, as a general rule."

Trump had, to some degree, comprehended this. Or at least he had blown hot and cold as to whether Kushner or Ivanka should come with him to Washington. "I don't even know that I will be involved with [Jared] . . . when I move to the White House," he told me in a phone conversation during the transition. A handful of people, including McGahn and right-wing media personality Ann Coulter, had warned Trump about this. "Nobody is apparently telling you this. But you can't. You can't just hire your children," Coulter told him. Michael Cohen, Trump's longtime attorney, was also against them coming. Trump heard about Cohen's objections. The difficulty, it was clear to Cohen, was that Trump hated telling Ivanka "no."

McGahn told Bannon and Priebus that a legal opinion, allowing Kushner to work in the administration, had been drawn up. It broke with historical precedent, overruling a string of Justice Department memos that had for decades concluded it was illegal for presidents to appoint relatives as White House staff. "Here it is," McGahn said, waving the document around. "This could go one way or the other. The Office of Legal Counsel really doesn't want to do this, but they can, if you think he's absolutely necessary." McGahn told Bannon and Priebus that the Obama-era Justice Department was leaning toward accepting the allowance for Kushner, albeit reluctantly: "Because you [Bannon] and [Stephen] Miller scare people more than Jared. They think Jared and Ivanka would be a calming influence."

Priebus was ambivalent about the ploy. Bannon took a deep breath and said he agreed with the Obama-era Justice Department: "I think we might

need them [Javanka]." He told McGahn and Priebus to think back to the
Billy Bush weekend crisis. "Our craziest moments of the campaign, the
really craziest moments, even Hope [Hicks] can't get to [Trump]. Only
Jared and Ivanka can talk him down off the ledge. We're going to have so
many of those. We're going to need Jared, to be able to talk to him like a
son-in-law, with Ivanka. I think we need that. I think it's worth it." On
January 20, the Justice Department released its opinion, approving Kushner
to start work in the White House.

Even as he green-lit the move, Bannon knew he was making trouble for
himself. Ivanka wanted Dina Powell, the Egyptian-born senior executive
from Goldman Sachs who had worked for the George W. Bush administration, to join her staff. Bannon found Powell, a lifelong Republican, deeply
impressive when he met with her. When they discussed Ivanka's proposed
women's economic empowerment initiatives, he told Powell: "Listen, I love
it. But I just don't want to embarrass Ivanka. None of the Republicans on
Capitol Hill care about this stuff. . . . You understand that, right?"

"I know," said Powell.

Powell later told me she did not recall that Bannon had any reservations about Ivanka's issues, but Gary Cohn told colleagues that it took Powell, who is famously politically astute, less than two months on the job to
get away from working with Ivanka, which was internally deemed a
thankless job, and to pitch her experience to National Security Adviser H. R.
McMaster, who thought she could be useful on the national security team.
She eventually got a new title: deputy national security adviser for strategy.

The timing of *The New York Times* report on the Anbang dinner published
on January 7 could scarcely have been worse for the image-conscious Kushner. It coincided with another publication, this one of a report by the U.S.
intelligence community detailing for the first time confirmation of what
had been speculated ever since WikiLeaks published hacked Democratic
National Committee emails: Russia *had* meddled in the 2016 presidential

election. Given Kushner's leadership role in the campaign, that had to concern him. But that was not his only difficulty: Jamie Gorelick, a widely respected lawyer who had served in the Justice Department under Bill Clinton, said Kushner would be resigning from Kushner Companies and divesting "substantial assets" in order to go into the government as an unpaid White House senior adviser. Her letter did little to assuage widespread concerns about Kushner's ethics—or apparent lack of them. The *Times* quoted Matthew Sanderson, a lawyer at Caplin & Drysdale who had been general counsel for Senator Rand Paul's presidential campaign, as saying that what Kushner was doing "strikes me as a half-measure [that] still poses a real conflict-of-interest issue and would be a drag on Mr. Trump's presidency and cause the American people to question Mr. Kushner's role in policy-making."

Cohn commiserated with Kushner, who kept moaning to people he bumped into in the hallway and in the morning meetings about how expensive it was to go into government. Cohn was abiding by the rules and selling off shares of Goldman Sachs. What neither he nor anyone else knew until months later was that Kushner sold only a tiny fraction of his real estate portfolio. According to *The Washington Post*, he still owned assets valued between $167.5 million and $569.5 million, placed in a trust with either his mother or brother, with whom, as previously mentioned, he was said to already share profits. An investor in Cadre, the digital real estate platform cofounded by the Kushner brothers, told me: "Jared and Josh own everything together, they're partners in everything—including [666 Fifth]. So, Jared saying he transferred the interest to his brother, and that somehow cleansed the deal, is a joke. Literally nothing's changed. He's not going to get the interest back when he leaves the administration? Are you fucking kidding me?"

A former colleague of Javanka's remembered: "The fact that it was reported that their businesses made money while they were in the White House caused a great deal of anxiety and strife among everyone else." It was felt to be unfair and unethical. "Everyone else had played by the rules."

CHAPTER TWELVE

The Secretary of Everything

"Jared never understands the details of anything.
He's just impressed by names."

—FORMER SENIOR WHITE HOUSE OFFICIAL

Ivanka Trump arrived in Washington, D.C., in a blaze of attention-seeking publicity. First, there was her dizzying array of designer outfit changes, each one chronicled on her Instagram feed. She deplaned from New York in a green Oscar de la Renta dress and matching coat, nude high heels, and— shrewdly, for a woman promoting a brand for working mothers—holding one child by the hand while cradling a baby. (Jared Kushner and their third child trailed her.) Next, there was the preinaugural candlelight dinner at D.C.'s Union Station. She posted herself on Instagram in another Oscar de la Renta number, this time a long white dress with a black waistband tied in a big bow at the back. She wore an asymmetrical Oscar de la Renta cream pantsuit for the inauguration and a golden, glittery Carolina Herrera ball gown for the evening balls. After the music had played for a few bars, she and her husband glided onto the stage at the Walter E. Washington Convention Center, just in time to save her father's ritual first dance from turning into his first national crisis. Donald and Melania Trump had shuffled about so awkwardly that there was speculation about their marital problems for months afterward. Ivanka and Kushner led the other Trump children and their spouses onto the stage, joining her father and Melania, and all eyes were now on them. Ivanka, it would later be reported, had said she wanted a "princess moment." And she got one.

It was still unclear, as she and her husband danced, what formal role Ivanka would have in the Trump administration. The couple had just announced they'd be renting a six-bedroom house for fifteen thousand dollars a month in the upscale Washington neighborhood of Kalorama, where their neighbors included the Obamas and Jeff Bezos. Ivanka had said she was officially taking a leave of absence from her business, now to be run by a lawyer, Abigail Klem. However, she did not *sell* the business. She claimed to be selling her common stock in the Trump Organization, but she would take equity payments.

It was an arrangement that ethics experts like George W. Bush's former chief ethics lawyer, Richard Painter, would find just as unsatisfactory as her husband's faux divestment. Painter told *The Guardian*, "The answer to avoiding conflicts of interest would be for Ivanka Trump to sell off her fashion business." Unlike the president, Ivanka's activities as an employee of the executive branch would be circumscribed by the Office of Government Ethics regulation that prevents government employees from using their position to profit themselves, their relatives, or their friends.

But why dwell on any of that when there was so much fun to be had in the immediate future? On inauguration night, her husband looked uncharacteristically emotional. Michael Cohen, who lived in the couple's building in New York, had once observed of Kushner that he is usually so calm, "he's almost like a flat line on an EKG." But that night, the couple was clearly euphoric. They had arrived at the apex of power—and they'd done it together. The author of *TrumpNation*, Timothy O'Brien, gave the couple the nickname Javanka, explaining, "I think of it as shorthand for the joint—and relatively unchecked—power they wield in the Trump White House, given their proximity to the president and the financial and familial ties that they share with him."

———

The day after the inauguration, more than half a million women marched along D.C.'s National Mall to the Washington Monument to protest the new president and his mistreatment of women. Josh Kushner slipped out of the Trump International Hotel to find out what was going on and was photographed walking among the protesters. It was widely interpreted that he was a not-so-secret member of the resistance. No such conclusions could be made about his brother or his brother's wife. During the campaign, Ivanka had championed women, yet today she remained silent. It would later emerge in longtime Planned Parenthood president Cecile Richards's memoir, *Make Trouble,* that the couple had already approached her and had tried to negotiate with Planned Parenthood, much as one would approach a real estate deal: you give up X, we give you Y. The difficulty was that Javanka wanted Richards to stop offering abortions, one of the many crucial services offered to women by Planned Parenthood, in exchange for federal funding. Richards was staggered by both the couple's naïveté and amorality. "It almost felt like a bribe," she wrote. From Richards's description, it was clear that whatever narrative they'd spun about being the liberal protectors of the president was false.

Steve Bannon skipped the inaugural balls and went with Stephen Miller to Bannon's new office near the Oval Office. Initially, he and Kushner had wanted a connecting door between their offices kept open. In his office, Bannon wrote out all the Trump campaign promises on a whiteboard, as a constant reminder of what had to be done. His plan had been to roll out the move of the U.S. embassy in Israel to Jerusalem—a promise to Sheldon Adelson, who had given twenty million dollars to a pro-Trump super PAC—on day one. But he'd later complain that when he arrived at his office, he found a draft of an interagency memo that claimed the change would cause outrage in the Middle East and result in rioting and an explosion on "the Arab Street." "Who fucking ordered this report?" he said to Miller. "If this thing gets in *The Washington Post,* we're done." He sent the memo back, but he feared its existence would mean delaying the embassy move a few months. According to a source close to J Street, a liberal, pro-Israel group that advocates for a two-state solution in Israel, a rumor went around that Kushner wanted the group to delay the embassy move—and that they had gone to the State Department. It was assumed by some that Kushner had feared the Palestinian reaction to the embassy move would sabotage his Middle East peace plans before he could even begin negotiating. He wanted the move to happen—but at a more expedient moment. Bannon was pissed, and everyone knew it.

Those first few days were chaotic for almost everyone in the new administration. A frantic Reince Priebus would quickly discover that it was impossible to impose any kind of order in this White House, in large part because Trump didn't like order. What Trump liked was having people fight in front of him and then he'd make a decision, just like he'd made snap decisions when his children presented licensing deals for the Trump Organization. This kind of dysfunction enabled a "floater" like Kushner, whose job was undefined, to weigh in on any topic in front of Trump and have far more influence than he would have had in a top-down hierarchy.

Several senior White House staffers thought Kushner meddled in *everything,* which led to his unofficial title as "Secretary of Everything." Gary Cohn had assumed that as the director of the National Economic Council, he'd handle U.S. trade agreements, but he hadn't accounted for Kushner. Luis Videgaray, who was now Mexico's secretary of foreign affairs, was frequently seen in Kushner's office, and Kushner told everyone: "We're making enormous progress with NAFTA, we are agreeing on everything." Two people who heard this wondered if Kushner knew that NAFTA was a multithousand-page agreement, and that renegotiating it would involve legal negotiations with U.S. trade representatives.

There was a setback to Kushner's scheme almost immediately. He and Videgaray planned for a public rapprochement at the White House between Trump and Mexican President Enrique Peña Nieto over trade and Trump's proposed border wall. One person remembered that the plan was for Peña Nieto to come to Washington, have a big ceremony at the White House, and then Trump and others would fly to Mexico and do the same thing there. Kushner, said this person, was more "caught up in the pomp and circumstance of saying we had an agreement than what the agreement was."

White House people quickly grasped that Kushner was a delegator and not a detail-oriented guy, and that he was more interested in headlines than in the substance of what followed.

Kushner's wall stunt never had a chance. Peña Nieto said publicly he would not be paying for the wall. Videgaray was at the White House when Trump retaliated, tweeting, "If Mexico is unwilling to pay for the badly needed wall, then it would be better to cancel the upcoming meeting." Kushner was livid, according to *Vanity Fair*.

Videgaray knew Cohn well from his years working with Goldman Sachs (he had been the Mexican finance minister then). "I'm just totally wasting my time with Jared, aren't I?" he asked Cohn, who replied, "I don't know if you're wasting your time, but you're not going to get a trade agreement done."

Priebus was deeply frustrated by Kushner's steadfast opposition to the idea of repealing the Affordable Care Act (Obamacare), put on the table at the start of the administration by Priebus's close friend Speaker of the House Paul Ryan. So, too, for completely different reasons, was Gary Cohn. Cohn, a Democrat, agreed with Kushner that repealing and replacing Obamacare the way the Republicans wanted—by, among other things, rolling back Medicaid expansion and cutting the taxes on the rich that helped pay for it—was wrong. But he completely disagreed with Kushner's approach to creating a workable alternative. He, and others, noticed that Kushner kept trying to get his younger brother involved. "Josh knows more about this topic than anyone else," he'd brag. He was referring to the fact that Josh had co-founded the online health insurer, Oscar, which was predicated on Obamacare: it could be purchased on the state exchanges that the Affordable Care Act had created. Cohn knew Josh, but he thought it would be completely inappropriate for the younger Kushner to be anywhere near the shaping of a new health care bill. (Jared denied attempting to involve his brother in health policy.) Cohn knew that the Kushner brothers had a partnership arrangement in Cadre, and this made him suspicious of Jared's motives on health care. Oscar's valuation around the time that the White House was considering replacing Obamacare was $2.7 billion—

higher than that of 666 Fifth Avenue—which meant that if new legislation rolled back Obamacare, it could be financially catastrophic. Someone close to the brothers pointed out to me that "no other asset [in the Kushner family] comes close [to Oscar]."

Josh never spoke to Cohn about the so-called repeal-and-replace efforts. However, Josh's chief policy and strategy officer at Oscar, former New York City schools chancellor Joel Klein, talked (and talked) to Cohn about it, to the point that Cohn felt uncomfortable. He felt Klein was blatantly trying to sculpt health care in a way that would be best for Oscar. (In an email, Klein said that Cohn had asked him for his views. "We publicly opposed the Administration's position and, like any other interested party, we wanted our views to be heard.")

Jared's next tin-eared move was to bring in Ezekiel Emanuel, a distinguished oncologist and academic, and the brother of talent agent Ari and Chicago mayor Rahm, as an ad-hoc consultant. Emanuel's ideas were even more radical than Obama's had been. There was no way they would garner any Republican support. Cohn felt Jared was not looking at the practical challenges of the puzzle they faced: of coming up with some kind of bill that could actually get votes. Jared was more impressed by famous names.

The first Friday of the Trump administration, Jared and Ivanka hosted their first Shabbat dinner in Washington. A florist, a rabbi, and a caterer were spotted arriving at their new home ahead of the notable guests: Commerce Secretary Wilbur Ross and his wife, Hilary Geary Ross; Treasury Secretary Steven Mnuchin and his then-fiancée, Louise Linton; Cohn; Dina Powell; and White House Director of Strategic Communications Hope Hicks. Around the time they all sat down to eat, the White House announced an executive order: a ninety-day travel ban on immigrants from seven majority-Muslim countries—Iran, Iraq, Libya, Somalia, Sudan, Syria, and Yemen. This had been one of the items on Bannon's whiteboard to-do list. Stephen Miller had been the person responsible for its implementation, which had been kept a closely guarded secret. Cohn was not supposed to hear about it, but word got around. Cohn was so concerned that he cornered Kushner at the dinner. "You need to get involved," Cohn told him. "Do you know we are doing this? Aren't your grandparents immigrants? Because mine are." Kushner told Cohn there was nothing he could do—Trump felt as strongly about the subject as Miller and Bannon did.

At first, it seemed to White House senior staff, Kushner and Ivanka were supportive of the travel ban. What they hated was the reaction to it. Airports around the country were flooded with protesters. The mainstream media went berserk. The night after the travel ban was announced, Ivanka posted on Instagram a photograph of the couple in full black-tie regalia heading out to the Alfalfa Club dinner, an exclusive annual event for the political elite. She wore a silver Carolina Herrera gown. A pairing of this picture with one of a refugee girl wrapped in a silver thermal blanket and the hashtag #letthemeatcake quickly became a meme.

After this, Ivanka told her father that the travel ban would never make him liked and he needed to fix it. Possibly, given all the nasty comments on the internet about her, what she probably meant was that *she* needed to be liked and he needed to fix this. She suggested crossing the aisle politically, "shaking hands" with Democrats to get Trump's poll numbers up. A source told me that Bannon was horrified. He hadn't come all this way to be liked; and he didn't believe that reaching across the aisle would help Trump be liked, either. "There's nothing you can do that's going to mollify [Democrats]," he told the president. "What you have to do is check the boxes on what you promised. You're going to keep your base, expand that another five percent. We'll win in [2020 in] a landslide."

He told Kushner that Trump won because of his agenda, and they had to deliver on their campaign promises if they wanted to be reelected. Kushner replied that Trump won because he was Trump.

Bannon now started to tell allies in and outside the White House that he was concerned that Kushner had no belief in the substance of what they had campaigned on. He feared they could no longer be partners and that, inevitably, he was in for a political knife fight with Javanka. Priebus was also deeply frustrated by the couple's political opposition to the Trump agenda. They opposed every executive order that was on Bannon's whiteboard and every policy Trump had campaigned on: the repeal of Obama-care, the exit from the Paris Agreement on climate change, immigration . . . on and on. Katie Walsh, Priebus's deputy, was utterly confused because her job was to try to put meetings on the calendar to advance the agenda, and she'd been told by Priebus and Bannon to move on repeal-and-replace and on executive orders, only to be told the exact opposite by Kushner.

For a couple of months, Kushner and Bannon confined their tension to arguments in front of Trump in the Oval Office. But some time after Bannon appeared on the February 13 cover of *Time* magazine with the headline THE GREAT MANIPULATOR, two sources say that he and Kushner got into a vicious argument in a cabinet room near Hope Hicks's office. It started when Bannon discovered Kushner was having secret meetings with Senators Lindsey Graham and Dick Durbin about DACA (Deferred Action for Childhood Arrivals), the Obama-era program that allowed young immigrants who had come to the U.S. as kids—the so-called Dreamers—to live and work in the U.S. Trump had vowed during his campaign that he would end DACA. But here was Kushner advocating for the exact opposite. According to someone Bannon confided in, Bannon asked for a minute in private with Kushner. As they sat across from each other, Kushner, according to this person's recollections, started off unctuously, "We were such great partners on the campaign and, you know, you did such a great job. But, you know, your ego is out of control; you want to be a puppet master," referring to the *Time* magazine cover.

"Jared, it has nothing to do with that," Bannon apparently said. "This is all about an agenda. We got here because this movement has got certain things that it has to have done, and Trump personified that. And what you want to do is so far off that . . ."

That was the end of the civil discussion, Bannon would tell a confidant. "We start shouting at each other. I could see his demeanor totally changed. He goes from a little boy to, like, this fucking devil. I was not pleasant, either."

There was no hope of rapprochement after that. The door between their offices was kept shut.

For Bannon and the populists, battling Ivanka would be even tougher than battling Kushner. Her relationship with her father was so tight it was nearly impossible for outsiders to intervene. Multiple people noticed that she'd regularly wander into the Oval Office, often with a child in tow, and talk to Trump in a singsong voice. He'd call her "baby" or pat her on the bottom. He sometimes stopped what he was doing to ogle her when she left the room. "Doesn't she look great?" he would say to others in the room. One person told me he found something about the dynamic sickening.

But their relationship was also more complex than anyone could fathom. Very, very occasionally Trump embarrassed Ivanka, deliberately showing White House senior staff—and her—the limitations of her brazen efforts to manipulate him. It was apparent that he sometimes thought she needed to be publicly reminded who was in charge. One example happened in early February, when the Chinese ambassador, Cui Tiankai, visited the White House, dropping in on Kushner. In turn, Ivanka took her daughter Arabella to a Lunar New Year party at the Chinese embassy in Washington. While Ivanka claimed to have nothing to do with her business, the brand badly needed the Chinese market to prop the business up; a former White House senior official told me he suspected Ivanka's courtship of Chinese government officials had something to do with the fact that sales in the U.S. had suffered a setback. Nordstrom, Neiman Marcus, and other retailers had dropped her brand after the inauguration. Her father was quick to tweet a response when this happened: "My daughter Ivanka has been treated so unfairly by @Nordstrom. She is a great person—always pushing me to do the right thing! Terrible!"

On February 9, counselor to the president Kellyanne Conway said in an interview on *Fox & Friends*, "Go buy Ivanka's stuff. . . . I'm going to give a free commercial here: go buy it today, everybody; you can find it online." This clearly broke an ethics rule that states a federal employee cannot use public office for endorsement of a product. Conway was formally counseled by the White House for that sales pitch, but instead of comforting Conway, Ivanka had a meltdown. She had been embarrassed by Conway's toadying. One source recalled, "Ivanka got really mad. She stormed into [Trump's] office."

In front of other people, Trump quickly deflated his daughter: "Honey, you sell shoes. Calm down."

On February 13, Ivanka attended a roundtable of a dozen female business leaders with Trump and Canadian Prime Minister Justin Trudeau. This was her first obvious foray into policy, and it was driven by her adviser, Dina Powell. The breakfast seemed a success—Ivanka and Trudeau appeared to forge a bond, albeit one that would be gossiped about in the White House. There were jokes that she had a "crush" on the handsome Canadian premier.

The roundtable also was a good tactical fit with Ivanka's policy position, announced during the campaign, that a child tax credit needed to be expanded beyond one thousand dollars per child. The problem with her position was that it was not the Republican one. Cohn liked the idea but tried to explain to her that it was going to be hard to get enough votes in Congress. But Ivanka would "not get off her ideas," it was said around the White House. Some Ivanka ideas were considered so "crazy" that her offices were nicknamed "HABI"—the Home of All Bad Ideas.

It didn't help that Ivanka had a reputation for being flighty. It was also noted that she wore a new designer outfit every day and came in late, at 10 A.M., usually with hair and makeup professionally done. She sometimes changed her outfit three times a day. She was also an attention-grabber. She sat next to German Chancellor Angela Merkel at a meeting on vocational training during Merkel's March visit to the White House, a move for which she was roundly criticized. *Politico*'s Annie Karni wrote that the bold gesture "essentially elevated a family member with no political experience to the level of Europe's most important leader."

Another issue was the remarkable number of vacations Javanka took—often at times of crisis. In late March, just as the White House–endorsed repeal-and-replace bill flamed out on the House floor—the first legislative disaster of the new administration—the couple was skiing in Aspen. One former government official observed that their mentality was felt to be extraordinarily entitled. "It's the whole concept that 'our lifestyles don't have to change just because we're working in government. . . . The American tax-payer owes us.'"

Bannon thought they were running away from political fights. "Any time there's a crisis, they fade," he said to people. Even Trump let it be known he was irritated by their many absences. Another senior-level person thought their vacations were a godsend. "It was always better when they were gone," this person said. "We loved it."

On February 13, Ivanka's favorite general, Michael Flynn, resigned, ostensibly for lying to Vice President Mike Pence about whether he had discussed U.S. sanctions with Russian Ambassador Sergey Kislyak. The media now asked who else Flynn had met with, where and when, but Kushner remained quiet about *his* meetings with Kislyak (one had been with Flynn) and with Sergey Gorkov, the Russian banker. His initial security clearance forms, filed on January 18, had no mention of these meetings—or, for that matter, of any that he'd had with the other dignitaries he had talked with secretly. He made zero mention of his meeting with Kremlin-linked lawyer Natalia Veselnitskaya with Don Jr. and Paul Manafort in Trump Tower. The "foreign contacts" section of his form was left blank. (His lawyer Jamie Gorelick later said the paperwork had been "prematurely submitted.")

All this would play out against the backdrop of investigations into Russian meddling in the 2016 presidential election conducted by the House and Senate intelligence committees and the FBI. During a House Intelligence Committee hearing in March, James Comey, the FBI director, confirmed that the bureau was conducting an investigation into whether the Trump campaign coordinated with Russia to sway the election. The same month, *The New York Times* broke the stories of Kushner's meetings with Kislyak and Gorkov. Kushner would try to explain them away as innocuous, but as William Saletan wrote for *Slate* at the time, it now seemed clear that Kushner was incapable of transparency. "Flynn, Sessions, Kushner . . . This White House never tells the truth."

In March, Bill Priestap, the FBI's assistant director in charge of the Counterintelligence Division, warned Kushner that he was seen as a target for influence by operatives from several countries—including Russia, China, and Israel. In the intelligence reports Kushner received thanks to his temporary security clearance, there was "chatter" about how it was possible to "manipulate or take advantage of Kushner" because of his family company's need to pay off the massive loan coming due on 666 Fifth Avenue and partly because he was naïve and inexperienced in foreign policy.

Kushner ignored Priestap's warning, and instead of pulling back, amped up his solo statesman act. On March 14, Saudi Arabia's deputy crown prince (and soon-to-be crown prince), MBS, was welcomed at the White House for a lunch attended by Trump, Kushner, Pence, Bannon, Priebus, and Flynn's replacement as national security adviser, H. R. McMaster. It is unheard of for a foreign official other than a head of state to be feted this way, but MBS and Kushner had already been introduced, and Kushner was lobbying hard on the prince's behalf in the White House. The two men needed each other. MBS, who was in his early thirties, wanted to reform the economic model of his country, whose oil would run out in some twenty years, and as a start he wanted to list the shares of Aramco, the Saudi state oil company, on the New York Stock Exchange. Kushner saw an alliance with MBS as the key to his Middle East peace plan in providing financing for the Palestinians and neutering Iran, which financed Hamas and Hezbollah, both foes of Israel. There was also discussion of a lucrative U.S. arms deal, with the Saudis willing to purchase billions in defense equipment and services. After this lunch, the two boy princes, as they would be nicknamed, communicated regularly on the encrypted messaging service WhatsApp.

When Ivanka officially joined the White House in March as an unsalaried adviser to the president, her assets were put in a trust overseen by Kushner relatives, but she remained the sole beneficiary. The day before she joined, one of her companies also applied for fourteen trademarks in China. On April 6, the same day Trump hosted Chinese President Xi Jinping at Mar-a-Lago, her brand received provisional approval for three new trademarks in China, which caused widespread criticism. It looked as if it had taken her less than a month to get them. Ordinarily it takes over a year.

Although their bank accounts were swelling, Javanka hated all the negative attention their unorthodox financial arrangements were attracting, and they figured it was essential to woo the media. Bannon was surprised to walk into the Oval Office one day to find *The New York Times*'s Maggie Haberman sitting with Ivanka in the president's small dining room. At least, he comforted himself, Haberman was seemingly impervious to the First Daughter's flattery.

Bannon scored a minor victory against Javanka on March 15, the 250th anniversary of the birth of the seventh American president, Andrew Jackson. Jackson was a general, a populist, and a slave owner who fought several duels, and everyone in the White House knew that Bannon was "obsessed" with the parallels between Jackson and Trump: "He was a man's man; he had a bad-girl wife." Trump loved hearing about their connection. Jackson's portrait had been hung near Trump's desk in the Oval Office. It was widely known that Bannon planned for Trump to visit Jackson's plantation, the Hermitage, in Tennessee, on Jackson's birthday and hold a rally in Nashville that night. But, according to White House sources, shortly before the visit, Trump asked him if they could go the following day. "Absolutely not," said Bannon, according to the same sources. "You're either there on the 250th birthday or you're not." Ivanka, it turned out, had tickets for the Tony Award–winning musical *Come from Away* and wanted to go with Justin Trudeau and his wife, Sophie, along with Kushner, Trump, and Melania.

Bannon gave Trump the list of reasons he thought this was a "stupid" idea. First off, Pence had just gone to see *Hamilton* and been booed by the audience and reprimanded by the cast. Second, "You can't get out," Bannon warned Trump. "If you want time in hell, go sit in a tiny theater seat and feel trapped while they're booing you." Third—and first, really, in Bannon's mind—the play was totally against Trump's immigration policy. "The reason everybody loves this show is because it's the anti-Trump musical, because it's a group hug at the end about how good open borders and immigration are—how we all really love each other after 9/11, right?"

Basically, said Bannon, you have a choice: "Jackson or Trudeau. Are you kidding me? That's not even a choice."

Trump looked at Ivanka: "Hey, baby. I think Steve's right. I think Jackson's my man." He went to the Hermitage. Ivanka went to the musical.

In April, Ivanka and Kushner hired a publicist, Josh Raffel, whom they knew from New York. He was considered to be an excellent publicist, but hiring him did little to endear Javanka to their colleagues. No one else on the White House staff had their own in-house dedicated public relations person.

Raffel had an impossible job. In this very leaky White House, everyone was aware that many of Javanka's colleagues found them tiresome and arrogant. It was quickly established that, for some people, the worst thing that could happen in their day in the White House was to be interrupted by Ivanka. "She walks in a room and everyone's just like, 'Ugh, we have to deal with this now?'" one person told me. "I'd better have an extra good smile when I wave at her." Another former senior White House official sarcastically described Kushner and Ivanka's earlier, privileged New York lives, where they never had to actually work for something: "They work long hours in their beautiful, marble offices with their drivers."

On March 27, *The New York Times* reported that the Senate Intelligence Committee wanted to question Kushner about his meetings with Russians during the transition. The story broke the news of his meeting with Sergey Gorkov, and Hope Hicks was also forced to answer questions as to why Kushner had not mentioned his meetings with Sergey Kislyak to senior White House colleagues during the conversations about firing Michael Flynn. She said these meetings were standard and inconsequential.

Kushner exchanged emails with Gary Ginsberg, the executive vice president of Time Warner, insisting that CNN, which is owned by a division of his company, needed to stop covering the Russia investigation. Ginsberg, who had met with Kushner in the White House early in the administration for a "very bizarre hour," during which Kushner bashed CNN's Trump coverage, felt Kushner's emails contained blatant falsehoods about Kushner's activities. "I just stopped talking to him," Ginsberg told people. In November, the Justice Department sued to block Time Warner's planned merger with AT&T, saying it would be bad for consumers. Ginsberg felt sure he knew why: "This lawsuit is 100 percent Kushner." (Ultimately, the suit failed.)

In late March, Kushner had better news to announce: he would be leading the White House Office of American Innovation—a group of officials and business leaders who would come up with ways to make the government more efficient. Kushner explained that "the government should be run like a great American company." Bannon was livid. The whole idea, he felt, was an extension of the technology roundtable during the transition: an example of "crony capitalism," and Kushner and Ivanka were the lobbyists. "It was a front," stormed Bannon to anyone who would listen, "for Jared to hang out with [Apple CEO] Tim Cook . . . and Lloyd Blankfein." Blankfein was then the CEO of Goldman Sachs, which was an investor in Cadre, the real-estate-investing start-up Kushner cofounded with his brother, from which Kushner had not divested, an arrangement which would draw the scrutiny of ethics watchdogs. Kushner should not have been meeting at the White House with one of Cadre's investors, if he wanted to avoid the appearance of a conflict of interest. (His stake in Cadre had not been mentioned on his financial disclosure form; instead, Gorelick would be later forced to explain, it had been housed as part of BFPS. His updated form would say he recused himself from Cadre-related issues.) On April 14, it was announced that the White House visitor logs would be kept closed. The official reason, White House Communications Director Mike Dubke said at the time, was "the grave national security risks and privacy concerns of the hundreds of thousands of visitors annually."

Bannon and two other senior White House officials felt certain that the directive had come from Kushner, who didn't want his frenetic networking exposed. Trump told press secretary Sean Spicer he had not even been looped in. "What the fuck have you guys done and why?" Trump asked Dubke upon learning of it. Bannon told Priebus he wanted visibility partly because it would have surprised a great many people who considered him a racist to know he was meeting with both black groups and unions. But Bannon was overruled, and it was not immediately clear to him—or to Spicer—by whom. Priebus would tell people the directive had not come from him, but he had not stopped it. He had not wanted to fight Kushner over issues he did not consider a priority. He was more concerned about the agenda.

At the end of March, Priebus's deputy, Katie Walsh, quit. Her job had become untenable because, even though she was the deputy to the White House chief of staff, she felt continually thwarted by Kushner. But Bannon heard that Javanka (he wasn't sure which half) had shown Trump a blog post by the right-wing activist and troll Charles "Chuck" Johnson that claimed Walsh had been leaking. It was surprising that Trump would even read it. Bannon asked White House personnel director Johnny DeStefano, "Who gave this to Trump?" The answer: Javanka.

On April 5, Ivanka appeared on *CBS This Morning* with Gayle King and responded to the suggestion, made on a recent episode of *Saturday Night Live,* that she was "complicit" in the draconian actions of her father. (The actress Scarlett Johansson had played Ivanka in the sketch.) "If being complicit is wanting to be a force for good and to make a positive impact, then I'm complicit." On staying silent, she said, "I would say not to conflate lack of public denouncement with silence. I think there are multiple ways to have your voice heard. . . . Where I disagree with my father, he knows it. And I express myself with total candor."

King broached the subject of Ivanka's potential financial conflicts. Ivanka pushed back, claiming no interest in "making money." It had been reported just the day before that Kushner's financial disclosures showed Ivanka's 7 percent stake in the Trump International Hotel in Washington, D.C., was worth between five million and twenty-five million dollars.

Even as Ivanka tried to burnish her image, Bannon found that in some ways he respected her. Ivanka, he felt, was at least trying to protect her father.

Bannon told colleagues he felt she was misguided in the way she tried to do it, but he understood where she was coming from and he admired it. He, too, had a daughter. What he—and other White House staff—felt was irritating was Ivanka's desire to have it both ways: She wanted to be taken seriously as a member of the White House staff but she also expected to be treated with greater respect, as the First Daughter.

The arrogance really got to Bannon. Just as he'd exploded with her husband, Bannon got into it with Ivanka. First there was a scene in front of Priebus, in which Bannon ripped Ivanka: "I realize, just as my daughter loves me, you love your father, and you're very supportive of him and that's terrific. But as a staffer, you're just another staffer here at the White House who doesn't know what the fuck you're doing."

Ivanka retorted: "I'm never going to be just another staffer. I'm the First Daughter."

Another epic Bannon/Ivanka fight came when Bannon was in the Oval Office dining room while Trump was watching TV and eating his lunch. The way White House insiders heard it—and hear it, they did—Ivanka marched in, claiming Bannon had leaked H. R. McMaster's war plan for Afghanistan. Bannon, according to people he talked to afterward, said mildly, "No, that was leaked by McMaster because they want to make sure it happens." (Trump had opposed McMaster's idea for adding troops; he wanted to withdraw. So did Bannon.) "It's obvious." According to multiple sources the conversation escalated quickly:

Ivanka: "No, you're the leaker."

Bannon: "You're the biggest leaker in this place. You leak all the time."

Ivanka: "I don't know anybody in the press. I wouldn't even know who to call."

Bannon: "Everybody knows you leak. You and Jared spend all day long leaking on people."

Ivanka: "You're a fucking liar. Everything that comes out of your mouth is a fucking lie."

Bannon: "Go fuck yourself. . . . You are nothing. . . ."

Trump, reading the offending news article: "Hey, baby, I think Steve's right on this one. I think they leaked it to make me look bad."

Bannon thought he would be fired on the spot. He was shocked—and impressed—by Trump's dispassionate attitude toward Ivanka in that instance. But he'd learned something important: much as Trump loved his daughter and hated saying no to her, he was not always controlled by her.

CHAPTER THIRTEEN

The Anbang Bang

"The president doesn't have really strange visitors.
Jared had the strange visitors."

—FORMER SENIOR WHITE HOUSE OFFICIAL

Charlie and Josh Kushner were present for Jared Kushner's swearing-in as a senior adviser to the president of the United States on January 22, 2017. And when Charlie got back to New Jersey, he showed Alan Hammer photographs of his grandchildren in the Oval Office and his sons walking down the halls of the White House residence quarters. Jared and Josh posed together under the portrait of John F. Kennedy, their idol. Charlie had always said the Kushners would be the Jewish Kennedys—and here they were! "He was incredibly proud of Jared," said Hammer. Father and son still spoke every day on the phone. Since Jared had undertaken only a limited divestment from Kushner Companies, what was happening with the loan on 666 Fifth Avenue and the rest of the portfolio must have remained of paramount importance to him. It was the empire to which he'd return when he was done with Washington, D.C. Of equal importance, it was what mattered to his beloved father.

Some of his meetings in the White House during the administration's early months were with people in a position to help his father, the sort of people Steve Bannon called crony capitalists. Kushner's visitors at the White House included Michael Corbat, the CEO of Citigroup, and Josh Harris, a founder of Apollo Global Management, whom Kushner had wanted to hire after the 2016 election to run Trump's Office of Management and Budget. Harris had also served on the Presidential Advisory Council on Infrastructure that Kushner had pushed for, and which Bannon thought achieved little. What not even Bannon knew while he was complaining about this showboating waste of time was that in March 2017, Citigroup loaned Kushner Companies $325 million to finance the mortgage on office buildings in Brooklyn. Later that year, Apollo lent the firm $184 million to refinance the mortgage on a Chicago skyscraper. The dots only got connected between Kushner's White House meetings and the deals with Kushner Companies a year later, shortly before John Kelly, the new White House chief of staff, insisted there be some level of transparency in the White House logs, which began to be released in April 2018.

When *The New York Times* broke the story of Kushner's meetings in 2018, it quoted Don Fox, the acting director of the Office of Government Ethics for two years in the Obama administration and its general counsel for five years. Before that, Fox was a lawyer for the air force and navy through Republican and Democratic administrations spanning three decades. "This is exactly why senior government officials, for as long back as I have any experience, don't maintain any active outside business interests," he said. "The appearance of conflicts of interest is simply too great." Senator John McCain saw the story of the loans on TV during a break between treatment sessions for his terminal brain cancer. He had never liked Kushner—he considered him a "pipsqueak"—and now he was appalled. He asked his adviser Rick Davis rhetorically: "Oh, my God, how can you have people come into the White House and then get a loan?"

But those deals were just a tiny blemish in the rash of questionable behavior by Kushner that would not have been tolerated in any other White House. On top of Kushner's continual pushing of his brother and Josh's knowledge of health care, there were his communications with Michael Fascitelli. Fascitelli had taken over the investment committee of the Kushner brothers' real estate technology platform, Cadre, as its chairman and senior adviser when Jared went into the White House. Cadre's investors included Goldman Sachs (Fascitelli's alma mater), Alibaba cofounder Jack

Ma, and Josh's Thrive Capital. But a Cadre investor told me he was startled to discover that after the election, Jared and Fascitelli remained in communication about the firm, from which Jared did not divest himself. (Fascitelli disputed this, saying that he "deliberately stayed away from Jared.") This investor felt that any such communication was not ethical. This person knew that Jared considered Cadre to have enormous potential. "This is what's going to make us all billionaires," he'd said in its early stages. Fascitelli was urging Jared to divest his stake in Cadre, because he believed (correctly) that Jared's new position would be a hindrance to raising foreign investment. But Jared was reluctant.

Meanwhile, the proposed terms of the Kushners' deal with the Chinese insurer Anbang for 666 Fifth, according to *Bloomberg*, would value the building at $2.85 billion. It was a figure that seemed far too expensive—at least twice the property's true value, according to a real estate expert. After *Bloomberg* reported that the deal seemed "unusually favorable" to Kushner Companies, five members of Congress—Senators Elizabeth Warren, Tom Carper, Sherrod Brown, and Gary Peters, as well as Representative Elijah Cummings—would write to Treasury Secretary Steven Mnuchin and White House counsel Donald McGahn to complain.

Meanwhile, the Kushners had stopped leasing office space in 666 Fifth so they could pitch the building to investors as a retail mall with luxury condos on the top. By the spring of 2017, 666 Fifth was down to 70 percent occupancy, and the Kushners were paying down the debt out of their own pocket. The floor plans and low ceilings were increasingly considered "obsolete," and a revamp would be hugely expensive. Office buildings had become much more densely populated than they used to be, which meant they needed more bathrooms and elevators, better HVAC, and higher ceilings. And those big corner offices had gone completely out of style.

An additional hurdle was that Anbang was met with skepticism in real estate circles. Its most infamous acquisition in the U.S. had been New York's Waldorf Astoria hotel, for which it paid $1.95 billion in 2015, an amount a major New York City real estate broker considered excessive by one billion dollars. The company's motivation in buying the building was also questionable. One person told me, at the time, that its chairman, Wu

Xiaohui, who had married a granddaughter of former Chinese leader Deng Xiaoping, seemed more interested in making a splash than in developing properties: "The Waldorf was his coming-out party." American brokers and developers were wary of Anbang and its buying spree.

After Anbang bought the Waldorf, two subsequent potential acquisitions—the Hotel del Coronado in San Diego and the company Starwood Hotels & Resorts—fell through. The U.S. government, specifically the Committee on Foreign Investment in the U.S. (CFIUS), had raised concerns about the San Diego acquisition, and the government could have had similar problems with the Starwood deal had it moved forward. Barry Sternlicht, Starwood's founder, also expressed serious doubts about Anbang. He wondered about Wu and believed Anbang was just a front; he suspected that the real buyer was the government of China. (In 2018, Wu was convicted of fraud and stealing ten billion dollars and sentenced to eighteen years in prison. Apparently, the Chinese government had turned on Wu, regardless of who he was related to.)

By the end of March, the Anbang-666 deal was dead. A spokesperson for Kushner Companies blamed all the criticism on the media, but in an interview with *The New York Times*, the firm's spokesperson sounded optimistic about finding funding elsewhere: "We are well on our way to lining up the $2.5 billion in equity needed to get this deal done, and we're confident that we'll get there."

Charlie knew what the rest of us did not—that some of his eldest son's foreign contacts were willing to take meetings with him.

CHAPTER FOURTEEN

St. Rex

"Rex Tillerson thought that he was secretary of state. . . . He didn't understand that the Trump chaos machine and the Trump family-loyalty machine were bigger than the U.S. Constitution."

—FORMER SENIOR WHITE HOUSE OFFICIAL

Rex Tillerson had a rough confirmation hearing on account of his long career as CEO of ExxonMobil: he was questioned in great detail about his dealings with countries like Russia and Saudi Arabia. He finally got confirmed as secretary of state on February 1. The vote had the most opposition of any secretary of state in half a century: 56–43.

He had assumed—understandably—that once he was in office, Jared Kushner would defer to him on foreign affairs. After all, he'd run a global firm for eleven years that, at the time of his confirmation, had a market capitalization of more than $350 billion—and he'd worked there for forty-one years. But Kushner told him to back off. First, he said to leave Mexico to him because he'd have NAFTA wrapped up by October. Tillerson would be startled to arrive with his wife for dinner at Cafe Milano in Georgetown in Washington, D.C., to find Luis Videgaray eating there, because he'd had no knowledge that his Mexican counterpart was in town. Normal protocol dictates that two foreign secretaries are each other's first point of contact when they travel to the other's home. Tillerson came over to say hello after he'd finished his meal. "Next time, do get in touch with me," he told Videgaray, who explained he was there to see Kushner. Tillerson was polite about the snub, but he told colleagues it was inappropriate.

Next, Kushner took the Middle East from Tillerson's portfolio. "I want Israel," is how he put it, according to a former Tillerson aide. The same day Tillerson was confirmed, it was reported that Israel planned to build its first new settlement in the West Bank in more than two decades. The U.S. issued a statement that suggested this might "not be helpful" in forging peace in the region, but Israel went ahead, clearly not fearing American action.

In the stay-in-your-lane corporate world Tillerson came from, Kushner would have been fired, but Tillerson, a former Boy Scout, tried to work with Kushner because he thought it was the right thing to do, said someone familiar with Tillerson's thinking.

Tillerson had more unpleasant surprises awaiting him. An adviser suggested that in order to receive budget approval for his department, he didn't just have to ask for it, he had to leak that he had asked for it. (He refused to do this, preferring to appeal directly to the vice president, but he never received budget approval.) He also became appalled by the culture he discovered at the State Department where, according to a former aide, there had been rampant sexual harassment—women cried in front of him as they told their stories. He decided to discuss the issue at every embassy he visited, and the unheralded legacy of his tenure at the State Department is, possibly, the great effort he made to try to right wrongs that were not of his making.

Kushner made such victories difficult for Tillerson, who figured that if he could get on Kushner's calendar—and the president's—as often as possible, they would start to understand that he had experience in the regions they were dealing with. He was wrong. The cabinet member who did listen to him—even though the two men did not always agree—was the one who, like him, had spent many years abroad: General James Mattis, the defense secretary. He and Mattis got so close that Mattis started calling him Saint Rex. They shared many of the same concerns: Trump, according to a Tillerson aide, relied on instinct and impulse. He didn't want to understand the historical rationale behind national security policy-making. Tillerson's meetings in the White House would be sometimes interrupted because, for example, Trump, who was always watching TV, saw Fox News host Sean

Hannity appear on his screen. "Look, look, Sean's coming on now," he once said in the middle of a briefing.

Tillerson worried that Kushner, like Trump, was not interested in details. Rather, like Trump, Kushner thought he could fix things by inserting himself as a "relationship person" and then delegate. He was also arrogant. "The one thing about Jared that I think is noticeable, is that he becomes quite self-confident, quite quickly," said someone involved in diplomatic negotiations who has known Kushner for years. "In areas that he has no experience. And that's a dangerous thing for anybody to do."

After reading the news reports of Kushner Companies' negotiations with Anbang, Tillerson feared that Kushner getting in the middle of negotiations with the Chinese could be catastrophic for national security. Tillerson thought Kushner might even topple the U.S.'s "maximum pressure campaign," said someone who spoke with him on the subject, referring to an effort to isolate North Korea diplomatically and economically through sanctions and restricting its trade, which required China's support. China comprises more than 90 percent of North Korea's trade economy, so Tillerson's job, as he saw it, was to remind China continually that its neighbor ultimately threatened China's stability by moving forward with its nuclear program. (Months later, Trump would tweet that Tillerson was "wasting his time" on North Korea.)

This administration, especially in its first six months, had no intention of relying on cumbersome, expensive government bureaucracies or advice that came from the principals atop them. Even the decision in April to bomb a Syrian air base after Assad's forces carried out a chemical attack on a rebel-held area was driven not so much by a cohesive policy as it was by emotion. Mattis presented Trump with tactical options, but as has been widely reported, Ivanka Trump and Dina Powell, a deputy national security adviser, persuaded Trump, who years earlier had criticized Obama for bombing Syria without congressional approval, to retaliate, by showing him horrific pictures of victims of the assault.

Populist, nationalist ideologues like Bannon believed the administrative state needed to be done away with, a premise that dovetailed neatly with the mentality of the Trump and Kushner families, who believed the government imposed unnecessary restraints on their schemes to make money. Foreign ministers relied so heavily on Kushner as their conduit to the government that foreign documents started showing up in meetings in the increasingly lean State Department, and no one knew where they'd come from. The answer was usually Kushner.

Whenever Tillerson met with Kushner, he was direct but respectful. Increasingly, however, he grew alarmed by Kushner's growing friendship with Mohammed bin Salman. Unlike Kushner, Tillerson was familiar with the Gulf and its players. He did not know MBS that well—he was from a different generation—but as he got to see more of him, he grew deeply concerned, because MBS could be hotheaded and vindictive. U.S. State Department officials knew he'd played a role in the 2016 execution in Saudi Arabia of Sheikh Nimr al-Nimr, a Shiite cleric who had publicly criticized the Saudi government and advocated for the rights of the country's Shiite minority. As defense minister, the prince had also pushed the Saudis deeper into the civil war in Yemen, which U.N. Secretary-General António Guterres called in 2018 "the world's worst humanitarian crisis."

MBS sold himself in the West as a friend of the U.S. and a reformer. He had a vision for a new Saudi Arabia, his so-called "Vision 2030." He talked of creating an economy built on entrepreneurship and foreign investment that would free his country from its dependence on depleting oil reserves. Liberalizing Saudi culture was key, and the first step, he said, was to allow women to drive. He looked for advice from his mentor, Mohammed bin Zayed, the crown prince of the secular, oil-rich Abu Dhabi, the most influential and perhaps most efficiently run of the seven United Arab Emirates, a country that borders Saudi Arabia. Analysts were concerned that MBS's "talk" was just a way to raise investment and that he had no real interest in addressing human rights abuses.

Kushner monopolized the U.S. relationship with the future Saudi crown prince, which meant MBS had phenomenal access to Trump. In March, when he visited the White House, neither Tillerson nor Mattis was present. Kushner had MBS to his home for dinner. Again, no Tillerson or Mattis. The prince and "prince" were still communicating on WhatsApp. Their private conversations alarmed the State Department and intelligence agencies, which are used to being looped in on back-channel exchanges. Tillerson also hated this arrangement.

Like Kushner, MBS appeared to love schmoozing with American innovators and business leaders. He hosted small groups of them at the Ritz-Carlton in Riyadh. One American financier told me that in 2017 he was part of a business group that included Tom Barrack, Steve Schwarzman, AOL cofounder Steve Case, SoftBank founder and CEO Masayoshi Son, and Boston Dynamics founder and CEO Marc Raibert. The men had been invited to a brainstorming session over Saudi Arabia's future. One topic was MBS's dream of a futuristic city on the Red Sea run by robots. The group saw a few obstacles: "How would you get people there?" one person asked. "What about women? Cities need women," said another. The answer was that, of course, there would be women. The new Saudi Arabia would be "free." So, Raibert asked, will the women be able to go to the beach in their bikinis? The stern answer was that the new Saudi Arabia would not be *that* free.

The Saudis had not liked dealing with Obama, but MBS saw in Trump a reflection of himself, according to a high-level diplomat who knows the prince. That bond could not have come at a better time for Saudi Arabia. Near the end of Obama's tenure, after the U.S. had signed the Iran nuclear deal without coordination with the Saudis, he had visited King Salman in Riyadh. Then–Secretary of State John Kerry had shown up late and asked MBS how it went. The future crown prince told Kerry, "You were lucky you weren't there." Kerry was surprised. "Our guys seem to think it went okay." MBS rolled his eyes and replied, "You know, John, I just want to close my eyes and go to sleep and wake up in January."

The rift between the two allies had come about because Obama had disliked Saudi Arabia's repressive regime and had openly stated that Tehran and Riyadh needed to figure out a "cold peace" on their own. The new alliance—Saudi Arabia (and by proxy, the UAE), Israel, and Kushner—shared a primary foreign policy goal. "Our plan was to annihilate the physical caliphate of ISIS in Iraq and Syria—not attrition, *annihilation*—and to roll back the Persians. And force the Gulf states to stop funding radical

Islam," Bannon told *The New Yorker*. "Jared and I were at war on a number of other topics, but not this."

Saudi Arabia was also the key to Kushner's burgeoning Middle East peace plan, being formed by his conversations with experts. (He learned by listening, not reading.) What Kushner wanted, according to multiple people who saw drafts of the plan, was for the Saudis and Emiratis to provide economic assistance to the Palestinians. There were plans for an oil pipeline from Saudi Arabia to Gaza, where refineries and a shipping terminal could be built. The profits would create desalination plants, where Palestinians could find work, addressing the high unemployment rate. The plan also entailed land swaps, so that Jordan would give land to the Palestinian territories. In return, Jordan would get land from Saudi Arabia, and that country would get back two Red Sea islands it gave Egypt to administer in 1950.

Despite a skeptical drumbeat from his father-in-law, who kept telling him, "You will never get this [trip] done," Kushner lobbied hard for Trump's first state visit to be not to a traditional ally with shared democratic values such as Great Britain, but to the autocratic Kingdom of Saudi Arabia. (According to Bannon, Kushner hoped Trump would win a Nobel Prize for bringing peace to the Middle East.) Trump agreed to go on the condition that the Saudis would buy a lot of weapons from the U.S. and agree to work harder on counterterrorism. Kushner believed he could get that done, too. What he did not know was that he was being played by both MBZ and MBS. Kushner had not yet learned what one American-born senior adviser to MBZ told me he'd learned from spending years around the Gulf state leaders: "When you deal in the Middle East, 'yes' always means 'maybe.' And then usually evolves into 'no,' but not for a while."

George Nader, a Lebanese-American and close adviser to MBZ, helped Kushner plan the trip while simultaneously communicating with MBZ, MBS, and venture capitalist and Republican fund-raiser Elliott Broidy, who around that time was named deputy RNC finance chairman. Nader, a convicted child molester, and Broidy, who had pleaded guilty for his role in a pay-to-play scheme in 2009, discussed lobbying American support for a project that was far more important to MBS and MBZ than Kushner's peace plan, which they privately derided as infantile. They wanted to use their newly won U.S. support to wage war with a close neighbor and nemesis: the independent emirate of Qatar.

A tiny monarchy (population 2.8 million) that shares a border with Saudi Arabia, Qatar has a long-standing rivalry with both that kingdom and the UAE for all sorts of reasons. It has one of the highest gross national incomes per capita in the world and the second-highest gross domestic product per capita. When the Egyptians toppled President Hosni Mubarak in Egypt during the Arab Spring uprisings of 2011, Qatar gave the new Muslim Brotherhood–led regime financial support, which alarmed the monarchs around it, who saw the well-organized Brotherhood members as revolutionaries who could unseat them. Qatar is also accused of being too close to both Iran (with whom it shares a gas field) and Hamas, the Islamist political organization and militant group that governs Gaza. It is also the home of the headquarters of the media conglomerate Al Jazeera, which is frequently critical of the monarchies around it. Its culture is strongly Islamic—a direct contrast with the increasingly secular UAE. Complicating matters further, it also houses the U.S. Air Force at its Al Udeid Air Base.

But because the Qataris are so rich, they always have friends in the U.S. Nader was alarmed when he learned that various Qatari leaders, including the country's foreign minister and the finance minister, had visited the White House. Both met with Kushner. Nader later told people he tried to "educate" Kushner on Qatar, telling him Qatar was "like a wounded snake that would turn around and bite you."

Kushner told Nader he knew Qatar and the UAE had a long-running feud, but Kushner and Trump had good reason to stay on friendly terms with Qatar's rulers. In mid-February, the same weekend Japanese Prime Minister Shinzo Abe visited Mar-a-Lago, Sheikh HBJ, the former Qatari prime minister who had considered financing 666 Fifth Avenue for the Kushners, was in the area. He and Trump had a private talk, after which he returned to Qatar and told Emir Tamim bin Hamad Al Thani, Qatar's ruler, that the people atop the new administration were heavily motivated by personal financial interest.

The more he heard about Trump's impending trip to Riyadh, the more Tillerson feared it was all a performance. "A huge percentage of the discussions about the trip [from Kushner] was, 'What cool stuff could we do visually?'" someone close to Tillerson told me.

Kushner always seemed more concerned with image than substance. On April 4, he had been photographed during a tour of Iraq wearing dark sunglasses, an open-collar button-down shirt, a navy blazer—under a flak jacket with his name on it—while accompanying General Joe Dunford, chairman of the Joint Chiefs of Staff, on an inspection of the troops. *The Tonight Show* host Jimmy Fallon lampooned the absurd outfit on *Saturday Night Live*, which irked Trump, who told Bannon he had not even been aware of Kushner's travel plans. Tillerson did not see much to laugh at here, either. Kushner had made the trip, so he said, to get to know Dunford, but the way he seemed to think that a brief visit would make him an expert on the region raised questions in the State and Defense Departments about his seriousness. Had it all been a photo op that misfired? "Jared will do things like wanting to go have a tour, and then he'll take one trip. And then he'll be like, 'Now I know about the waste in our Defense Department.' It's as if he watches a YouTube video," said someone who talked to Tillerson about it.

On May 1, Kushner met with a Saudi delegation in Washington to push a $110 billion sale of U.S. defense equipment—a plan they wanted to finalize in time for the Riyadh summit. *The New York Times* reported him as saying, "Let's get this done today." During the meeting, the Saudis asked about buying a radar system, and, sensing cost was an issue, Kushner phoned Marillyn Hewson, the top executive at Lockheed Martin, who said she'd look into it. She was being polite. The reaction inside the senior ranks of Lockheed Martin and the Defense Department was that there was no chance that deal would be renegotiated just like that. What Kushner had done was both ignorant and potentially harmful. "Arms deals are very carefully calibrated, complicated things," someone inside Lockheed explained. They also require congressional approval.

In fact, Bruce Riedel, the Brookings Institution senior fellow and former CIA and Pentagon official, wrote for Brookings later that spring that the announced deal had still not closed—and probably never would. "There is no $110 billion deal. Instead, there are a bunch of letters of interest or intent, but not contracts. . . . None of the deals identified so far are new, all began in the Obama administration." The whole thing was a charade, a PR stunt, and Kushner looked absurd. A leading Republican strategist told me he believed Bannon must have leaked the item to the *Times*, because where was the upside? (Bannon said he had nothing to do with it.) It portrayed Kushner as "a ham-handed manipulator," the strategist said. "I mean, who the fuck does that [calls an executive during a meeting] and tells them to lower their price so they can announce it on the trip? That is so weak. So weak."

On May 20, Trump made his first overseas trip as president. His destination: Saudi Arabia. His hosts reportedly planned to spend nearly sixty-eight million dollars on the festivities. The author Michael Wolff would write in *Fire and Fury*, his book about the first nine months of the Trump White House, that Trump told an associate right before he left Washington, "Jared's gotten the Arabs totally on our side. . . . It's going to be beautiful." During the trip, billboards lined the streets of Riyadh with images of Trump and Saudi Arabia's King Salman and the phrase "Together We Prevail." The main purpose of the trip, which Trump outlined in a May 21 speech to the Arab Islamic American Summit, was to bring the Muslim world together to fight Iran and Islamic terrorism. "If you choose the path of terror, your life will be empty, your life will be brief, and YOUR SOUL WILL BE CONDEMNED" (emphasis in White House transcript), Trump said.

But there was also business to do: on the first day of his visit, Trump and King Salman signed the arms deal Kushner had supposedly negotiated. The deal reportedly could be expanded over the next decade to as much as

$350 billion and "includes tanks, combat ships, missile defense systems, radar and communications, and cybersecurity technology," according to the Associated Press. The same day, the Saudis announced a twenty-billion-dollar bid investment in the American firm Blackstone's infrastructure fund, with the proviso that Blackstone had to match that with money from other investors. Following the business announcements, the festivities continued with a ceremony later in the day that included drumming and dancing with swords. That evening, King Salman, Egyptian President Abdel Fattah el-Sisi, and Trump gathered around a huge, luminous globe and placed their hands on it, in a scene that observers said made them look like comic-book villains. Kushner and Ivanka had dinner with MBS at his home. The trip seemed like an unadulterated triumph.

At a security session on the summit's second day, at which some fifty countries were invited to talk about combating terrorism, Qatar, which Trump hailed as an ally in his speech that day, was noticeably absent, although it was at the summit and the theme was cooperation. Someone close to the Qatari leadership told me the country was not invited. "It was a Saudi thing," said this person. Qatar's senior families believed the Saudis and Emiratis were plotting military action against Qatar. The Americans, they believed, either were kept ignorant of the scheme and/or, according to one person, at least were supporting the plan. This person told me it was believed in Qatar that at the summit the Saudis "bought and paid for Jared." Since he was now a government official, he could not accept gifts, but "you can get them under the table," the person said. "They're very good at giving big, rich diamond-encrusted medals in Saudi Arabia." (There is no report that Kushner received such gifts.)

On June 5, while Tillerson and Mattis were in Australia attending an annual forum with their counterparts, they were astonished to learn that Saudi Arabia, the UAE, Bahrain, and Egypt had announced a blockade against Qatar. The ostensible excuse was pro-Iranian statements supposedly made by Sheikh Al Thani. In fact, the emir had made no such statements. U.S. intelligence would determine they were fabricated by the UAE. But Trump, who has repeatedly made it clear he does not trust U.S. intelligence and does not always read his briefings, was duped. He tweeted his support for the blockade the next day. "During my recent trip to the Middle

East I stated that there can no longer be funding of Radical Ideology," he wrote in a morning post. "Leaders pointed to Qatar—look!"

Tillerson was "horrified," according to a former State Department official. The way Tillerson saw it, the official said, the Saudis had decided to count on "U.S. support, and instead of addressing problems within the Gulf community and marshaling the Gulf community to face Iran, the Saudis instead turned on the royal family in Qatar." Another Tillerson aide told me, "The Saudis would not have risked moving forward without permission from somebody. Now, if you . . . get a phone call that says, 'Hey, we're thinking about doing this,' you might not have the experience and the capability and the maturity to know how hard to push back. Part of the issue is if you put yourself in as the point of contact and you're not actually capable of being the point of contact." This person concluded, "That person must have been Jared."

Until now, Kushner's dalliances in world affairs had been ethically questionable. With Qatar, Tillerson believed they had become alarming. Threatening Qatar, with the U.S. presence at its air base, was tantamount to threatening the U.S. "Qatar was when [Kushner's interference] became dangerous for the United States," said a Tillerson confidant. "The United States security architecture in the Middle East is what we have in Kuwait [at the Ahmed al-Jaber Air Base] and what we have in Qatar. . . . It's not like, 'Oh, we have something in Saudi [Arabia] that protects us.' It's a web there, and you break that apart, that's our national security that's at risk. It's not theirs [at risk]. It's ours."

Trump, according to two sources, had no idea there was a U.S. base in Qatar—a fact that would alter his perspective somewhat when he was informed of it, probably after his morning tweets. Tillerson, Mattis, and a specially appointed envoy, Middle East specialist Tim Lenderking, immediately flew to the region to try to get the aggressors to back down. But there was a limit to how much they could do, because the Saudis and Emiratis already had their tentacles into the White House and they felt the U.S. secretary of state had been neutered by Kushner. Even Tom Barrack, Qatar's old beneficiary, reportedly failed to persuade the administration to back down when he argued on behalf of his most staunch business patron. "The ambassadors of Saudi Arabia, UAE, and others were quite convinced that the State Department had been marginalized on Gulf politics and that these issues were all going to be resolved through the White House and through the president," said a former senior State Department official.

The two crown princes began belittling Tillerson, both in Washington and abroad, and MBZ reportedly pushed Kushner to get Tillerson fired. This came after the secretary reportedly intervened to stop a Saudi invasion of Qatar, and because MBZ did not think Tillerson was tough enough on Iran. The secretary of state read some of the negative chatter about himself in the intelligence reports he received. At some point, according to a Tillerson aide, he told Kushner that his interference had endangered the U.S. Kushner quickly left the room. "He's the type of person who lights the firecracker and then realizes it's going to blow up and hands it off," said a person familiar with their conversations.

Tillerson thought Ivanka was less dangerous than her husband but acted even more entitled. A Tillerson colleague in the State Department told me: "All of her murders are done from someone else's hands." Thankfully, her transgressions were mostly annoying and petty. Many taxpayer dollars were spent burning up phone lines while deciding absurdly trivial things such as who should go on State Department–funded trips. "Jared and Ivanka [wanted to] decide who's allowed and who's not allowed [on trips]," said a Tillerson colleague.

Ivanka also wasted time by asking to travel on an air force plane when it was not appropriate. John Kelly, then secretary of homeland security, was quite helpful to Tillerson in turning her down. "It's Tillerson's trip. It's not Ivanka's trip," he explained. When officials rebuffed their requests, Kushner and Ivanka would ask a cabinet secretary, most often Treasury Secretary Steven Mnuchin, to accompany them, and thereby get a government plane.

The time-suck of these machinations was viewed by State Department staffers as Ivanka's biggest transgression.

She also found a way to be near Trump when he received phone calls from foreign dignitaries—while she still owned her business. "When the president spoke to the leader of India, she'd say, 'Thanks so much for the CD you sent me,' . . . and something about yoga, and then the president says, 'All right, all right, all right,' and she got off," according to someone who heard one of these calls and was struck by the unethical nature of it. "It was not what was said," said this person; rather, it was the concept. "The law states that you can't even be standing on the Capitol grounds and ask for a political contribution over your personal cell phone . . . but there was Ivanka benefiting from that conversation."

While Ivanka's behavior was irritating, Kushner was playing a game on a whole different level: he was playing for serious money. What Tillerson did not know at the time of the Qatari blockade—indeed, few knew then—was that in April, Kushner's family had been courting the Qataris for financial help and had been turned down. When that story broke—almost a year later—the blockade and the Trump administration's response to it suddenly all made sense. As one Tillerson aide said about the blockade, "It must have been [Kushner]."

CHAPTER FIFTEEN

He'll Take Anything

"Trump has made it safe for people not to obey rules. Trump has made it safe for people . . . not to have ethical considerations."

—AMERICAN ADVISER TO SHEIKH MOHAMMED BIN ZAYED

In April 2017, Qatari Finance Minister Ali Shareef Al Emadi, a member of the Qatar Investment Authority (QIA), the country's sovereign wealth fund, flew to New York City. According to *The New Yorker*, he rented a suite in the St. Regis hotel in Manhattan and emptied out the furniture to create a reception room for the line of American businessmen who would soon come seeking money. Charlie Kushner and his thirty-four-year-old daughter, Nicole Kushner Meyer, were in that line. The next day, Qatar representatives went over to 666 Fifth Avenue and met with the Kushners in a conference room. According to *The New Yorker* and another source, Charlie asked for just under one billion dollars. A source close to the QIA explained that Al Emadi was never really interested in 666 Fifth, given that Qatari sheikh HBJ had already been in discussions with the Kushners, and because HBJ is a business partner of the father of the emir of Qatar. But, he added, "they're not ungracious people," and so they will "take any meeting that someone wants to have." In other words, they politely turned the Kushners down.

A financial analyst with knowledge of the meeting told *The New*

Yorker's Dexter Filkins, "Here's a question for you: If they had given Kushner the money, would there have been a blockade? I don't think so."

That same week, after reportedly receiving advice from a lawyer, Josh Kushner met with Al Emadi. According to Josh's spokesperson, Jesse Derris, the meeting lasted thirty minutes. Derris denied assertions made by *The Intercept* that Josh had solicited funds for his firm, Thrive Capital. The firm, Derris said, was not doing a capital raise at the time.

The truth was that Charlie was desperate to get out from under 666 Fifth—and both his sons knew it. One New York businessman told me, "Charlie has asked everybody in New York for advice, including me. I mean, not that he's a stupid man, but this is way above his capability. . . . He'll take anything, or try anything, or talk to anybody. He doesn't care, because he knows [the building] could really undo the family."

On March 13, *Bloomberg* reported that Kushner Companies had asked for $850 million in EB-5 funding for 666 Fifth. The EB-5 program was created in the 1990s to encourage investments in rural areas or neighborhoods with high unemployment. The idea behind the government-sponsored program is that companies can receive funding from foreign investors—who in exchange receive U.S. green cards—to spur growth in economically disadvantaged places, not in the center of Manhattan. One major developer told me that abuse of the program by wealthy developers has become a "joke."

That was also the view of three Democratic U.S. senators, Dianne Feinstein, Patrick Leahy, and Mazie Hirono, who sent a joint letter on April 21 to White House counsel Donald McGahn questioning Kushner Companies' actions. They wrote: "Many of the projects funded by the EB-5 Regional Center program are large real estate developments—the cornerstone of both the Trump and Kushner business empires. As public reporting indicates, the potential for conflict is real. For example, *Bloomberg News* has reported that, as chief executive officer of the Kushner Companies, Jared built a Trump-branded luxury tower in New Jersey that relied on $50 million of EB-5 dollars from wealthy Chinese investors. Additionally, according to *Bloomberg*, Kushner Companies is reportedly seeking $850 million in EB-5 funding for redevelopment of their marquee Manhattan skyscraper at 666 Fifth Avenue. This would mark the largest single EB-5 investment in the history of the program."

In May, the Kushners did something arguably far worse than applying for that EB-5 funding. Charlie sent his daughter Nicole to China to pitch more than one hundred Chinese investors at the Ritz-Carlton hotel in Beijing, asking for $150 million in EB-5 funding for the One Journal Square project in Jersey City, where Kushner Companies is planning to develop two sixty-six-story towers. As the presentations got under way, journalists were told to leave the hotel ballroom because the event was "private," despite being advertised to the public. Nicole stood in front of a screen on which, at one point, flashed a picture of Trump. She told guests the project "means a lot to me and my entire family." She referred to Jared's previous role at Kushner Companies and how he had gone to work in the White House. A slide in her presentation mentioned that Trump was a "key decision maker" in the EB-5 program.

Touting her family connections in an attempt to woo foreign dollars was outrageous, and there was an immediate outcry. Noah Bookbinder, who heads Citizens for Responsibility and Ethics in Washington, a government watchdog group, told *The New York Times* that the sales pitch was "highly problematic" and exhorted Jared to recuse himself from any decision-making concerning the EB-5 program.

Risa Heller, the Kushner Companies spokesperson, told Charlie that the correct thing to do was to apologize. And on May 8, Kushner Companies issued a statement: "In the course of discussing this project and the firm's history with potential investors, Ms. Meyer wanted to make clear that her brother had stepped away from the company in January and has nothing to do with this project," the company said. "Kushner Companies apologizes if that mention of her brother was in any way interpreted as an attempt to lure investors. That was not Ms. Meyer's intention."

Three months later, Charlie fired Heller. In his mind, there had been no transgression in China and no need for an apology. One person who spoke to Charlie about the firm's trips abroad to garner EB-5 investments remembered Charlie saying that it would be smart *not* to send a translator with Kushner Companies representatives, "because if we don't know what is being said, we cannot get in trouble for it."

That May, Kushner Companies was subpoenaed by the U.S. attorney's office for the Eastern District of New York, in Brooklyn, over its use of the EB-5 program in developing the One Journal Square project in Jersey City. That same month, the U.S. Securities and Exchange Commission also opened an investigation.

With every passing day, it seemed less likely Charlie would find a way to pay off 666 Fifth's mortgage, which, with interest, had risen to $1.4 billion. And the family name was getting pummeled. On April 26, *The New York Times* reported that the Kushners had once partnered with the nephew of an Israeli billionaire, Beny Steinmetz, whose firm the federal government now suspected of bribing foreign officials. In May, it emerged that Jared had not reported that he still had a stake in Cadre. Then *The New York Times Magazine* and *ProPublica* jointly published a deep dive into Kushner Companies' management of fifteen apartment complexes outside Baltimore. Residents complained of neglect and intimidation—over five hundred lawsuits had been filed against tenants by a Kushner Companies subsidiary called JK2 Westminster, in an effort to collect back rent of, in most cases, just a few thousand dollars. The financial difficulties of some of the tenants were harrowing. One former tenant, Kamiia Warren, had received a summons for $3,014.08 while she was pursuing her bachelor's degree in health care administration and raising three children on her own. When she was unable to pay the judgment against her, JK2 Westminster got a court order to garnish her wages and her bank account. She had to borrow money from her mother to buy food for her children. "How could it possibly be worth Kushner Companies' while to pursue hundreds of people so aggressively over a few thousand dollars here and there?" the authors asked.

The spotlight was not only on Charlie. Jared's lawyer, Jamie Gorelick, was "getting hell," according to one of her friends. She was being roasted in her social and professional circles over her client: Why was he apparently incapable of filling out his security clearance forms properly, even after multiple attempts? (She had said this was due to an administrative error.) How had he omitted his meetings with Russians and other foreigners during the transition? And then there was the fact that he and his wife had apparently clung onto assets worth hundreds of millions of dollars. A recent financial disclosure had showed that Jared and Ivanka Trump were still worth between $144 million and $740 million.

An April 19 public opinion poll by Quinnipiac University's polling center showed that a majority of Americans did not think either Jared or Ivanka should play a significant role in the White House. Trump told Reince Priebus that the negative attention the couple was generating "was not worth it." He told senior staffers that an investigation into Kushner Companies' business practices would make it easier to investigate his own. "That was not something he was excited about," said a former senior White House adviser.

On April 24, Ivanka shared a stage in Berlin with German Chancellor Angela Merkel, and it did not go well. The audience booed when Ivanka called Trump "a tremendous champion of supporting families." The moderator asked Ivanka about attitudes her father had shown that "might leave one questioning whether he's such an empowerer for women." Ivanka blamed the media: "I've certainly heard the criticism from the media, that's been perpetuated." There was a report the next day, for which she could not blame the media, indicating that workers for G-III, the company that manufactured Ivanka's fashion line in China, earned just sixty-two dollars per week for almost sixty hours of work.

It was fortunate, given so much bad news, that Javanka now had their own publicist, Josh Raffel. Raffel started to get very busy doing damage control, which was not always easy. "Raffel has had to do more deals with the devil than anyone should have to," a former senior White House colleague observed.

CHAPTER SIXTEEN

The Shock Felt Around the World

*"Jared was one of two people in the White House who knew
the Comey thing was coming. It was his idea. That was one
of the times where he actually put his balls on the line,
which is something he doesn't ever do."*

—FORMER SENIOR WHITE HOUSE OFFICIAL

On April 6, *The New York Times* ran a damning report on Jared Kushner's many omissions on his SF-86 security clearance form. The article pointed out that the "form warns that 'withholding, misrepresenting, or falsifying information could result in loss of access to classified information, denial of eligibility for a sensitive job, and even prosecution; knowingly falsifying or concealing material facts is a federal felony that may result in fines or up to five years imprisonment.'"

Kushner's lawyer, Jamie Gorelick, called the omissions innocent errors, but Kushner would be questioned about his meetings with Sergey Kislyak and Sergey Gorkov by both the House and Senate intelligence committees and the Department of Justice, as part of their respective investigations into Russian interference in the election. Meanwhile, he still had an interim security clearance.

Trump was also wrangling with suspicions involving Russians who may have helped him win the election. In March, FBI Director James Comey had confirmed to Congress that his agents were investigating possible contact and coordination between Moscow and Trump's campaign. Weeks later, in early May, an aide to Gary Cohn, who had an office on the second floor of the West Wing, noticed a document on his printer. It appeared to be a letter from Trump, firing Comey. It also appeared to have been sent to the wrong printer.

Comey had led the FBI for nearly four years and had a mixed reputation. Hillary Clinton blamed him for her election loss because eleven days before the election, he had announced there was new material related to the previously completed investigation into her use of a personal email server while she was Obama's Secretary of State. But now the bureau's investigation into whether the Trump campaign had colluded with the Russians was dominating the headlines. Trump was livid about the attention the FBI investigation was attracting, but to fire the head of the FBI while it was investigating him was an extraordinarily risky move. The FBI is part of the Justice Department and falls under the executive branch of government, but only once in the history of the bureau had a president (Bill Clinton) ever fired its director.

Cohn told his aide to take the letter straight to Donald McGahn, who also had an office on the second floor of the White House (and whose printer it had clearly been meant for). Upon receiving it and realizing it had been printed in the wrong place, McGahn said, "Oh, fuck!"

Cohn now waited for the news to break.

Days later, on May 9, Trump fired Comey. As the images of Comey's plane, sitting on the tarmac on the West Coast, flashed across TV screens, Cohn huddled with his former colleague from Goldman Sachs, Dina Powell. "Dina, what do you think the fallout is?" Cohn asked. Using strong language, Powell said not good. Later that day the duo was seen in Kushner's first-floor office; Powell was clearly emotional. According to sources within hearing distance, she told Kushner that firing Comey was a huge political mistake. But Kushner was unmoved. "No, no, this is what should be done," he said. "The guy is not on our team."

What Cohn and Powell did not yet know was that Kushner was behind the decision to fire Comey, and he and Steve Bannon had had a huge fight over it. Kushner had, to quote a former White House senior adviser, "put his balls on the line." And this time, Bannon had lost.

The backstory: In January, Bannon had argued in front of multiple people that Comey needed to go—immediately. He thought the FBI director had behaved improperly and with clear political bias during the transition. On December 29, when Obama expelled thirty-five suspected Russian spies and issued sanctions in retaliation for Russian interference in the election, Bannon declared, "Whoa. That's a game-changer. Why didn't they give the president-elect a briefing on it?" Bannon told Reince Priebus to call Obama's chief of staff, Denis McDonough, and get the "exact same presentation" from the intelligence agencies that Obama had gotten in order to make his determination for the expulsions.

On January 6, the director of national intelligence and the heads of the CIA, NSA, and FBI arrived at Trump Tower to make their presentation. Bannon figured Priebus could handle the meeting. Everyone was stretched—they were fourteen days away from regime change—so Bannon was sitting on the twenty-sixth floor when Priebus and Representative Mike Pompeo (Trump's pick for CIA director), Trump, and others returned from the briefing on the fourteenth floor. The consensus was that the information had been a non-event. "It's interesting, it's compelling—but not necessarily mind-blowing," was the group's summation. Trump suddenly said, "[What about] that dossier thing?" Bannon asked around: "What dossier?" Priebus explained that during the briefing, Comey had asked to speak alone with Trump about a document in the FBI's possession. Priebus had asked Trump if he wanted someone to stay with him. Trump said no. Bannon was upset that Priebus had let Trump do that. If a dossier was not part of the official record, he suspected a trap.

Within four days, the thirty-five-page dossier, which had been compiled by a former British spy, Christopher Steele, and commissioned privately, was published by *BuzzFeed News*. Among other things, the dossier alleged that Trump was a Russian asset and that in 2013 he had prostitutes urinate on a bed in his Moscow hotel—allegedly because the Obamas had slept in the same suite. "We just got played because we're a group of clowns, and they think that we're a group of clowns," Bannon complained later. He suspected that Comey had masterminded the setup, but Trump wanted to give him another chance. He invited Comey to dinner. Bannon volunteered himself or Priebus to sit in on their dinner as "a witness," but Trump said, "I don't need it."

The morning after that dinner, Trump said it had gone very well and that Comey was going to stay on as FBI director. Comey, who made careful notes of the conversation as soon as he left the White House, would later describe the dinner as an attempt by Trump to gauge his loyalty and establish what Comey would call a "patronage relationship."

Three months later, Kushner was exposed by the media as someone who would almost certainly have an increasingly prominent role in the Russian collusion investigation. Not only had he met with Russian government officials or connected officials, but he also had left those meetings off his security clearance forms. "That is a cardinal sin," said a former senior government official and security expert. "Ordinarily, that would be considered a crime. Game over."

Bannon and others noticed that Kushner became "gung-ho" about firing Comey. Bannon would tell colleagues: "We're sitting in the Oval Office and Jared is arguing [the following] to the president: Number one, Comey is hated by all the agents. You fire him, you'll be the greatest thing that ever happened. Number two, the Democrats hate him. If you do it, it'll be the biggest bipartisan thing. They'll love you. Number three, the 'deplorables'"—Bannon's ironic nickname for the Trump base ever since Clinton used the word at an event to describe his supporters—"will raise more money off of it anyway."

Bannon disputed each point in front of multiple people. "Let's say that the agents all do hate him [Comey], because of his behavior during the election," Bannon began. "The moment you fire him, he's J. Edgar Hoover," meaning they'd rally behind him, because he was their leader.

"Let's say the Democrats all do hate him," he continued, again referring to the Clinton investigation controversy. "The minute you fire him, he's Joan of Arc."

Bannon's final point: "The deplorables don't give a shit."

Bannon made his appeal in front of Trump and others: "You fire Comey, you're going to get a special counsel. Comey's thing [on Russia] is so boring that right now, it's the third segment on Anderson Cooper's [CNN show]. Even CNN is running out of juice on this thing. They can't book guests anymore because there's no interest. This is boring. This is going to run its course. Let's just let it play out."

Priebus agreed with Bannon. Trump, Bannon and Priebus could tell, had made up his mind. He viewed the Russia investigation as a "witch hunt." On May 4, Trump went to his private golf club in Bedminster for the weekend with Kushner and Ivanka, Stephen Miller, Hope Hicks, then–Deputy National Security Adviser K. T. McFarland, and White House social media director Dan Scavino. Priebus stayed in the White House to work on health care repeal, and Bannon was fearing the worst: "They were gung-ho on firing Comey, and I didn't want to be any part of it. I had taken my best shot and essentially been dismissed," he told anyone who would listen.

After Comey was fired, the media reaction was the exact opposite of what Kushner had predicted. There was an outcry, including numerous assertions from Democrats and even some Republicans that what the president had done was unconstitutional. "It is an abuse of power if the FBI was in fact investigating the president of the United States," said Senator Richard Blumenthal of Connecticut on CNN. "For the president to fire someone who has him under active investigation without better cause is, in my view, an abuse of power." The shock felt around the world only worsened when Trump told NBC News anchor Lester Holt, "When I decided to just do it, I said to myself, I said, 'You know, this Russia thing with Trump and Russia is a made-up story, it's an excuse by the Democrats for having lost an election.'" In other words, he admitted that the FBI investigation into the Trump campaign's potential ties to Russia factored into his decision to fire the FBI director.

Quickly, Trump realized he'd made an error, and blamed Kushner. When Kushner piped up during a subsequent meeting that Joe Lieberman, the former senator and 2000 Democratic vice presidential nominee, should replace Comey, Trump was openly annoyed: "You've told me that ten times, Jared. I know who you want." It seemed clear to Trump's advisers, and not for the first time, that he wished Kushner were not in the White House. He said to Kushner in front of senior staff: "Just go back to New York, man. It's so much better there than here. I mean, why do you want to put up with this stuff? I told you this was going to be horrible. Look at this."

Attorney General Jeff Sessions had recused himself from the Russia investigation back in March following a report that he had met with Sergey Kislyak during the campaign and failed to disclose the contact during his confirmation hearing, so oversight of the FBI's investigation fell to Deputy Attorney General Rod Rosenstein. On May 17, Rosenstein announced the appointment of Robert Mueller as special counsel to oversee the inquiry. Mueller was revered within the Justice Department; he had been the longest-serving director of the FBI since J. Edgar Hoover. *The New York Times* reported that Trump accepted the announcement calmly but wanted to "fight back." Kushner agreed and urged Trump to go on the offensive. But Trump ultimately listened to his other advisers, who suggested he take a calmer approach. The White House released a statement that didn't attack the inquiry but still asserted Trump's innocence.

Just eight days later, *The Washington Post* reported that Kushner was a focus of Special Counsel Mueller's investigation. A few weeks after that, it was reported that his business dealings were also being investigated by the special counsel. It would emerge months later that Mueller wanted to know all about Kushner's—and his family's—meetings with representatives of the governments of Qatar, Turkey, the UAE, Russia, and China. Separately, Mueller's Justice Department colleagues at the U.S. attorney's office in Brooklyn would look into a Deutsche Bank loan that Kushner Companies had received as part of a refinancing package right before the election. The Senate Judiciary Committee requested more information about Kushner's security clearance in June. Mueller would also look into whether Kushner's advice to Trump to fire Comey was part of an effort that could be interpreted as obstruction of justice.

In New York, Charlie Kushner phoned an old friend, Robert Torricelli, the charismatic former U.S. senator from New Jersey, and asked for the best white-collar defense lawyer Torricelli knew in Washington. Torricelli gave him a list, but he was confident the Kushners would pick Abbe Lowell, who had made his name as chief counsel for the House Democrats during the Clinton impeachment hearings and who was the only Orthodox Jew on the list. Lowell had also represented the former senator and onetime Democratic vice presidential nominee John Edwards, disgraced lobbyist Jack Abramoff, and Bob Menendez, the senator from New Jersey who would beat corruption charges in January 2018. Lowell was known as a gossip, a Washington "character" who liked dealing with the media. "Very smart, very driven, a little too much ego," is how a friend described him. "Do I think Abbe is ethical? Yes. But you know, he is where the bar is. You may not like where the white-collar defense bar now is in America. . . ."

As her husband faced growing legal threats, Ivanka's carefully spun narrative that the couple's presence in the White House was justified because she was a moderating influence on her father seemed risible. She was clearly ineffectual in that role. Trump would not—and could not—be reined in by anyone, even his favorite daughter.

A clear example of that: On June 1, Trump announced from the Rose Garden that the United States would pull out of the Paris Agreement on climate change. Neither Kushner nor Ivanka was present. This had been Ivanka's battle, and she'd lost; it was reported that she'd been given a copy of the climate change documentary *Before the Flood* by the actor Leonardo DiCaprio, who later came to Trump Tower during the transition to brief her and Trump on how green jobs can boost the economy. She'd also welcomed the former vice president turned global-warming activist Al Gore to talk to her and her father about climate policy. "It's no secret that Ivanka

Trump is very committed to having a climate policy that makes sense for our country and for our world," Gore told MSNBC after the meeting. She had reportedly also encouraged Apple CEO Tim Cook to speak to her father about climate issues.

Trump's decision to pull out of the Paris Agreement, which signals a reduction in the likelihood that the U.S. will provide funding for renewable energy and climate conservation to developing countries, was her first major policy loss. Following the withdrawal announcement, Gore called the move "a reckless and indefensible action."

Reince Priebus knew Trump's gut instinct had always been to exit the Paris Agreement. So did Bannon. About a week before Trump made his decision, Bannon had deputy strategist Andy Surabian pull together a list of all the times—seven or eight—when Trump had promised to pull out of the agreement during the campaign. Bannon left it on the president's desk and knew better than to push the issue.

In the ultimate principals meeting chaired by Cohn in the Situation Room, there was a "food fight," remembered someone present, which was typical of what Trump liked to see before he made a decision. While Cohn, Rex Tillerson, and National Security Adviser H. R. McMaster wanted to stay in the agreement, stressing the importance of international relations, EPA head Scott Pruitt, Attorney General Sessions, Bannon, Priebus, and McGahn all wanted out. Rob Porter and Dina Powell inhabited a shifting middle ground. Complicating matters, the departments' various legal representatives—lawyers from the EPA, the Department of Justice, the White House Counsel's Office, and the Department of State—could not agree on whether it would be legal to pull out, or what legal restrictions the U.S. might be bound by if it did.

Someone who was in the room observed that Trump did not seem concerned about the legal arguments. "He doesn't care if something's lawful or unlawful, or constitutional or unconstitutional, or if he has authority or not. He'll just say, 'Well, let's just do it anyway and we'll sue in the courts.'" What swayed him was the argument made by Bannon and Pruitt that the agreement's financial burden was disproportionately borne by the U.S.: that the climate targets negotiated for China were far less than the level of the U.S.'s, and that the accord was harming the U.S.'s GDP and costing it a great deal more than it was costing other countries.

Bannon watched Trump listen to Tillerson and McMaster reiterate their concerns about the "international community," and in that moment Bannon knew he'd beaten Ivanka. "As soon as you say 'international community' to Trump, it's game over," he said to Priebus and others later. You get a predictable reaction, which is to say: no.

Cohn, who had argued against exiting the Paris Agreement, thought Ivanka had not played her Trump card. Cohn had gotten the Business Roundtable, a business lobby group, to take out full-page ads in national newspapers supporting the accord. He had also asked the group's chair, JPMorgan Chase CEO Jamie Dimon, and longtime Dow Chemical CEO Andrew Liveris to talk to Trump about it. Ivanka supported Cohn's actions, but several White House aides heard him say to her more than once: "Ivanka, I can do all of this, or you can walk in there and tell your father he's just dead wrong. You could tell him that the paper of facts that [EPA head] Pruitt is using is all lies."

Ivanka told Cohn, "No, I can't really do that."

Her reluctance to speak frankly to her father was the antithesis of the story she had been pushing in the media. For example, *The New York Times* had reported on May 2 that father and daughter "trade thoughts from morning until late at night, according to aides." Ivanka had told Gayle King on *CBS This Morning* on April 5, "Where I disagree with my father, he knows it. And I express myself with total candor."

It was after she lost the fight over the Paris Agreement that Ivanka told *Fox & Friends* that politics in Washington involved "a level of viciousness that I was not expecting." One of the people who'd firmly supported Bannon and the Paris Exiteers was euphoric: "She knew she would be drummed out of the New York elite if she did not deliver Paris. . . . She had to deliver for the Trudeaus."

CHAPTER SEVENTEEN

"That Would Be a Felony"

"They talk to you as if they grew up in an ivory tower,
which they did—but they have no idea how normal people
perceive, understand, intuit."

—MEMBER OF TRUMP'S LEGAL TEAM

Once Robert Mueller was appointed as special counsel in charge of the investigation into whether the Trump campaign had colluded with the Russians, the president had to lawyer up. He had often worked with Marc Kasowitz, of the New York firm Kasowitz, Benson, Torres, and he was comfortable with "Kas," as the snowy-haired lawyer is affectionately known, and another partner at the firm, Michael "Mike" Bowe, who is the blunt son of a New York City firefighter. Trump used to reminisce about his New York lawyers to his senior staff. "I was 12–0 with this one; I was 10–0 with that one."

Now that there was an official investigation, White House personnel were advised not to discuss the Russia probe with the president because that would both taint his attorney-client privilege and could make them witnesses. But dodging him on the subject was not easy, according to multiple people. He'd start up with almost anyone: "This Russia thing . . ."

Kasowitz and Bowe were not planning to leave New York full-time, so they cast around to beef up their ranks. Bowe knew John Dowd, who had retired two years earlier from a D.C. law firm; he volunteered to work pro bono. Dowd introduced them to another Washington lawyer, Ty Cobb. The plan was to copy the strategy of Bill Clinton's legal team when he faced an investigation by independent counsel Kenneth Starr. White House lawyers would represent the president as the president, and outside attorneys would represent him personally. Jay Sekulow, an attorney from the American Center for Law and Justice, would be the lawyers' public spokesperson. The person in charge of communications strategy would be Mark Corallo, a Washington PR veteran who had run communications for the Department of Justice under former Attorney General John Ashcroft. And Ned Ryun, a former speechwriter for George W. Bush, would help Corallo with messaging.

A month earlier, Corallo, a telegenic, churchgoing former army infantry officer, had been asked if he would consider becoming the White House communications director. (The previous incumbent, Michael Dubke, exited on May 18, 2017, after only three months on the job, citing "personal reasons.") Corallo said no. He had promised his wife that he was done with full-time government service after he left the Justice Department. He has three daughters and a son who was a budding professional baseball player, and he needed to be on the road often. Before accepting the role of outside spokesperson for the legal team, he warned an intermediary who had reached out to him on behalf of "the people who have the power" at the White House that, although he'd voted for Trump, he had said some "unkind things" about Jared Kushner and Ivanka Trump, who, he presumed, considered themselves to be "the people who have the power."

After Kushner's sister had solicited EB-5 funding in China while invoking Jared's name and his role in the Trump White House, Corallo had tweeted: "Dear Mr. President, this is worse than just 'bad optics.' It's sleazy. You could start draining the swamp by removing your in-laws." And he had criticized Ivanka when she hired a chief of staff, writing, "Since when does a senior advisor to the President need a chief of staff?" Corallo took a screenshot of all of these tweets and sent them to the White House. He was expecting to be rejected, but he and Ryun were invited to a meeting in Steve Bannon's office in May, where he found himself explaining that Mueller was his hero—they had worked together at the Department of Justice after 9/11. "If you watched him and John Ashcroft, and the guys I worked with at Justice in those eighteen months after 9/11, dealing with what they dealt with on a daily basis and the way they dealt with it, taking so much crap, keeping their heads down, and if you know anything about Bob Mueller, I mean, he is Mr. Integrity."

Bannon was fascinated and said, "You must know Jim Comey." Corallo did, and told Bannon not to assume Comey and Mueller were close friends just because they'd worked together. They weren't. Next, Corallo went with Kasowitz, Bowe, Bannon, and Priebus into the Oval Office to explain this all over again to Trump. Corallo, a formal type, was mortified because he was not wearing a tie when he met the president.

The group persuaded Corallo to accept the job as an outside consultant, in charge of running communications strategy for the legal team. He had one proviso: he would never be part of anything that knocked Mueller, who, he said, "walks on water."

Corallo enjoyed working with fellow New Yorkers Sekulow, Kasowitz, and Bowe, as well as Ryun. But Corallo, who already had White House experience, was immediately dismayed by the feuding and chaos around him now. "Where's the schedule?" he had asked in his first meeting, thinking back to the Bush days, when even the president's three-minute bathroom breaks were planned. Instead, the place was more like a fraternity house with anyone wandering in and out of offices, including the president's.

As they pored over media reports and testimony, Kasowitz and Bowe began to form a plan. They figured that the special counsel's office would look at essentially three buckets: first was Flynn and Manafort and whatever their foreign connections were; second, there was the interference on Facebook and other social media platforms through microtargeting; third was the firing of Comey. It was their view that there was just one individual with a possible hand in each of those buckets: Kushner. What gave them the most concern on his account was the microtargeting, because Kushner had taken all the credit for that in his *Forbes* cover article. They were also bothered by the negotiations over 666 Fifth Avenue and the impending mortgage payment due on it, as well as the many omissions (later corrected) on Kushner's security clearance forms. It would have been easier to explain these if he had forgotten a meeting with, say, the British ambassador. But to forget meetings with Russian officials? "If it was found he omitted that deliberately, that would be a felony," said Corallo.

In June, the lawyers learned there were emails not yet in the public domain concerning the meeting in Trump Tower in June 2016 requested by a Kremlin-connected lawyer, Natalia Veselnitskaya. (This was the one for which a British publicist, Rob Goldstone, had emailed Don Jr. that he had a lawyer with ties to the Russian government who had "dirt" on Clinton. Don Jr. replied, "I love it." Kushner and Manafort attended the meeting; Ivanka talked to Veselnitskaya on her way out of Trump Tower.) The consensus among the lawyers was that they should be prepared to advise the president that Kushner might have to leave the White House. Sekulow told Corallo he should prepare talking points in case it came to that. Dowd, a former Marine Corps lawyer who knew Mueller—and would later assure Trump, "I can get [the Mueller investigation] done in three weeks"—was the only one who expressed any reluctance. "He was charmed by Jared and Ivanka," Corallo recalled. Meanwhile, the legal team was negotiating with Congress as to when they needed to produce campaign-related documents. They figured they had until after Labor Day.

According to a member of the legal team, Kushner's new lawyer, Abbe Lowell, told Trump's lawyers that before emails regarding that Trump Tower meeting were provided to Congress, he wanted to leak them to the media, and he wanted Don Jr. to do it, presumably as part of a strategy to associate the meeting with Don Jr. rather than Kushner. (Lowell denied this.) Jamie Gorelick argued for an almost immediate release, but she was overruled by Lowell. (She was still representing Kushner but was slowly extricating herself from that relationship, having been "nudged out by Kushner [for] not being aggressive enough with the press," according to Corallo.) What the president's lawyers and spokesmen did not know—and felt Lowell omitted to tell them—was that Kushner had, for the third time, updated his SF-86 forms, this time including the Trump Tower meeting. (Lowell said he never shares details of his clients' security forms.) Bowe and Kasowitz told Lowell that at the appropriate time—and they would give the signal—he could manage the publicity around the emails. Kushner and Don Jr. were not their clients. Even so, they had some reservations. They did not trust Lowell.

It quickly became apparent to Kushner and Ivanka that they were not universally liked by the new team of presidential lawyers and their spokesman. One strong clue: they kept being asked to leave the room. The lawyers noticed that the couple, one or the other of them, mostly Ivanka, interrupted pretty much every meeting they had with the president. One member of the group said Ivanka would just "mysteriously" happen by for every meeting. "We'd just be sitting there awkwardly, like, Okay, well, we can't really talk until she leaves." Corallo explained to me that Kushner and Ivanka appeared not to have any understanding of the difference between a regular PR issue and a federal criminal investigation, and how you cannot get between the president and his lawyers without becoming witnesses and ruining the privilege of the conversations. "They were reckless," said Corallo. "They were omnipresent."

Corallo was so concerned about Kushner and Ivanka's intrusions that he warned Donald McGahn, "Make sure people are not discussing this case." McGahn said, "Trust me. It's the bane of my existence, having to get people to understand the importance of this."

Corallo was open about how horrible a precedent he felt the behavior of Kushner and Ivanka was, and how difficult it made it for the rest of the White House staff to function. But Kushner and Ivanka seemed oblivious—another aspect of their personalities that rankled the outside legal team. "They talk to you as if they grew up in an ivory tower, which they did—but they have no idea how normal people perceive, understand, intuit," someone close to the legal team told me. They seemed like "the type of people who, if you don't pretty much indicate quickly that you're happy to shove your head up their ass, you're immediately a threat."

It was also difficult to get Trump's attention when Kushner and Ivanka were around. "You can't have a conversation without him talking about her,"

Corallo complained to me, doing an imitation of Trump. "'Isn't Ivanka fabulous? I mean, is she not one of the best-looking women you've ever seen? And they're good kids, and I just think it's crazy. They've got a nice life in New York. What do they want to do this for? God, they're fabulous, though. Aren't they fantastic? I mean, have you ever seen a better-looking couple?'"

Corallo is fastidiously polite, and widely respected in Washington Republican circles, but Kushner saw a tougher side of him in mid-June, when he again tried to persuade Corallo to take the White House communications director job. A group of senior White House staff, including Corallo, was discussing possible options to replace Dubke. Kushner walked in and said, "Well, if Mark would just say yes, we wouldn't have to have these discussions."

Corallo demurred politely, saying that he had made a promise to his wife after leaving the Justice Department to make sure he had enough time for his family.

Kushner didn't let it go. "Don't you want to serve your country?"

Corallo paused. "Young man, my three years at the butt end of an M16 checked that box."

As things soured between Corallo and Javanka, he learned they were out to get him—behind his back. Some days after that conversation about public service, Corallo got a call from a reporter, an old friend. "Dude, what did you do to Jared and Ivanka? They've sicced this Joshua Raffel on you; he's trashing you all over town."

Corallo heard from six or seven reporters that his integrity was being attacked. He was indignant. A mutual friend of the Trumps and of Corallo had warned him, "Keep your head down, be careful. I'm worried about you, because the minute one faction perceives that you are on somebody else's team, the knives are going to come out, and they're going to try to kill you."

Corallo replied, "Hey, buddy, I'm too old for that. If I feel like I'm being attacked, I'm out of there. I mean, life's too short."

The pressure continued to mount on Corallo when he found himself on the phone with Dowd, who was telling him to "make peace with Jared and Ivanka." Corallo said he had not done anything wrong. Instead of apologizing, he quit. Bowe asked him to reconsider. "We need you," he said. Corallo reluctantly agreed to return. Dowd, in turn, told Corallo he would talk to Kushner and Ivanka, and tell them to call off their PR attack dog.

On June 19, *The New York Times* ran a story about Corallo's tweets—the ones he had given to the White House before accepting the job. When Ivanka saw him, she sniffed, "Nice tweets, Mark." He shrugged. "Well, I am a conservative. Sorry." Next, Trump grilled him. "What are you? One of these Never-Trumpers?" Corallo was matter-of-fact. "Mr. President, it is your privilege to dismiss me at any moment. . . . I support you and voted for you . . . but I don't agree with everything you've done. That doesn't mean I am not loyal."

The weekend after July 4, Corallo was at a fireworks celebration when his phone rang. A reporter from *Circa*, a Sinclair-owned news website, had gotten fragments about the June 2016 Trump Tower meeting. Corallo and the others presumed the leaks were from congressional committees reviewing campaign material handed over by Manafort as part of their investigations of Russian meddling in the election. The reporter didn't have the email correspondence about the meeting, but knew Don Jr. had attended. When Corallo got that call, Trump was at the G20 summit in Germany with Ivanka and Kushner.

Corallo brainstormed with the president's legal team and drafted a statement he wanted to give to John Solomon, a journalist at *Circa* he knew well. It said: "We have learned from both our own investigation and public reports that the participants in the meeting misrepresented who they were and who they worked for. . . . Specifically, we have learned that the person who sought the meeting is associated with Fusion GPS, a firm which according to public reports was retained by Democratic operatives to develop opposition research on the president and which commissioned the phony [Christopher] Steele dossier. These developments raise serious issues as to exactly who authorized and participated in any effort by Russian nationals to influence our election in any manner."

They asked Solomon to delay publishing his story, partly because the Trump lawyers wanted to avoid having this news hit the Sunday morning TV circuit, but also because *Circa* had asked for a statement from Don Jr., and Bowe could not get hold of Don Jr.'s lawyer, Alan Futerfas. While Bowe was still waiting on Futerfas, *The New York Times* published an article about the meeting.

The team had no idea *The New York Times* had been looking into the story. What's more, they were blindsided by a statement in the article, purportedly from Don Jr. (It would later be reported that it had been dictated by his father from Air Force One.) Don Jr. had told the *Times:* "It was a short, introductory meeting. I asked Jared and Paul to stop by. We primarily discussed a program about the adoption of Russian children that was active and popular with American families years ago and was since ended by the Russian government, but it was not a campaign issue at the time and there was no follow up. . . . I was asked to attend the meeting by an acquaintance but was not told the name of the person I would be meeting with beforehand."

That evening, Hope Hicks phoned Corallo and, according to him, started berating him for the statement he had released. "What are you guys even doing talking to *Circa*? We had *The New York Times* handled." Corallo was astonished: "You had it handled? You just made yourself a witness in a federal criminal investigation, because the statement you guys put out is not accurate." Corallo said Hicks started crying and hung up.

The next day, a Sunday, Corallo was folding laundry when he got another call from Hicks, who put Trump on the line. They accused him of making a one-day story "bigger . . . than it is." Corallo said, "Well, Mr. President, *The New York Times* is not going to stop reporting on this. This is not a one-day story, because the truth is going to come out, because there are documents, as I understand it, that will prove that the statement you guys put out was not accurate, and it'll make it even bigger."

Hicks said, "Only a few people have [the emails]. They will never get out."

Corallo had had enough. "Mr. President, we can't have this discussion without the lawyers. I am urging you to talk to your attorneys. . . . Please do not talk to me about this. Please protect the privilege."

Trump told him, "I don't know what the hell you are talking about."

Corallo was correct. The *Times* published the emails on July 11 and Don Jr. had to scramble. Corallo had by now heard that Lowell had been seen lunching with a *New York Times* reporter the previous Thursday. He also heard that Lowell had been seen in the *Times* building. The legal team figured Lowell must have handed the emails to the *Times*. "Abbe's timeline [to leak them] just got fast-forwarded by leaks," one of the legal team members said. (Lowell denied leaking the emails.) They believed Lowell's strategy was to sacrifice Don Jr. to give Kushner some cover. Over the weekend, Kushner had issued a statement stressing that he had only been a peripheral participant in the meeting.

"It was exactly what Abbe wanted," speculated someone close to the president's legal team. The story ran and ran. Trump was livid and kept asking who had leaked the emails. Bowe and Kasowitz heard that Kushner and Ivanka blamed them—and Corallo, who had never even seen the emails, heard they blamed him, too.

Don Jr. would be summoned to testify to the Senate Judiciary Committee about the Trump Tower meeting. He testified that it had not only been about an adoption program; rather, it also concerned a claim that "business people who were supporters of the DNC, and perhaps Hillary Clinton, were in some sort of tax scheme to avoid paying taxes in both the United States and Russia," something he had not disclosed in his initial statement to the *Times*. In his testimony, he also said he did not know if his father had any involvement in his statement to the media.

Corallo was exasperated by this mess. "All to protect Jared and Ivanka," he sighed. "Because if [Kushner] has to leave, then [Ivanka] has to leave."

Hicks also had to testify before the Senate and House intelligence committees. Her lawyers would ultimately recommend she leave the White House, it was speculated, because she knew more than she ought to about the Russia investigation. She managed to stay on through the end of the year, but left at the end of March 2018.

On July 19, Corallo read an interview Trump gave to the *Times* "ripping" Mueller. He quit the next day. Ryun, who was disgusted that Corallo had been treated so badly, also walked. It appeared that Kushner and Ivanka had a new plan—and that Kasowitz's strategy had been rejected and they wanted him gone.

On July 11, *ProPublica* published a lengthy investigation of the culture at Kasowitz's law firm—and into Kasowitz's personal life. The article claimed that Kasowitz could have problems getting a security clearance if he applied for one because, it was alleged, he had struggled with alcohol issues—for which he'd spent some time in rehab—and that in the past he had been seen under the influence at his law offices. (A spokesman for Kasowitz denied the allegations.)

But two days after the article was published, Kasowitz responded in an inappropriate fashion to a retired public relations expert who had emailed him saying, "Resign Now." His responses: "I'm on you now. You are fucking with me now Let's see who you are Watch your back, bitch. . . . Call me. Don't be afraid, you piece of shit. Stand up. If you don't call, you're just afraid." And later: "I already know where you live, I'm on you. You might as well call me. You will see me. I promise. Bro."

"It was bad," said a friend of Kasowitz's.

Bowe advised his partner to finish setting up the team, then return to New York, and let Dowd, Cobb, and Sekulow stay in Washington. Kasowitz and Bowe would still represent the president, but they would quarterback, as needed, from New York.

But the nastiness of what had happened stayed with the group. They felt that it was now clear that Trump's greatest weakness was his daughter. "Doesn't this presidency feel like he's now the advance team for [Kushner and Ivanka]?" Corallo would ask.

One member of Trump's legal team told me: "General [John] Kelly said it best in a private conversation: '[Jared and Ivanka] are just playing government.' I think most people find that offensive."

CHAPTER EIGHTEEN

First Family

"Get rid of my kids. Get them back to New York."

—PRESIDENT DONALD TRUMP

Despite the steady drip of damning information about Jared Kushner's meetings with Russians, Javanka carried on, still imperious, still pushing their fists into every pie.

On June 21, Kushner arrived in the Middle East for meetings with Israeli Prime Minister Benjamin Netanyahu and Palestinian leader Mahmoud Abbas. According to reports, the talks did not go well. A Palestinian official told the Israeli newspaper *Haaretz* that Kushner and Jason Greenblatt, the former Trump Organization lawyer who was now the president's Middle East peace envoy, "sounded like Netanyahu's advisers and not like fair arbiters."

The Palestinian diplomat Saeb Erekat told Kushner that his people were having difficulty setting up meetings with their Israeli counterparts. Kushner implied he knew that. "We told them they shouldn't meet with you now," he reportedly told Erekat. The diplomat complained: "It's much better for us to meet with the Israelis. . . . You're not going to make peace for us."

In one of their conversations, Erekat told Kushner that it felt like he was dealing with real estate agents, not U.S. officials. Kushner's comeback: "You haven't made peace with politicians. Maybe you *need* a real estate agent."

On July 8, Ivanka Trump broke protocol at the Group of 20 summit in Germany. In a much worse echo of when she sat next to German Chancellor Angela Merkel, she briefly took her father's seat when he had to step out, sitting between British Prime Minister Theresa May and Chinese President Xi Jinping. The gesture seemed to send the message that the U.S. government was now run on nepotism. Senior State Department officials and a senior White House official agreed it was inappropriate. "I'm a better person than this, but I sneeringly called her the Princess Royal," said Mark Corallo. "Because that's how she behaves. Ivanka Trump should not be representing the United States at the G20. Ivanka Trump should not be representing the United States in any official capacity."

On July 14, *The Washington Post* published "Ivanka Inc.," a scathing deep dive into the labor practices behind her fashion line. Her company, the paper reported, "lags behind many in the apparel industry when it comes to monitoring the treatment of the largely female workforce employed in factories around the world." Workers at three factories described harsh conditions and low pay. These practices were the antithesis of what Ivanka preached about women's rights and empowerment.

A few days later, Ivanka dropped in on her father while he was doing an interview with *The New York Times*, saying she "just wanted to come say hi." (She did the same thing during an interview that summer with *The Wall Street Journal*.) A report in the paper two days later showed that Ivanka—or her trust—had raked in at least $12.6 million since early 2016. While working in the White House, the *Times* found, Ivanka would continue to collect at least $1.5 million a year from her business.

On July 21, New York financier Anthony Scaramucci arrived at the White House, potentially as the new communications director, reporting directly to the president—and not to Chief of Staff Reince Priebus. This was widely construed by White House colleagues as part of a "Javanka" plan to drive Priebus out. Back in May, Kushner had explained to a colleague that they needed to shelve a plan to restructure the communications department as more of a decentralized communications shop comprised of Cliff Sims, Andy Surabian, and Steven Cheung—all Jason Miller deputies from the campaign. "We cannot do anything dramatic," Kushner explained. "We have to let Reince make his own bed. We have to let Reince and Sean [Spicer] kill themselves." It turned out he meant the opposite of this. What he meant, according to this person, was that Javanka would bring in a henchman from their world. "Scaramucci was their hit man," the former official explained. The couple knew he was a big talker. "We will have to muzzle him," they told a confidant. "But he is someone we can deal with."

It was widely known that Scaramucci hated Priebus. The talkative, media-friendly hedge fund manager blamed Priebus for blocking him from the White House job he'd wanted, which was running the Office of Public Liaison. Priebus would claim he had not blocked Scaramucci from anything and that the White House counsel's office would not clear Scaramucci for the job because the Committee on Foreign Investment in the United States, a government body that can block foreign investments it deems threats to national security, had an objection to the planned sale of Scaramucci's company, SkyBridge Capital, to a Chinese conglomerate, and until that was resolved, the counsel's office could not clear him. Scaramucci was told it was felt that the price offered was too high, which might mean the Chinese would expect favors from the administration if the deal went through. Scaramucci was livid.

At least one senior White House official thought this was just an excuse not to hire Scaramucci: "The great irony is that the conflicts of interest and [issue of] divestitures for Jared and Ivanka are way more significant and serious than what Scaramucci was dealing with."

Priebus claimed he tried desperately to avoid a war with Scaramucci. Priebus put Stefan Passantino from the White House counsel's office on the phone with Scaramucci and himself to try to explain their position. Priebus also put Bannon on the phone with Scaramucci and himself. He even came up with the idea of a different job for Scaramucci: senior vice president and chief strategy officer of the Export-Import Bank of the United States and ambassador to the Organization for Economic Cooperation and Development (O.E.C.D.) in Paris. In June, Scaramucci took the Export-Import post.

But Ivanka brought Scaramucci into the White House without telling anyone and said to her father, "He'd be a great communications director." Priebus's biggest mistake, he'd say later, was not moving faster to fill that slot. Every time he mentioned it to Trump, Trump pushed back against meeting candidates. "Maybe next week," he'd say. And then, the way Priebus saw it, Ivanka did an end run. "Jared and Ivanka's plan was to have Scaramucci become chief of staff," said one person who was close to it all. They felt Scaramucci would be loyal to them, whereas Priebus tried to keep them from randomly walking into the Oval Office. "I get to decide whether what you think is sufficiently valuable that you get to personally pass it on to the president," Priebus told colleagues. "And that was something that was not acceptable [to Jared and Ivanka]."

Priebus was not the only person in the White House concerned about the arrival of Scaramucci. Spicer, the press secretary, had not been warned of his appointment and did not want to work under him. He immediately resigned. According to *The New York Times,* Trump tried to get Spicer to stay on, but he could not be won over. Initially, Priebus did not think Scaramucci's ascension meant he'd be out, but on Scaramucci's sixth day on the job, after it was reported that he had assets worth up to eighty-five million dollars, a figure that was publicly available, he lashed out. "In light of the leak of my financial disclosure info which is a felony," he wrote on Twitter, "I will be contacting @FBI and the @TheJusticeDept." He added #swamp and Priebus's Twitter handle. He later deleted the post and said it was "Wrong!" to assume that he was blaming the chief of staff for the leak. But Priebus realized that gasoline was being poured onto a combustible situation. He and Trump had discussed his departure on July 28. Priebus quietly resigned and thought Trump had agreed to wait a day or so before Priebus announced the news. But almost immediately after their conversation, Trump tweeted that his secretary of homeland security, General John Kelly, had been named the new chief of staff.

On July 24, Kushner testified before the Senate Intelligence Committee behind closed doors. In his prepared remarks made public before the hearing, he said, in part:

> *I am not a person who has sought the spotlight. First in my business and now in public service, I have worked on achieving goals, and have left it to others to work on media and public perception. Because there has been a great deal of conjecture, speculation, and inaccurate information about me, I am grateful for the opportunity to set the record straight. . . . Over the course of the campaign, I had incoming contacts with people from approximately 15 countries. . . . With respect to my contacts with Russia or Russian representatives during the campaign, there were hardly any.*

He also said he had no memory of having spoken with Sergey Kislyak twice by phone, as had been reported, and that he was "highly skeptical these calls took place." He added: "I had no ongoing relationship with the ambassador before the election, and had limited knowledge about him then. In fact, on November 9, the day after the election, I could not even remember the name of the Russian ambassador."

He discussed the June 2016 Trump Tower meeting, saying Don Jr. had asked him to attend and that he did not know who would be present:

> *When I got there, the person who has since been identified as a Russian attorney was talking about the issue of a ban on U.S. adoptions of Russian children. I had no idea why that topic was being raised and quickly determined that my time was not well-spent at this meeting. Reviewing emails recently confirmed my memory that the meeting was a waste of our time and that, in looking for a polite way to leave and get back to my work, I actually emailed an assistant from the meeting after I had been there for ten or so minutes and wrote, "Can u pls call me on my cell? Need excuse to get out of meeting." I had not met the attorney before the meeting nor spoken with her since. I thought nothing more of this short meeting until it came to my attention recently.*

In those same remarks, Kushner also said that during the campaign and the transition, he had contacts with more than fifty people from at least fifteen countries, including two Russians: Kislyak and Sergey Gorkov. He said he didn't solicit those conversations. He said that during the Kislyak meeting, the ambassador asked whether there was a secure line at the transition office for Russian "generals" to call, and that he said there was not. "I did not suggest a 'secret back channel.'"

About Gorkov, he claimed:

> He said that he was friendly with President Putin, expressed disappointment with U.S.-Russia relations under President Obama, and hopes for a better relationship in the future. As I did at the meeting with Ambassador Kislyak, I expressed the same sentiments I had with other foreign officials I met. There were no specific policies discussed. We had no discussion about the sanctions imposed by the Obama Administration. At no time was there any discussion about my companies, business transactions, real estate projects, loans, banking arrangements, or any private business of any kind. At the end of the short meeting, we thanked each other and I went on to other meetings. I did not know or have any contact with Mr. Gorkov before that meeting, and I have had no reason to connect with him since.

That same day, Kushner also made a rare public statement on camera outside the White House, echoing his written statement. "The record and documents I have voluntarily provided will show that all of my actions were proper and occurred in the normal course of events of a very unique campaign," he said. "Let me be very clear: I did not collude with Russia, nor do I know of anyone else in the campaign who did so. I had no improper contacts. I have not relied on Russian funds for my businesses. And I have been fully transparent in providing all requested information."

Some of the cable news panels thought Kushner had acquitted himself well—though his high-pitched, whiny voice was lampooned on the late-night talk shows. A source close to Trump's legal team did an impression of it for me and opined that anyone who begins a statement, "My name is Jared Kushner," while reading from notes in front of the White House "really does not belong there."

What got buried amid all the television coverage was a report by *The Guardian* concerning a "sealed real estate deal" done by Kushner in 2015 with a company owned by Lev Leviev, the Soviet-born Israeli diamond tycoon who was close friends with Putin—and with Trump and Kushner. Kushner had bought four floors at the base of the former *New York Times* building for $295 million from Leviev. But Leviev had done business with a Russian-owned company, Prevezon, that was then at the heart of a money-laundering case being investigated by Democrats in Congress. The whistle-blower had been the accountant Sergei Magnitsky, whose death in jail in Moscow led to U.S. sanctions against Russia.

On July 31, John Kelly officially took over as chief of staff and immediately bounced Scaramucci after he gave a profanity-laced interview to *The New Yorker*'s Ryan Lizza that was published on July 27. It was reported that Kushner and Ivanka were in favor of Kelly taking the job and hoped he'd impose some order in the White House, including controlling who went in and out of the Oval Office. They did not know that Kelly had orders from Trump to get rid of them.

Gary Cohn was involved in some of the discussions the president had with Kelly just days before he officially started, and he heard Trump tell Kelly, essentially: "Get rid of my kids, get them back to New York." (The way Trump usually put it was: "It would be best for them . . .") Trump complained to Kelly and Cohn: "They don't know how to play the game. They waffle on answers." Another source said Trump waffled about sending the couple home. "It came in cycles and waves," said this person. "[He wanted them gone] when the lawyers would tell him it was going to be problematic or he was dissatisfied because he thought that Jared or Ivanka was proving to be a liability, getting a lot of bad press, whatever it was, then it would kind of flare up and he'd have a couple of those conversations with Kelly and others. And then things would die down. . . . Jared or Ivanka would do something that was helpful, et cetera. And it was as if he had totally forgotten about it."

Kelly told Trump in front of Cohn that it would be difficult to fire them. Instead, Kelly and Trump agreed he would make life so difficult for them that they would resign—and the president would accept their decision.

The couple could have spotted the signs. For example, Ivanka had set herself up as a supporter of people of all sexual and gender identities, and had tweeted during Pride Month: "I am proud to support my LGBTQ friends and the LGBTQ Americans who have made immense contributions to our society and economy." On July 26, Trump announced he would ban transgender troops from the military, a move that apparently took her by surprise.

The first weekend of August, Trump was in Bedminster, along with Kushner and Ivanka. The following Tuesday, Trump—who had not commented on the upcoming special Senate election in Alabama—tweeted his support of Luther Strange, the tall, silver-haired state attorney general of Alabama who had been appointed to the Senate seat vacated when Jeff Sessions was sworn in as U.S. attorney general. But Strange was unpopular in Alabama for accepting the appointment, because it had been offered to him by Governor Robert Bentley, then under investigation by Strange's office on corruption charges.

Bannon left the White House on August 18. (He would always say he had only wanted to serve a year since joining the campaign.) Many would speculate that he was fired, but he was almost as influential, if not more so, outside of the White House. He resumed his old post as the head of *Breitbart*, the go-to media outlet for the Trump base. Bannon told multiple people he detected the hand of Kushner behind Trump's tweet about Strange. He had heard that Senate Majority Leader Mitch McConnell had asked the political consultant Jeff Roe, who was friendly with Kushner, *not* to run the senatorial campaign of U.S. Representative Mo Brooks, Strange's opponent in the Republican primary, who seemed the person most likely to win. Bannon liked Brooks and his politics. Originally a staunch supporter of former presidential candidate Senator Ted Cruz, Brooks had given

Trump money and helped rally House Freedom Caucus votes for Trump. "Mo Brooks had been the one congressman that went out of his way to support Trump," Bannon told people. But Strange was McConnell's "guy," according to Bannon. "He got him picked [to replace Sessions] and . . . he's beholden to McConnell." Roe wound up as the top strategist on Strange's well-funded campaign.

Roe, Bannon knew, had sent Kushner emails loaded with polling data that suggested Strange would win easily over Brooks and a third candidate, Roy Moore, an extremist whom even Bannon privately called an "oddball." Kushner also passed on printouts of statements Brooks had made when he'd been fighting for Cruz. Brooks had called Trump a "serial adulterer." Trump was immediately turned off. Bannon was livid when he heard all this. (I reported on this at the time for *The Huffington Post,* and a White House official denied that Kushner ever spoke about Brooks or the Alabama race to the president.)

Bannon and his allies, and another senior White House source not part of that group, thought Kushner was backing Strange for self-serving reasons: partly to improve his tenuous standing with Republican leaders in the Senate. "He's going to need them if things go south in the Russia investigation," one explained. And, partly, to look good in front of Trump.

On August 15, Brooks lost the Alabama primary. The two top finishers in the primary, Strange and Moore, both got less than 50 percent, triggering a runoff between them in late September. On September 22, Trump went to Alabama to campaign for Strange; Bannon broke with the president and campaigned for Moore, mostly as a protest, because he could not tolerate the idea of letting the establishment win and partly because he felt he had to support the state's evangelical voters. The way he justified it, he was—in a circuitous way—being loyal to Trump. He was sending a subliminal message to McConnell, whom he viewed as Trump's enemy, that he had not—and would not—forsake Trump's base.

On September 26, Strange lost the runoff in a landslide. In December, Moore, facing ugly allegations that he had sexually assaulted teenage girls many years before (and reportedly had been banned from a mall for harassing teenage girls), lost to Doug Jones, the Democratic candidate. It was a humiliation for Trump, who had won the state by twenty-eight points just a year earlier.

According to a source close to the president, Trump went "ballistic" on Kushner for advising him so badly on this fight.

The Senate race in Alabama would become corrosive and diverting, but it was not the top item on the minds of most White House staff on August 12, when a far-right rally in Charlottesville, Virginia, turned violent, resulting in the death of a young woman, Heather Heyer. Trump condemned "hatred, bigotry, and violence on many sides," a statement that caused widespread outrage. Kushner, typically, said nothing. Ivanka tweeted: "There should be no place in society for racism, white supremacy and neo-nazis."

Kushner and Ivanka then went on vacation in Vermont so Rob Porter, Gary Cohn, Hope Hicks, and White House Press Secretary Sarah Huckabee Sanders worked with Trump on a new statement, which he put out on Monday, in which he specifically condemned the racist far-right groups involved. But a day later, when taking questions following a press briefing in the lobby of Trump Tower, Trump reverted to drawing moral equivalency between racist far-right groups and the counter-protesters they clashed with at the rally. He said there were "very fine people on both sides."

That Friday, Cohn went to Bedminster to resign, on principle. Before seeing Trump, he stopped at Kushner and Ivanka's house there. According to colleagues he later confided in, the couple told him they could not understand why he was resigning. "My dad's not a racist," Ivanka said. "He didn't mean any of it; he's not anti-Semitic."

Cohn would tell colleagues he was flabbergasted by this. His subsequent conversation with Javanka was so surprising it became legend among a small group of senior staff. Cohn had told the couple: "There were not good people on the other side carrying tiki torches, saying 'Jews will not replace us.' I don't know about you, but most of my family got killed in the Holocaust; my grandfather got over on a boat at thirteen, thank goodness, but all his relatives are gone. I'm first-generation college-educated in this country. We haven't been here that long. My grandma is still alive and tells me lots of stories. This is too close to home for me."

He had been totally frustrated when Ivanka answered him with two Trumpian responses. Instead of understanding what he was saying, Ivanka said:

First: "My dad didn't mean any of that."

Second: "That's not what he said."

Cohn then walked the couple through what had happened while they'd been away. It had not been easy for the crisis team to persuade the president to walk back his first remarks. But once he'd done it, they'd come up with a plan for the press conference following Tuesday's infrastructure briefing. Trump was supposed to say: "I stand by my statement of yesterday," and then get into the elevator. Cohn, Mnuchin, and Elaine Chao, the secretary of transportation, would handle questions from the press, Cohn told the couple. Instead, Trump whipped out a piece of paper with quotes from the statements he had made on Saturday and Monday. In other words, Trump *had planned* to say what he said about there being very fine people on both sides.

Ultimately, Cohn did not resign, but no thanks to Javanka. Rob Porter persuaded him that they could get past this and that he was essential to the administration in so many ways, not least because he was needed to get tax reform through Congress. But Cohn's view of Kushner and Ivanka was deeply affected by that exchange on Charlottesville. He mentioned this to Porter, among others. Porter's view was that the couple was conditioned to understandably defend Trump. But for Cohn, that was not good enough. He was upset that they were not sufficiently upset. And he was upset that they seemed to think, as they always did, that this was one more public relations problem that needed to be massaged. In his mind, Kushner and Ivanka were not the Trump whisperers they claimed to be. They really were complicit. They only *pretended* to be the good guys.

CHAPTER NINETEEN

The Newspaper Industry
Is Out to Get Me

*"I wouldn't want to do business with Jared now. . . . It's a shame what
happened. He would have been a star."*

—KUSHNER BUSINESS ASSOCIATE

In July, while Jared Kushner was facing scrutiny from both Robert Mueller's investigators and Washington lawmakers, Charlie Kushner released a statement saying Kushner Companies was "reassessing the financing structure" of 666 Fifth Avenue. And on August 1, Vornado's Steve Roth reaffirmed that sentiment on a conference call with analysts, telling them, "We have been internally debating what the business plan is for the asset and that debate continues, and so we don't have an update on that right now."

The reality was that the building was stagnant—or worse—and most New York developers and brokers knew it. The debt was current, but about a quarter of the office space sat vacant. Meanwhile, costs mounted and the clock ticked.

Bloomberg reporters David Kocieniewski and Caleb Melby laid out exactly what was at stake. The tower was described as "the Jenga puzzle piece that could set the [Kushner] empire teetering." They reported that Kushner Companies was extracting as much cash as possible from its other properties and refinancings to prop up the building. Had Jared used his White

House connections to help in this desperate effort? The Kushners denied it, but the *Bloomberg* article pointed out that because no "short- or medium-term return can be expected from" the Kushners' plans for the building, the likely buyer would be "a foreign firm looking to get capital out of its country or seeking a trophy Manhattan property."

Tom Barrack told *The Washington Post* that Jared's entering the White House had "just about completely chilled the market [for 666 Fifth], and [potential investors] just said, 'No way—can't be associated with any appearances of conflict of interest.'"

Because of his son's White House position, every move Charlie made—or had made—was now scrutinized and publicized, and, in some cases, prosecutors followed the bread-crumb trail left by reporters. Charlie complained to Alan Hammer that "the newspaper industry is out to get me."

On August 15, Jesse Drucker reported in *The New York Times* that a lawsuit had been filed in New York State Supreme Court against Kushner Companies by tenants in a Brooklyn building, alleging the firm was violating state regulations for rent-stabilized leases. A nonprofit group that researched the alleged violations said similar issues were noticed in more than fifty Kushner Companies properties in New York City.

Next, the *Post* reported that Jared had not divested from One Journal Square in Jersey City until three days after his sister's very public and controversial EB-5 pitch in China.

By October, the Maryland attorney general's office had opened an investigation into management practices at apartment complexes owned by Kushner Companies, following reports about issues at the firm's Maryland properties by *The New York Times Magazine*, *ProPublica*, and *The Baltimore Sun*. Charlie was appalled by the coverage. "I try not to focus in my life on the haters, but it's just—I have never seen anything like this," he told the *Post* a few months later.

In addition to the legal issues and the negative coverage, Charlie was tormented by Roth (publicly, he denied this). In October, Roth stated on an earnings call that he was not on board with the Kushners' elaborate renovation plans for 666 Fifth. "It's likely that those are not feasible. So, it's likely the building will revert to an office building," he said. Around that time, Charlie and his daughter Nicole went to see Jeff Blau, the CEO of Related Companies, and asked if his firm would raise all the money and be their developing partner. Blau pointed out that since Kushner Companies didn't own the whole building and that there was no chance Roth would sign off on the Zaha Hadid/Jared vision for the building, he wasn't interested. Blau did not believe the building could be saved.

In December 2017, it was reported that the U.S. attorney's office for the Eastern District of New York had requested records relating to the $285 million loan Deutsche Bank gave Kushner Companies as part of a refinancing package for its retail space in the lower floors of the former *New York Times* building. The loan came a month before the election and provided Kushner Companies with seventy-four million dollars more than it had paid for the space; it was guaranteed by both Kushner brothers.

What appeared to be happening, one of Trump's legal advisers at the time told me, was that Mueller's office was farming out issues it came across and thought worthy of investigation but were extraneous to the narrow question of Russian collusion in the election. "I think Mueller does not want to be doing this forever. . . . And he also does not want to be accused of exceeding [his] mandate and going on a political witch hunt. And so, I think all this stuff other than Russia has probably been sent to other offices," the person said.

Charlie was defiant in private—and in public. He told a friend it was all so "unfair." He didn't see why Jared should be penalized because he had gone to work for the government. Charlie was not just whining; he was still fighting, still raging against the system, the rules that seemed to be in his way—and his eldest son's. Hammer told me Charlie thrives on pressure: "I've seen him in very high-level things over the years, because he didn't get there without taking great risks at times when those great risks were maybe bigger than this one. And he's just manned up and done what he's had to do. . . . He's put himself under pressure like this since the beginning."

A leading real estate developer who did not want to be quoted by name told me that regardless of Mueller's findings on Jared, if the litigation against Kushner Companies and other matters kept going, Jared's future as a star in the world of real estate was over. "No one will want to do business with him," said the source, who knows him well. "It's a shame what happened. He would have been a star. He was so ambitious, right from the beginning. . . . He backed Trump, obviously, because it's his father-in-law. But that's totally opposite everything he ever believed in. But he loves that next level [of power] that it took him to. And so, in a way, he got himself in trouble. . . ."

CHAPTER TWENTY

Trump Is Different and I'm Different

"They caught the Saudis talking to each other about how Jared would give them information."

—U.S. POLITICAL CONSULTANT IN THE MIDDLE EAST

During the fall of 2017 and the winter of 2018, Jared Kushner and Ivanka Trump appeared unable to stop the torrent of negative press coverage ravaging them. Articles in *Politico* and *Newsweek* reported that Kushner and Ivanka had used private email accounts for government work—exactly what Trump had pounded Hillary Clinton for during the campaign, using the moniker "Crooked Hillary." The email stories greatly upset Trump and John Kelly, who complained about them incessantly. Kelly felt sufficiently emboldened to say in meetings, "Well, this is why we can't have four different people who all think they're secretary of state." (*The Washington Post* would report more than a year later that Ivanka had continued using a personal account for hundreds of emails related to her government work "throughout much of 2017." The report said aides were "startled" by the large number of emails. She was apparently indifferent to the rules.)

One of the most hard-hitting articles about the couple was by Sarah Ellison in *Vanity Fair*. "Exiles on Pennsylvania Avenue" focused on the couple's elitist mind-set and quoted Kushner discussing in a previous interview with *Forbes* "exfoliating" people who criticized him for supporting Trump. It showed how they had alienated many people in Washington,

D.C., and that some of their former New York friends did not want them to come home. "What is off-putting about them is they do not grasp their essential irrelevance," one person told Ellison.

Vanity Fair had been, to use Bannon-esque terminology, "their base." In their former lives, they'd attended the celebrity-filled parties hosted by the magazine. That it had turned on them was a sign of how anchorless they now were: scorned, according to Ellison, in both Washington and New York.

The couple tried to slip from the spotlight. Kushner spent hours in the weekly meetings helmed by Rob Porter to discuss trade policy. Those meetings were tempestuous, with people often trading personal insults, since Trump had told all the principals who had a stake in trade that they could do whatever they wanted. Commerce Secretary Wilbur Ross and the economist Peter Navarro, director of the Office of Trade and Manufacturing Policy, were, like Trump, against free trade, trade deficits, and the Trans-Pacific Partnership. Gary Cohn's views were pretty much the opposite. Also joining in because their agencies were affected by U.S. trade policy were Treasury Secretary Steven Mnuchin, Agriculture Secretary Sonny Perdue, National Security Adviser H. R. McMaster, Labor Secretary Alexander Acosta, Kevin Hassett, chairman of the Council of Economic Advisers, and, of course, U.S. Trade Representative Robert Lighthizer. Porter had trouble keeping the meetings to ninety minutes on account of the widely diverging views. Everyone wanted to speak. Except Kushner. Two people in those meetings reported that he never said much. It was understood that, unlike everyone else at the table, he didn't know much about trade.

The couple focused on their "pet projects"—a term Kelly used dismissively to describe their political goals. "They want 'deliverables,'" he'd say, sarcastically quoting Ivanka. She was focused on job creation and women's empowerment, including paid family leave and childcare tax credits, while Kushner was involved with modernizing the government, prison reform, peace in the Middle East, and NAFTA. The problem was that neither had any understanding or background in policy. Further, most of the issues they cared about were either not priorities for Republicans or things the party was split on. Ivanka's childcare tax credit was viewed by some Republicans as an annoyance, since it didn't further the GOP's agenda. One person who attended dinners at the couple's home to debate Kushner's pet project of criminal justice reform described his attitude as: "Well, even though it's been debated in previous years and it's torn Republicans apart, they just need me to come in and help explain it to them, and help negotiate. . . . No political history, even recent political history, matters, because everything is different, because Trump's different and because *I'm different*."

Rex Tillerson was working long hours trying to break the Gulf standoff, while Trump was now spending more time going after North Korea. In late October, Tillerson complained bitterly and loudly to John Kelly about Kushner's refusal to abide by protocol and run his activities by the State Department. Tillerson pointed out it was a fundamental principle of the National Security Council that communications from foreign government officials go through its operational center. Kelly did what he could to help. Tillerson was livid that Kushner was still trying to run the Middle East—or at least the parts he cared about—on his own. The blockade against Qatar was still in place—and the ruling family no longer viewed Tom Barrack or his investment firm so favorably after he lobbied during the campaign, and at the start of the administration, at least, so hard on behalf of Saudi Arabia. (This would later reportedly have a negative impact on his business.) In late June, the Saudis and their partners had issued a list of thirteen demands, including the closure of Al Jazeera, ending the Turkish military presence in Qatar, and the shuttering of Qatari diplomatic posts in Iran. Qatar, which had taken steps to weather the blockade, did not budge. Against this backdrop, Kushner made his third trip of the year to Riyadh to visit MBS, who was now the crown prince of Saudi Arabia. *The Washington Post*'s David Ignatius reported that the two were said to have "stayed up until nearly 4 A.M. several nights, swapping stories and planning strategy."

A few days after Kushner's October visit, MBS had around two hundred prominent Saudis, including at least eleven senior princes, rounded up. They were accused of corruption and detained in the same Ritz-Carlton hotel where, just weeks prior, MBS had been hosting Western business-men and talking about how "free" the new Saudi Arabia would be. The hostages—who were not tried, just expected to hand over billions in ex-change for their release—included Prince Alwaleed bin Talal, a prominent investor in Western companies, who had feuded with Trump via Twitter. At least seventeen of the captives reportedly needed hospital care during their house/hotel arrest, and one died, according to several accounts. Dexter Filkins reported in *The New Yorker* that the kidnappers and interrogators were heard speaking English—the implication was that foreigners had been involved in MBS's roundup and shakedown.

In March 2018, *The Intercept* reported that Kushner may have shared U.S. intelligence on Saudis disloyal to the crown prince with MBS. A spokesperson for Kushner's attorney denied this, but someone with knowl-edge told me: "They caught the Saudis talking to each other about how Jared would give them information." This was confirmed to me by intelligence sources focused on that part of the world. Democrats in Congress de-manded an investigation.

Tillerson also received intelligence that none of the Saudis who had been rounded up and asked to hand over their allegedly ill-gotten wealth were from MBS's immediate branch of the royal family. "There's seven houses," he told Kushner, according to an aide—presumably referring to seven power-ful branches making up part of the Saudi royal family. "Yet no one in his family was corrupt. That's statistically unlikely, don't you think?" Kushner replied, "Well, that's what you think. We'll see . . ." According to a Til-lerson aide, Kushner tried to avoid discussion of the arrests, "so that he couldn't get pinned down on the issue."

The prominent Saudi journalist Jamal Khashoggi, living in exile in the U.S., commented to *The New Yorker,* "It's an interesting form of dictator-ship that is being created in Saudi Arabia. . . . MBS is now becoming the supreme leader." *The New Yorker* pointed out that only North Korea and Iran, Saudi Arabia's adversary, use that title.

Bruce Riedel, the Brookings expert on the Middle East, said that, aside from asserting control, the motive behind MBS's roundup of Saudi royals was the same as that behind the blockade of Qatar: a need for money. "The

Saudis have spent an awful lot of money since King Salman ascended the throne—on war in Yemen and on various other things," said Riedel. "They have suffered from a significant decline in oil prices, [although] there's some recovery now. Nonetheless, they took a big hit. I think the purpose of the blockade and boycott was for the Saudis to essentially take over Qatari finances. . . . But when the Qataris didn't fold, Mohammed bin Salman then went after other targets that were easier to shake down, namely, Saudi citizens."

The day of the roundups, Trump tweeted that Saudi Arabia should list the state oil company Saudi Aramco on the New York Stock Exchange. Soon after, he tweeted his support of the arrests. "I have great confidence in King Salman and the Crown Prince of Saudi Arabia, they know exactly what they are doing. . . . Some of those they are harshly treating have been 'milking' their country for years!"

According to *The Intercept*, MBS remarked to Abu Dhabi Crown Prince Mohammed bin Zayed that Kushner was "in my pocket."

A Christie's auction on November 15, 2017, showed how rich and petty Kushner's new best buds were, and how reckless and feckless. A painting, *Salvator Mundi*, supposedly by Leonardo da Vinci (experts were divided as to its authenticity), was put up for auction by Russian oligarch Dmitry Rybolovlev. That night, it fetched $450.3 million, a price that beat all records for art sold at auction by $270.9 million. (Rybolovlev had paid $127.5 million in 2013.) It was reported in December that MBS had been the buyer (the Saudis denied it), and according to two well-placed sources, it was a fantastically expensive mistake. MBS had thought he was bidding against Qatar—the ruling family, the House of Thani, has a world-famous art collection—which is why he'd gone so high. In fact, he'd been bidding against MBZ, who had wanted the painting for Louvre Abu Dhabi, but, more important, was determined to make sure Qatar did not get it. (Qatar's ruling family had not bid on the painting. It thought it was a fake.) When the mistake was uncovered, MBS offered to swap the painting for

MBZ's yacht, the *Topaz*, since he did not want the painting, which depicts Christ holding an orb.

On December 6, Trump issued a proclamation recognizing Jerusalem as the capital of Israel and instructed the State Department to prepare to move the American embassy there from Tel Aviv. Tillerson had reportedly told Trump, "You are making a huge mistake."

A former senior Tillerson aide explained his concerns: "What's the strategy? Other than keeping a campaign promise?" Another former senior State Department official explained that normally, "you don't give a concession without getting something in return." Israeli Prime Minister Benjamin Netanyahu could have been asked to stop the expansion of settlements in the West Bank, for example. But there didn't appear to be any interest in seeking that kind of concession.

A further problem, Tillerson and Defense Secretary James Mattis warned Trump, was the chance that upon hearing the pronouncement, the Palestinians would revolt and "all hell's going to break loose." When that didn't happen, Trump mocked his advisers: "Yeah, you guys are geniuses."

The embassy move seemed like a big victory for Kushner, who was already thinking aloud about the ceremony that would take place in Jerusalem in May. The Palestinian leader, Mahmoud Abbas, was not able to tell Trump what he felt about the move because the line reportedly kept getting dropped when Trump phoned him. But Arab leaders had warned Kushner that if the move were announced, they would no longer be able to pressure Abbas to come to the table for peace talks.

Kushner, meanwhile, continued to work to get rid of Tillerson. Around this time, the UAE's ambassador to the U.S., Yousef Al Otaiba, went to a dinner party in Washington and claimed Tillerson was on his way out. "Things will be much better when Mike [Pompeo] is installed," Otaiba told the group, according to a European diplomat who spoke with *New York Times* columnist Roger Cohen. Presumably, he was talking about the standoff with Qatar. The implication, according to Cohen, was that Otaiba must have heard this from Kushner. (Otaiba clearly had inside information, or was a very good guesser, because Pompeo did replace Tillerson a few months later.)

That winter, Ivanka did get a political win, albeit a small one: on December 20, she finally got the expanded childcare tax credit of two thousand dollars through the House and Senate as part of the GOP's tax bill. But it didn't change the general impression that she was out of her depth on policy. On December 21, she got basic facts about the tax reform bill wrong in an interview on *Fox & Friends*.

Although Javanka had racked up a few minor victories, they remained under siege. As winter progressed, in the wake of Mueller indictments of Paul Manafort and his longtime deputy Rick Gates (who had been Barrack's consultant), and charges against and then guilty pleas by Michael Flynn and former Trump campaign adviser George Papadopoulos, the news was full of rumors about Mueller's interest in Kushner. Much of that speculation came as court documents in the Flynn case said a "very senior member" of the Trump transition had directed Flynn to reach out to Russia. It was widely reported that Kushner was that unnamed senior member, and Chris Christie told MSNBC that all this new scrutiny of Kushner was deserved.

An unexpected event gave John Kelly fresh impetus to curtail Javanka's access to the president. On February 1, DailyMail.com ran a story about Hope Hicks's romance with Rob Porter. The two had been photographed together out on a Saturday night. The Mormon son of a Harvard professor—his father had taught Kushner—Porter had warned Donald McGahn at the start of the administration that one of his two ex-wives "had an axe to grind." Porter knew the FBI would interview both his exes as routine procedure, but he was not that concerned. He'd already been through the process. Years earlier, when he was a law clerk on the D.C. circuit, Porter's first wife had been interviewed by the FBI, and no concerns had been raised. McGahn had told him to let the FBI do its investigation and that if anything serious was found, his security clearance would be revoked and he'd be asked to leave.

Five days after the DailyMail.com story of Porter's romance with Hicks was posted, the site published another article, in which both of his ex-wives stated that Porter had been abusive—although the second wife, Jennifer Willoughby, a motivational speaker, issued a strange caveat. "I want to be very clear when I say this: I don't want to be married to him. I would not recommend anyone to date him or marry him. But I definitely want him in the White House and the position he is in. I think his integrity and ability to do his job is impeccable. And the majority of the issues he suffers from are very personal and intimate."

The first ex, Colbie Holderness, issued a one-sentence statement, telling DailyMail.com that Porter was "verbally, emotionally, and physically abusive and that is why I left." Porter said, "Many of these allegations are slanderous and simply false," and both Kelly and Sarah Huckabee Sanders leapt to his defense. "Rob Porter is a man of true integrity and honor, and I can't say enough good things about him," said Kelly. "He is a friend, a confidant, and a trusted professional. I am proud to serve alongside him."

"I have worked directly with Rob Porter nearly every day for the last year and the person I know is someone of the highest integrity and exemplary character," said Sanders. "Those of us who have the privilege of knowing him are better people because of it."

That night, *The Intercept*'s Ryan Grim tweeted several photographs. In them, Holderness had a black eye, which she claimed was given to her by Porter in 2005. The day after Grim's tweet, Porter resigned, still refuting the claims made against him. He said he wanted to fight the allegations privately.

A few days later, Holderness, ordinarily a very private person, published an article in *The Washington Post* in which she recalled "living in constant fear" of Porter's anger. "An abusive nature is certainly not something most colleagues are able to spot in a professional setting," she wrote.

The Porter affair confounded people in Washington. Everyone with whom I spoke who had worked with Porter either in the White

House or in Congress thought he was one of the most thoughtful, clever, careful—and gentle—people they had dealt with. He never showed any signs of a temper, a rare quality in the Trump White House. Gary Cohn had found Porter extraordinarily helpful in convening the weekly meetings on trade, and liked him. But he told Hicks, "If he lays a hand on you . . ." Hicks assured Cohn that Porter was kind and sweet.

On February 16, Kelly issued a memo tightening the sloppy system that had enabled Porter and dozens of others in the White House to have interim top-secret security clearances without being quickly and permanently cleared. Encouraged by the new head of homeland security, Kirstjen Nielsen, who was horrified by the large number of interim security clearances that had been issued, Kelly stated he wanted a new system in which the FBI quickly reported to McGahn if issues were found. "We should—and, in the future, must—do better," Kelly said. Meanwhile, all those working on interim clearances, and whose background checks had begun prior to June 1, 2017, would have their clearances downgraded until they were cleared. This included Kushner. On February 9, Deputy Attorney General Rod Rosenstein had told McGahn there would be a delay to Kushner's security clearance process, due to "significant information requiring additional investigation," according to *The Washington Post*. Rosenstein did not say who had discovered this information, but it was speculated that it was Mueller.

Abbe Lowell said in a statement: "The new policy announced by Mr. Kelly will not affect Mr. Kushner's ability to continue to do the very important work he has been assigned by the president." But without a top-secret security clearance, Kushner could not see the President's Daily Brief, unless the president handed it to him.

The New York Times reported that Kushner saw what Kelly was doing as a snub and fought back. "It wasn't," said a former senior White House official. "It was Kelly just doing his job."

On February 27, *The Washington Post* reported that Mueller was investigating the protocols—or rather, lack of them—that Kushner had followed when interacting with foreign officials. The paper reported that H. R. McMaster had talked to Kushner about how his freelancing with foreign officials, presumably from the UAE, China, Israel, and Mexico, had led to chatter in McMaster's intelligence briefings about Kushner's malleability and vulnerability.

That same day, the Trump 2020 campaign announced that Brad Parscale would be its campaign manager, and multiple sources told me the appointment offered Kushner an easy way out of the White House—he could go back to working with his old wingman on the 2020 campaign. But what they did not know was that Charlie Kushner, according to someone who knows him well, was telling his son to stay in Washington. The worse his situation got there, Charlie argued, the more imperative it was that Kushner stayed close to Trump. According to this source, Charlie's thinking was, who knew what Trump might say to prosecutors about his son-in-law otherwise?

By spring, the news started to catch up to at least some of the Kushners' meetings from the year before. Democrats demanded information about the loans to Kushner Companies from private equity firm Apollo Global Management and Citigroup. The revelations about the loans and the story of the meeting almost a year earlier, between Charlie and Qatari Finance Minister Ali Shareef Al Emadi, caused Jed Shugerman, Fordham Law professor and contributor to *Slate,* to ask whether the partial sale of Rosneft—the Russian oil company—to Qatar around the time of the election "may have been a quid pro quo of Russian oil money for Trump policy change on sanctions."

Around this time, NBC News reported that Qatari officials considered handing over evidence to Mueller of allegedly illicit influence by the UAE on Kushner and other Trump associates, although the Qatari ambassador to the U.S., Sheikh Meshal bin Hamad Al Thani, denied this. "It was a badly worded statement," said an adviser to Qatar. "What they actually meant was, unless asked, we're not going to give Mueller anything because we don't have anything." Even without Qatar's help, Mueller and anybody else was able to see the attempted manipulation of Kushner by the UAE via the hacked email correspondence of the RNC deputy finance chairman Elliott Broidy, which was leaked in batches to various news outlets.

The emails showed how Broidy had plotted with George Nader, an adviser to MBZ (and a convicted child molester) to lobby the president, Kushner, and the press against Qatar. (Broidy was known in Republican circles for always being on the periphery of intrigues. As one Republican operative put it, "He's like the Forrest Gump of political things, he's just everywhere.") The duo agreed to spend more than twelve million dollars on the effort, which involved publicly linking Qatar to Iran and hard-line Islamist groups. They got an April 2017 opinion piece in *The Wall Street Journal* and a May 2017 conference hosted by the Washington think tank Foundation for Defense of Democracies, both linking Qatar to the Muslim Brotherhood. Broidy also claimed to have gotten U.S. Representative Ed Royce, chairman of the House Foreign Affairs Committee, to support legislation to sanction Qatar. Meanwhile, Broidy and Nader were both visiting the White House and meeting with Kushner. Nader helped Kushner plan the Riyadh summit, and Broidy had meetings with Kushner and Trump, during which he used anti-Qatar talking points supplied by Nader. On the back of that campaign's success, Broidy also sought multimillion-dollar intelligence contracts from the UAE and Saudi Arabia and had been paid one installment.

It was all going well for this dynamic duo until FBI agents greeted Nader when he landed in the U.S. on a flight from the UAE in 2018, and he started cooperating with Mueller's investigators. It appeared Mueller thought Nader might be connected to Russia's election meddling. After all, Nader had been at a January 2017 meeting in the Seychelles between Erik Prince, the founder of private military contractor Blackwater, and Russian banker Kirill Dmitriev, that MBZ reportedly arranged.

The news of Nader's cooperation suggested that the scope of the investigation was larger than previously thought and that countries besides Russia might have sought to influence the Trump administration, countries whose crown princes Kushner was still wooing.

There was more bad news for Kushner in this mess: Nader's emails made it clear that Kushner's friends in the Gulf mocked him behind his back: "You have to hear in private my Brother what Principals think of 'Clown prince's' efforts and his plan!" Nader wrote, referring to Kushner's peace plan. "Nobody would even waste cup of coffee on him if it wasn't for who he is married to."

CHAPTER TWENTY-ONE

The Passover Revelation

"Go knock yourselves out for the next ten years. . . .
We didn't do anything wrong."

—CHARLIE KUSHNER

On March 18, the Associated Press reported that for three years while Jared Kushner was nominally running Kushner Companies, the firm filed false paperwork with the New York City Department of Buildings that, tenants alleged, helped the company push them out of buildings and later make millions when they were sold. (The documents maintained there were no rent-regulated units in the buildings, although there were hundreds.)

Three days later, the Department of Buildings confirmed it would be investigating potential "illegal activity" involving documents filed by Kushner Companies. Around that same time, the U.S. attorney's office in Brooklyn issued a grand jury subpoena relating to the false paperwork. (Kushner Companies told the AP it has paperwork of the type in question drawn up by third parties, and that Kushner's signature was not on any of the documents.)

Five days after the Department of Buildings launched its investigation, it was reported that officials in the Office of White House Counsel were looking into whether five hundred million dollars in loans from Apollo and Citigroup to Kushner's family's company had led to federal ethics violations or even crimes. (A day later, the White House denied that Kushner was being formally investigated.)

The New York Times reported that some investors were now shunning Kushner Companies and that two of the firm's properties had ended up on creditors' watch lists. The paper also cited a family friend who said Charlie Kushner hoped Jared's position in the White House might result in a pardon for his past crimes. (Charlie told the *Times* that he did not want a pardon for his felony conviction because of the attention it would draw— even though the Kushners were already attracting plenty of attention.)

On April 6, hours before Passover's end, Vornado's Steve Roth said in a letter to investors, filed with the Securities and Exchange Commission, "I believe we now have a handshake to sell our interest [in 666 Fifth Avenue] to our partner." He added: "While not the outcome we expected going in, it's now the appropriate outcome for us and for our partner." He said Vornado would still own the retail space at 666 Fifth. A person with knowledge of the talks between Roth and Charlie told me: "Here's a guy who's older, tired of dealing with Kushner, tired of . . . his name being bandied about with Kushner. . . . And he said, 'Fuck it. I'll just get out.'"

Around the same time, Josh Kushner was temporarily split from his girlfriend, Karlie Kloss, and, according to a friend, was feeling low and deeply upset about his father's troubles. He offered to fly to China to find an investor who would bail out 666 Fifth, according to someone with direct knowledge of his conversations. Aryeh Bourkoff, founder of the investment and merchant bank LionTree, gently intervened, telling the younger Kushner that the optics would be terrible. Josh heeded Bourkoff's advice.

Charlie, always pugnacious, decided to talk to the *Times*, and was characteristically blunt and defiant. "Go knock yourselves out for the next ten years," he said of the investigations. "We didn't do anything wrong."

In the same story, the *Times* also reported that there was friction between Josh and Jared over Josh's opposition to the Trump administration. (Josh was open about not having voted for Trump.) During a party at the Oscar offices, while describing the obstacles the company had faced in 2017,

Josh reportedly said: "We survived Donald Trump. Don't tweet that. Really, don't tweet that. I'll get in so much trouble."

When asked about the brothers' relationship, Jesse Derris, Josh's spokesperson, told the *Times* that Josh and Jared were "just as close as ever."

That spring, however, there was a rift between the brothers, but it had more to do with business than politics. Cadre's young CEO, Ryan Williams, told people that the SoftBank Vision Fund was thinking of investing at least one hundred million dollars in the company. But Jared's holding in Cadre—worth between twenty-five and fifty million dollars, according to his 2018 White House financial disclosure—was becoming a problem for stakeholders, said two people with knowledge. The Vision Fund is a private fund largely backed by the governments of Saudi Arabia and the UAE. Mike Fascitelli, the chair of Cadre's investment committee, hoped Jared would sell his stock, or give it to his brother or one of his sisters, in order to remove SoftBank's conflict. He was deeply frustrated that Jared would not do it. "They think they are above it," Fascitelli complained to people.

When initial reports of SoftBank's interest in Cadre appeared in *Bloomberg*, one investor in Cadre heard from someone close to Fascitelli about his discussions with Jared. In fact, the investor was told that Fascitelli and Jared had talked about Cadre since the election. "That's not appropriate," this person told me. Fascitelli disputed this: "For the avoidance of conflict, I have deliberately stayed away from Jared. I've deliberately stayed away from the White House," he said.

When it was reported that the SoftBank Vision fund might invest in Cadre, Abbe Lowell issued the following statement about Jared: "For more than a year and a half, Mr. Kushner has removed himself from the operations and direction of Cadre. . . . Like many others, he is merely a passive investor, and has not taken part in any negotiations for any investments. His passive investor relationship with Cadre was reviewed and approved by the Office of Government Ethics when he entered government and part of his ethics agreement which was written and reviewed by outside attorneys and with which he has complied with every provision."

CHAPTER TWENTY-TWO

The Double-Dipper

"The Saudis are dismayed by how transactional Jared has turned out to be. They think he's just the worst human being they've ever met."

—SENIOR U.S. POLITICAL CONSULTANT FOR THE MIDDLE EAST

On March 20, 2018, Saudi Crown Prince Mohammed bin Salman and an entourage of bodyguards traveled to the White House in armored limousines. MBS was there to meet with President Trump, Jared Kushner, and John Kelly, ostensibly to discuss weapons sales. Trump said after the meeting: "We've become very good friends over a fairly short period of time." He later boasted that various deals with the Saudis would create 120,000 American jobs. The meeting was exactly one week after Trump announced the firing of Rex Tillerson. (Trump tweeted the news shortly after Tillerson had returned from a trip to Africa—and before he told Tillerson.)

But the meeting, according to several sources briefed afterward, was not as successful as Trump's amiable tone and statements implied. MBS balked when Trump asked him to pay some of the anticipated costs associated with rebuilding Syria. Trump said he wanted four billion dollars, the same amount he had reportedly asked for from MBS's father, King Salman, three months earlier. MBS responded that he didn't have that kind of money. MBS looked visibly offended at the gauche way in which Trump produced storyboards to show what benefits Saudi investment would reap in the U.S. (Trump even used MBS as his human easel.) According to a source close to MBS,

Trump refused to believe the Saudis were broke and challenged MBS on the subject. The thrust of his questions were, according to this source: "Well, how did you fly here? Did you fly in commercially, or did you come in on your several airliners? Who paid to transport your five-thousand-people delegation, and these four hundred limousines?" He may even have mentioned the story of the auctioned painting and the yacht, said this person. "It became very heated."

Almost three weeks later, Emir Tamim bin Hamad Al Thani of Qatar met with Trump at the White House. Afterward, Trump described the emir as "a friend of mine" he had known "long before I entered the world of politics." Trump added, "He's very popular in his country. His people love him." He also mentioned Qatar's purchasing of military equipment from the U.S. The emir then described the military relationship between the two countries as "very solid, very strong," and added, "I want to make something very clear, Mr. President: we do not and we will not tolerate people who fund terrorism," a dig obviously meant for the UAE and Saudi Arabia, as much as for Iran.

The meeting had been a stark contrast to the one with MBS. According to a source with knowledge, Al Thani even thought carefully about what to wear and came in a suit. (MBS had worn his robes.) A tennis player who is six feet, five inches tall, with a fifty-inch chest, Al Thani has an imposing physique, and he knew Trump reacted strongly to people's appearances. He also knew that MBS had been embarrassed by his meeting with Trump, and he knew what to say, in contrast, which was essentially: "I want to help you with Iran. I can't, because I've got these four other countries [the UAE, Saudi Arabia, Bahrain, and Egypt] who have barred us from their airspace. So, I have to have an ambassador to Iran, because that's my only over-fly."

"I want to help you with Syria," he basically said, according to the source. "I've got money ready for rebuilding Syria . . . but I can't do it because of these other four countries [and their blockade]."

Trump's response: "We've got to get this sorted out."

Trump then phoned Mohammed bin Zayed, the crown prince of Abu Dhabi, and asked him to visit. But MBZ deferred any meeting. "MBZ said if it is about bending or changing our position on Yemen and Qatar, no, thanks," said a well-connected source.

Trump then wrote a letter to MBS, which he gave to his new secretary of state, Mike Pompeo, to deliver.

According to a source who was talking with MBZ often, the letter basically said: "You need to embrace [Al Thani] and put the Gulf [Cooperation] Council back together. Knock off everything you're talking about. And by the way, I calculated what we've given you guys as far as support over the last few years. It's seven trillion dollars. And we're going to cut you off if you get late [on payments for arms deals]. If you don't make good with this guy, I don't want to hear anything more about it. Signed, Trump."

MBZ heard about the letter and found a way to suggest to Pompeo, who was due to visit Saudi Arabia at the end of April to discuss the impending repeal of the Iran nuclear deal, not to hand it to MBS. MBZ explained that MBS would not appreciate being put on the spot like that. If MBS accepted the letter, he would be forced to say yes or no, and the consequences of either response were untenable for him. A yes would cede victory to Qatar. A no would put him in a standoff with the U.S.

When Pompeo landed in Saudi Arabia, he kept the letter in his pocket, but he did talk with MBS and reportedly warned him to stop the blockade.

MBS and MBZ were now extremely frustrated. They had lobbied for Tillerson's removal, but now his replacement was also being tough with them. And where was Kushner? Whose side was he on?

MBS started to wonder if Kushner Companies' financial situation meant that the "clown prince" was now leaning more toward Qatar and its deeper pockets. It was noticed that the lawyer Alan Dershowitz, who had met Kushner at Harvard and remained in touch, had visited Qatar in January. Former Arkansas governor Mike Huckabee was also on the trip, which had been arranged by a U.S. lobbyist. Dershowitz later refused to disclose whether he had been paid for the visit, but told me, "I spent two days with Jared in the spring [on the Middle East peace issue]. . . . We had long talks about Qatar. . . . I don't think he's anybody's pawn. . . . I don't think Jared needs the money."

According to a source who is close to MBS, the Saudi crown prince's view was different: He now thought Kushner was a "double-dipper." This did not mean he viewed Kushner as a wasted connection, but he understood whom he was dealing with. "If you're Jared Kushner . . . you've got dollar signs in your eyes as you look at MBS and say, 'That dude cannot cough up four billion dollars for defeating the enemy in Syria. How is he going to pay for whatever we are ambitious together on?'"

Even newspapers in Lebanon, where Qatari money rebuilt much of the country a decade ago, now talked about Kushner being in bed with Qatar.

In May, a source who has spent significant time with the Saudi royal family told me the Saudis hate Kushner "because [he] sold [them] out to Qatar. . . . Obama was so awful to them, but at least his people were not personally corrupt. But here, they're shocked about the finality of it all." (He meant Trump's decisive move of writing that letter.) "They are dismayed by how transactional Jared has turned out to be. They think he's just the worst human being they've ever met."

And none of these countries liked being dragged into the Mueller investigation, which they were, because it was now looking into Kushner's communications with so many foreign government officials. Rick Davis, Senator John McCain's former adviser, who knows the players in this conflict, told me, "Nobody's happy right now. The Saudis aren't happy with the U.S., the UAE guys aren't happy, the Qataris aren't happy. . . . It's a shit-show of self-interest."

While this Gulf feud raged on, Kushner and Ivanka Trump faced challenges at home. Spring brought an exodus of many of their allies from the White House: Gary Cohn, Josh Raffel, and Reed Cordish. Senators began asking the White House for records of the meetings held by Kushner's Office of American Innovation (OAI). In one letter, Senators Catherine Cortez Masto and Gary Peters, Democrats from Nevada and Michigan, respectively, wrote that "recent reports suggest that rather than encouraging efficiency in government, the office is potentially a vehicle for cronyism and waste."

In April, Kushner sat for a seven-hour interview with Mueller's team, though this was not reported until the following month.

Later that same month, the Pentagon published a damning evaluation of the multibillion-dollar Veterans Affairs digital health care plan Kushner, in his capacity as director of OAI, had supported. People could die, said the report, because of glitches in the software that attempted to link the electronic health records of both the Department of Defense and the VA. "The systems did not talk to each other," someone involved in the overhaul explained. Two software providers had wanted the contract, but Kushner pushed Secretary of Veterans Affairs David Shulkin to choose Cerner, the software provider currently servicing the DoD, to also work with the VA and link the two—without putting it out to bid. His argument was that it was the cheapest solution.

According to two people involved in the talks, the thing grew political in the spring of 2018, with Cerner's rival, Epic, lobbying for a sliver of the contract. And on March 28, Trump fired Shulkin. That same day, Shulkin published an op-ed in *The New York Times* criticizing the White House's push to privatize the VA. "I am convinced that privatization is a political issue aimed at rewarding select people and companies with profits, even if it undermines care for veterans," he wrote. But his replacement, Robert Wilkie, stuck with Cerner; during his Senate confirmation hearing, he said it would be his top priority.

A government official told me that in many ways, the negative press about Cerner's problems had been unfair: Kushner's involvement had been critical in getting any reform under way at the VA, something that had been needed for years. The Obama administration had talked about reform but achieved nothing. The official added that it had been very clever of Shulkin to get the White House (and Kushner) involved. "If the White House puts an arm around [the issue] and even just asks a question, the bureaucracy will wake up. So, [Kushner] wanted to fix [administrative problems at DoD]. I think that's good for the fucking country. . . . I liked that he was unwilling to sit and wait for the VA to do yet another study for another ten years."

———

On May 14, Kushner and Ivanka accompanied Deputy Secretary of State John Sullivan to Jerusalem for the official opening of the U.S. embassy. They sat next to Israeli Prime Minister Benjamin Netanyahu during the ceremony and took a selfie with him. Kushner's speech reiterated comments he made in December at the Saban Forum about Israel and Arab countries aligning against Iran. He said: "Iran's aggression threatens the many peace-loving citizens throughout the region and world. From Israel to Jordan to Egypt to Saudi Arabia and beyond, many leaders are fighting to modernize their countries and create better lives for people. In confronting common threats and in pursuit of common interests, previously unimaginable opportunities and alliances are emerging."

As he was speaking, riots broke out near the Gaza border. More than twenty-seven hundred Palestinians were injured and sixty-two were killed. Hamas claimed that fifty of its members were among the dead. Kushner alluded to what was happening by saying that those "provoking violence are part of the problem and not part of the solution."

Deputy White House Press Secretary Raj Shah said later that day: "We believe that Hamas is responsible for these tragic deaths, that their rather cynical exploitation of the situation is what's leading to these deaths, and we want them to stop." Israeli Ambassador Ron Dermer thanked him personally for the comments.

The next day, the chief negotiator for the Palestine Liberation Organization, Saeb Erekat, wrote an op-ed for the Israeli newspaper *Haaretz* criticizing the embassy move and claiming that U.S. officials were acting like "spokespeople" for Israel. Trump's special representative for international negotiations, Jason Greenblatt, responded in his own *Haaretz* op-ed a few weeks later, criticizing Erekat's "unhelpful rhetoric" and blaming Hamas for the escalation of violence.

But someone who worked with Kushner for many years told me that Erekat was probably right. Kushner had always held strong pro-Israel views, although he was less vocal about his stance than his father. Charlie Kushner had gone berserk when New Jersey Senator Cory Booker had supported the Iranian nuclear deal. In front of people on a job site, he had shouted at Booker on the phone, saying he had "betrayed" him. The

Charles & Seryl Kushner Foundation has given hundreds of thousands of dollars to groups connected to Israel, including those supporting the Israel Defense Forces and some West Bank settlements.

As the deadly protests continued along the Gaza border and Israel carried out air strikes, Qatar kept cozying up to the U.S. It even paid for the Washington, D.C., Metro system to stay open an hour past its usual closing time when the Washington Capitals hockey team was playing in Game 4 of the NHL Eastern Conference finals. "It was very nice of them to do that, and I don't think it actually cost Qatar all that much money," Bruce Riedel, the Brookings expert, explained. "But it was all about marketing Qatar as the good guys."

In April 2018, a Washington lobbyist showed me a chart depicting the amount of money and number of lobbying firms Qatar has deployed in the U.S. On that date, the country had twenty-two firms on retainers, and some of those raked in more than one hundred thousand dollars a month. Corey Lewandowski's firm, for instance, was being paid five hundred thousand dollars a month. It was reported that Kushner was shocked when he heard this. He should not have been. Lewandowski was hardly the only beneficiary of Qatar's wealth.

CHAPTER TWENTY-THREE

Charlie Barks and Bites

"Charlie used to tell me he had the Qataris. . . . I never really believed the Qataris were really there. . . . Apparently, they were, because this [Brookfield deal] didn't come out of the blue."

—A KUSHNER BUSINESS ASSOCIATE

On May 17, 2018, *The New York Times* reported that Kushner Companies and Brookfield Asset Management, a Canadian firm that invests in real estate, were approaching a deal whereby Kushner Companies would get a "bailout" on 666 Fifth Avenue. In the very first sentence of their article, the reporters lasered in on Brookfield's ties to the government of Qatar. The Qatar Investment Authority is the second-biggest investor in Brookfield's real estate arm—it bought a $1.8 billion stake in that part of the firm in 2014. A spokesperson for the Qatari fund told the *Times* it had "no involvement whatsoever in this deal."

Brookfield Property Partners chairman Ric Clark told attendees at a real estate conference in May 2018 that the firm had a strategy to enhance the value of 666 Fifth, and it had taken on ventures like this "multiple times."

On June 1, Vornado announced it had agreed to sell its 49.5 percent stake in 666 Fifth to Kushner Companies for $120 million. The statement declared that the outstanding debt would be repaid, and the firm would continue to own the building's retail space. This left Charlie Kushner free to do a deal with Brookfield—but at what price? He was already paying $120 million to get Roth to go away in order to cut a deal with a developer who wanted to do to the building what Roth had wanted to do all along, that is create a gleaming office tower with retail at the base.

Also, on June 1, *The Real Deal* published an interview with Charlie in which he was rude to the reporters and scornful of the people criticizing him and his eldest son for their ethics:

> *You want to know what I think about ethics watchdogs? . . . I think they're a waste of time. They're guys who can't get a real job. . . . All they want to do is assure that poor, not successful people go into government . . . Because if you're successful, you shouldn't be penalized by stupid ethics watchdogs.*

A financier who was talking with Charlie at the time on the deal for 666 Fifth told me that that interview "was a 'contained'" version of Charlie. His other, "uncontained side," is documented in email evidence, apparently. As he got older, Charlie seems to have gotten more careless about leaving a paper trail. "You don't know what unhinged means," this person said. "This guy is a real wolf in his decked-out clothes. . . . He is a demented guy who is much more dangerous than Trump. This guy doesn't care anymore; he's been to prison. . . . He's not even smart enough to do things in his best interest. He will snarl and bark and bite at things, which will hurt his immediate interest. That's how crazy and stupid he is."

A few days after the *Real Deal* interview was published, Brookfield's Ric Clark told a colleague that he'd been horrified. He thought Charlie's interview was "insane" and damaging to the Brookfield brand. However, Brookfield remained set on the deal, claiming the value of the real estate deal was the only motivation. Many real estate experts did not believe it. For example, it was pointed out to me, the two had already been partners on the Monmouth Mall in New Jersey, so the Kushners were not exactly unknown to Brookfield. Why wait so long to do a deal if the building was so enticing? Someone close to the talks explained that if the Qataris wanted to spend unlimited amounts of money on the building, it would not be in Brookfield's shareholders' interest to upset them. "If the Qataris say [to Brookfield], 'We're giving you our money, you've got to spend it,' Brookfield isn't giving it back, they're spending it."

This same person remembered that for several years Charlie implied he had the Qataris in his back pocket. "Charlie used to tell me he had the Qataris. . . . I never really believed the Qataris were really there back in the day. Apparently, they were, because this [Brookfield deal] didn't come out of the blue."

On August 3, *The Wall Street Journal* confirmed that Brookfield and Kushner Companies had closed a deal in which Kushner Companies leased the building's office space for ninety-nine years to Brookfield. In an unusual arrangement, Brookfield would pay the entire rent up front, thus enabling Kushner Companies to pay off the debt of more than $1.1 billion on the building and buy out Vornado. (Charlie reportedly negotiated a reduction of the final debt with the lenders.) Some East Coast developers did not think the math made sense. "Is the consideration for the lease," meaning the amount Brookfield was offering, "worth more than most people think the building is worth?" asked one of the former Kushner lenders rhetorically.

The Brookfield team likely agreed to do it this way "as a favor" to accommodate the Kushners' tax requirements, according to someone familiar with the talks. A sale would force them to pay the "recapture"—the total amount of taxes they deferred over the years—which could have been hundreds of millions of dollars, partly because the building had generated tax shields and partly because the Kushners had invested so much into the building over the years. This way, they avoided paying taxes—legally. Such loopholes are not available to regular homeowners.

The New York Times noted that the Kushners might not make money from the deal, although Charlie later told a friend that he "had upside" that was not reported. Presumably this came in the form of a fee, which is customary in these sorts of transactions. Meanwhile, Brookfield planned to invest about seven hundred million dollars into revamping the building, including updating the lobby, façade, and mechanical systems. The Kushners would have no management role.

So, to sum up the 666 Fifth investment: The Kushners had initially put fifty million dollars down in 2007 for a building worth $1.8 billion. More than a decade later, they got a lease that would help take care of the $1.4 billion mortgage, and likely pocketed a fee on top of that. For an initial bet of fifty million dollars, Charlie had delivered the Kushners from New Jersey to Manhattan—and, as a result, propelled them to the White House. Looked at this way, the deal was a success.

Though Josh Kushner was rarely in 666 Fifth, he paid careful attention to what was going on with the building. It was, after all, his inheritance, too. Even before Jared had gone to the White House, when he was still nominally in charge of Kushner Companies, Josh Kushner asked other people (not his family) about numbers and performances. It seemed apparent to people he spoke to that he wanted to do his own due diligence, not be wholly reliant on his brother and father for information.

His independence was even more clearly manifest in July 2018, when Karlie Kloss, his girlfriend of six years, announced their engagement. He knew his parents would struggle with this. For years, people told me, the whole family spoke horribly about Kloss behind her back. A family friend referred to her as "the lingerie model." Josh told Gary Cohn and others he was not allowed to bring Kloss to holiday family gatherings. For six years they refused to even meet her.

Soon after the couple announced the engagement, I wrote to Charlie Kushner to congratulate him, and he wrote back: "We are very excited about Karlie and Josh." But a friend of Charlie's who spoke to him the day after the announcement was hesitant to offer congratulations because he wasn't sure how Charlie would react. Alan Hammer told me in July 2018 that he and his wife had been talking to Charlie and Seryl Kushner over and over, trying to persuade them to ease up on Kloss. "Just because you want things to be a certain way doesn't mean they're going to be," he recalled telling Seryl.

Hammer also talked to Josh about his dilemma often. "It has troubled him deeply," Hammer told me, "but he doesn't want to hurt his parents."

But once he made it clear he intended to marry Kloss, his parents met with her and even had her stay with them in their beach home for a long weekend that summer. "It's a gigantic step forward," observed Hammer, while admitting that "it shouldn't be."

To marry Josh, Kloss had to convert to Judaism, just as Ivanka had. In fact, it appeared that she worked on it longer: well over a year before she and Josh were officially engaged, she was seen walking alone, with a bodyguard, to Barry Diller's annual Oscar party in Beverly Hills in order to avoid driving on a Saturday.

Despite Kloss's efforts, the fissure was not closed by the nuptials. Charlie and Seryl admitted to a friend that they had not been asked to play any part in planning the wedding, a small Jewish ceremony in front of around eighty people in upstate New York, on October 18. Charlie was noticeably restrained when he talked about the wedding to a family friend.

A Kushner family member told me Seryl likely saw Josh's marriage to Kloss as her biggest failure, "like it was Seryl's job to make sure the kids married the right people and perpetuated the stream, and obviously Ivanka and Karlie don't match that." A New York rabbi's wife, who asked to remain anonymous, explained Seryl and Charlie's Orthodox mind-set to me: "I think there is this feeling that once you marry out [of the faith], that you have sort of doomed your family chain . . . that you have lost something tremendously valuable. It is a source of tremendous shame for someone like Charles Kushner, who sets so much store in Jewish identity, in Jewish education, and Jewish continuity."

The sad irony is that Charlie and Seryl have got it backward: in the liberal circles in which they travel, Kloss is a far more admirable role model and champion of women in the workplace than Ivanka. When she was just twenty-two, she set up what would become a nationwide program, Kode with Klossy, a summer camp for teenage girls interested in technology. It now offers one thousand scholarships in twenty-five cities. In May, her YouTube channel, which has more than seven hundred thousand subscribers, started posting interviews with pioneering women in STEAM (science, technology, engineering, the arts, and mathematics). In 2016, Kloss made the *Time* 100 list honoring the year's most influential people.

"Karlie isn't who most people picture when they hear the words *computer nerd*, but that's exactly what helps her reach the girls she does," Melinda Gates recently told *Vogue*.

Kloss has made her political positions clear—and has acted on them. She attended the pro-gun-regulation March for Our Lives protest in March and spoke out against family separations at the border in June. On November 5, 2018, the day before the midterm elections, she wrote to her fans on Instagram: "96 Americans are killed by guns every day. Bring your thoughts and prayers to the polls tomorrow #VOTE."

There was zero ambiguity in what she wrote. While Ivanka postured on social media, Kloss was authentic and passionate. Who she was now related to wasn't going to change that.

CHAPTER TWENTY-FOUR

Prison Reform, Mommygrams, and NAFTA

*"If Josh and Jared's last name weren't Kushner and they were just,
you know, like me . . . Josh would have found a way
to be successful. Jared? I don't think so."*

— KUSHNER FAMILY FRIEND

On May 16, as *The New York Times* would soon report, Mark Inch, a retired army major general who had been appointed by Trump to run the Federal Bureau of Prisons, quit. He was replaced almost immediately. Two days after his resignation, he was scheduled to be attending a White House meeting on federal prison reform hosted by Jared Kushner, but instead he was packing up his office.

Inch had been caught in the middle of what the *Times* called "an ideological turf war" about sentencing and prison reform between Kushner and Attorney General Jeff Sessions.

The backstory: Soon after Kushner arrived in Washington, D.C., he began holding meetings to discuss criminal justice reform. He was open about his motivation: his father. "I think he saw through his father and other inmates that they are still human beings [despite their incarceration], and they can still contribute to society," Inch told me.

But White House colleagues noticed that Kushner had little knowledge of either the issue or its political history. There had been a growing debate in the last two years of the Obama administration about criminal justice reform, which could be divided into two buckets: prison reform (which could include creating and improving job training and other programs to reduce recidivism) and sentencing reform (such as softening sentencing on first-time offenders and creating exceptions to mandatory sentencing rules).

Senate Majority Leader Mitch McConnell hated the issue because it united Democrats—almost all of whom were in favor of both prison and sentencing reform—but divided Republicans. Hard-liners like Sessions and Senator Tom Cotton of Arkansas were dead set against sentencing reform.

Inch was keen to educate Kushner on all he did not know. He "was attentive in trying to learn," said Inch. "I saw passion and compassion."

By late March, Kushner and Sessions met in the middle. Kushner would push for bipartisan legislation on prison reform and leave the sentencing aspect out of it.

On May 22, a bill Kushner and the White House had supported passed the House. The bill added federal funding for in-prison educational and vocational training, but it did not include sentencing reform. McConnell announced in December that the Senate would vote on the bill before the end of the year. A former congressional aide told me that the chances of the bill reaching a vote in the Senate were "still pretty slim." But on December 18, the Senate passed its version of the legislation, which included sentencing reform. Trump signed it into law three days later. The news reports afterward touted Kushner's involvement, and it seemed obvious—and, in this instance, appropriate—that he would take credit for the rare bipartisan victory. "So proud of my husband!" Ivanka wrote alongside a photo of him on Instagram.

Another policy area where Kushner and Ivanka thought they could exert influence was immigration—particularly after Bannon's departure. They held several brainstorming bipartisan dinners on the subject. But these did not seem to make much difference. In April, it was reported that, since October 2017, hundreds of children had been taken from their parents while attempting to cross the U.S.-Mexico border and detained separately. Websites and news shows everywhere showed heartbreaking images of young children being detained. The next month, Ivanka posted on Instagram a photograph of herself holding her youngest child, Theodore, in his pajamas. Not for the first time, her tone-deaf social media post was slammed as being isolated in her elitist, insulated, wealthy world.

One of the most trenchant critics was MSNBC *Morning Joe* cohost Mika Brzezinski, who had once been friendly with Ivanka. "When you have babies being taken away from their mothers," she said on-air on June 15, "you have to ask why the counselor to the president—who was brought in to help the president perhaps create good policies surrounding women, parental leave, domestic policies that are important to women in this country—you have to ask why Ivanka Trump is so tone-deaf to post a picture about her special day yesterday with her daughter.

"Again, [she's] just missing the mark every step of the way, because this is about who we are as a nation. It's also about women and their vital role as mothers, and we're losing . . . a sense of who we are," she went on. "And it's wrong and we need people in [the White House] with stronger voices."

Melania Trump got in front of the First Daughter this time, issuing a statement on June 17 that she "hates to see children separated from their families" and that she hoped Congress could pass immigration reform.

On June 20, Trump signed an executive order that apparently ended the border separations. Minutes later, Ivanka finally spoke publicly on the issue: she tweeted her gratitude to her father for making this humanitarian gesture. By now, the media was familiar with Ivanka's public relations strategy. Her tactic here was an echo of the one she employed during the travel ban and after the violence in Charlottesville: tell the public you care about an issue; watch silently while your father does the exact opposite; and when he moves a little, take all the credit.

But neither Kushner nor Ivanka was eager to talk to reporters when ancient history caught up with Kushner that summer. On August 6, *BuzzFeed News* reported that back when Kushner owned the *Observer*, he had tasked Austin Smith, the software engineer, to go around Kushner's editors and secretly delete stories from the *Observer*'s website. His former editors—except Kurson—gave public statements critical of Kushner. "Jared doesn't care about ethics," former *Observer* editor Elizabeth Spiers told *The Washington Post*. "It's not an issue of him not understanding what the ethics are. It's him deciding they don't matter."

Kushner and Ivanka received top-secret security clearances in May. It was later pointed out in *The Washington Post* that a "top secret" clearance is not the highest level of clearance. A senior intelligence official told me there was not a chance Kushner would receive a "sensitive compartmented information" clearance, or SCI, of the sort that Jim Mattis and Mike Pompeo had.

Meanwhile, the spotlight was back on Cambridge Analytica and its CEO, Alexander Nix. In the spring of 2018, Christopher Wylie, a former director of research at Cambridge Analytica, testified in a hearing at the British House of Commons about how the company's use of personal data could have influenced the Brexit vote. As for the U.S. presidential election, he theorized that the data Cambridge Analytica collected on American voters could have fallen into the hands of Russian intelligence because Aleksandr Kogan, the data scientist in charge of collecting the data, made frequent trips to Russia.

Nix was suspended from the company in March after he was videotaped by an undercover Channel 4 News investigation suggesting to a phony potential client that they could entrap political opponents with honeypots. In that same recording, he mocked the U.S. House Intelligence Committee, which had interviewed him the previous year about Cambridge Analytica and the election, saying, "They're politicians, they're not technical. They don't understand how it works." It would also be alleged that Nix embezzled eight million dollars from Cambridge Analytica.

By May the U.S. Justice Department and the FBI, as well as British authorities, had begun investigating the company. On May 2, thirteen days before reports of the FBI investigation appeared, the company folded.

Ivanka, too, seemed to be of interest to investigators. In March, the financing and negotiations for Trump International Hotel and Tower in Vancouver, in which she had played a part, came under the scrutiny of the

FBI. Trump's friend/attorney Rudy Giuliani opined that if Mueller's team went after her, "the whole country would turn on them." He added, cryptically, "Jared is a fine man, you know that, but men are disposable."

A Republican operative I talked to scoffed at the claim that Ivanka had the whole country behind her. "Who is Ivanka's base? If she ran for president, neither of her brothers would vote for her." He was alluding to the fact that conservatives do not consider her one of them, the far right scorns her as a "globalist," and Democrats are troubled by her ethics.

On May 7, just days before Trump announced he was working with Chinese President Xi Jinping to save jobs at the Chinese telecommunications company ZTE after it had been slapped with penalties for violating American sanctions, Ivanka's brand received approval for five new trademarks. She would receive two more later in the month. When she was asked to comment on this by a journalist on a White House media call, she left the room.

On July 24, she closed her business and issued a statement: "After 17 months in Washington, I do not know when or if I will ever return to the business, but I do know that my focus for the foreseeable future will be the work I am doing here in Washington. So, making this decision now is the only fair outcome for my team and partners."

A former White House colleague and friend speculated that the real reason for the closure was the business's poor performance. According to Rakuten Intelligence, which looks at aggregated receipts of online purchases, the brand's online sales through Amazon, Macy's, Bloomingdale's, and Zappos had fallen about 55 percent from the previous year, *The Wall Street Journal* reported. In October 2017, a YouGov consumer perception survey had found that Ivanka's fashion line was in the bottom ten of more than sixteen-hundred brands ranked by favorable consumer opinion.

Despite the closure, Ivanka still raked in trademarks. In October, in the midst of a U.S.-China trade war, she received initial approval for sixteen new Chinese trademarks. As of this writing, she had seven more Chinese trademarks pending. And yet again, there was a report showing the couple's steady accumulation of income while they worked in the White House. In June, it was reported that Kushner and Ivanka pocketed eighty-two million dollars in 2017. And on October 13, *The New York Times* noted that though he had amassed a net worth of $324 million over the last decade, Kushner, apparently, had paid almost no federal taxes.

But who cared about Jared Kushner's taxes when the headlines were filled with far more sensational allegations regarding Trump's sex life? In March, Stephanie Clifford, a porn star from Baton Rouge, Louisiana, known professionally as Stormy Daniels, had gone public with the claim that she'd had sex—very bad sex, she'd later say—with a very married Trump. Months earlier, her agent had tried to sell her story to the *National Enquirer,* run by a friend of Trump's, David Pecker. Over the years, Pecker had done many favors for Trump, who was a longtime source of gossip and dirt for the *Enquirer.* He would also get unflattering stories about himself killed. So, naturally, when Trump was campaigning for president of the United States, Pecker offered to quash any negative stories that surfaced. When Pecker learned that Daniels and another woman, former *Playboy* model Karen McDougal, were shopping their allegations, he alerted Trump's personal attorney, Michael Cohen, who arranged a payment for Daniels—killing the story. Both women were paid to sign NDAs that would prevent them from talking again about having sex with Trump. In January 2018, *The Wall Street Journal* reported that Cohen had arranged to pay Daniels $130,000 to stay quiet in October 2016—just one month before the presidential election.

Cohen was loyal to Trump, often cartoonishly so. In the summer of 2017, amid revelations that he had contacted the Kremlin regarding plans for a Trump Tower in Moscow, Cohen declared that he'd take a bullet for the president—but then, as the feds closed in, he changed his mind. (Pecker and another executive close to the *Enquirer* also cooperated with prosecutors.) The *Enquirer*'s parent company, American Media, Inc., would get a non-prosecution agreement, meaning it would not be charged for its role in the case. On August 21, Cohen pleaded guilty to eight criminal counts, including tax evasion and campaign finance violations. Cohen admitted he had been involved in plans to bury the *Enquirer*'s story about Trump's alleged affair with McDougal in 2006–07. Cohen had set up a shell company in August or September 2016 evidently with the intent to buy the rights to McDougal's non-disclosure agreement. The deal to purchase the rights ultimately fell through. Cohen also admitted to negotiating and making the Daniels payment. He had acted, said the Justice Department, with "one or more members of the campaign" when he offered to help deal with the negative stories. The other member was reportedly Trump.

But Steve Bannon was not alone in speculating that Kushner had played a part in all this, because "Kushner controlled all the [campaign] money." On December 12, 2018, Cohen was sentenced to three years in prison. Two days later, *The Daily Beast* reported that soon after the 2016 campaign, Kushner had taken over for Cohen as the liaison between Trump and Pecker.

Both Bannon and his ideological nemesis, Gary Cohn, agreed that it was partly Kushner and Ivanka's fault that Cohen, the most loyal of Trump's consiglieri, had turned on his boss by pleading guilty and agreeing to cooperate with Mueller. Cohen had wanted a job in Washington (he'd later say this was not so); Bannon, Priebus, and Javanka had wanted him to stay away. Trump had been fond of Cohen, but he also treated him condescendingly. "No funny business, Michael," he'd say in front of people, wagging his finger at the lawyer. "No funny business." Even so, Cohn told colleagues he thought Kushner and Ivanka were "stupid" to keep Cohen out. He had been privy to so many secrets during the decade he'd worked at the Trump Organization that it was suicidal to alienate him. "Had he been in the administration, they could have invoked executive privilege, not have to testify, and they could have protected him a lot better," Cohn told colleagues.

On August 29, Trump tweeted that White House counsel Donald McGahn would be leaving. *The New York Times* reported he was pushed out partly by Kushner and Ivanka, who were upset about the thirty hours he had reportedly spent talking to Mueller's team. Someone close to the president's legal team told me it was possible they feared McGahn had talked about Kushner's recommendation that Trump fire James Comey. If it could be proved Kushner did that out of self-interest, that could be obstruction, this person told me.

Following the news about McGahn, a *Washington Post* report said Trump and his advisers had discussed having Kushner's lawyer, Abbe Lowell, join Trump's personal legal team. That would have been problematic. In addition to representing Kushner, Lowell was representing the Moroccan diplomat Jamal Benomar as a defendant in Elliott Broidy's lawsuit, which claimed Benomar acted as an agent for Qatar and played a role in the hacking of Broidy's emails. Given that Mueller was investigating Kushner's dealings with both the Qatari and Emirati governments and that that investigation almost certainly encompassed the Broidy emails, it's hard to see how Lowell would not have been conflicted out. Lowell did not join Trump's legal team.

On October 1, Kushner took credit for a major political achievement when the U.S. announced a reworked NAFTA deal. Kushner stood in the White House's Rose Garden alongside U.S. Trade Representative Robert Lighthizer as the president spoke about the agreement. The day before—the deadline to strike a deal—Kushner had skipped the Jewish holiday Sukkot in order to help finish the negotiations.

Publicly, both Lighthizer and Mexican Foreign Minister Luis Videgaray credited Kushner with leading the parties to the agreement. "The deal fell apart more than once. And on every occasion, it was one person that always found a way to put it back together: Jared Kushner," Videgaray said.

The reality was somewhat different, according to two people closely involved with the NAFTA negotiations. They said Lighthizer did all the heavy lifting. "Jared was Lighthizer's sidekick and didn't have a whole lot to contribute. He spent hundreds of hours being in meetings and trying his best to contribute," said one. "He deserves partial credit."

CHAPTER TWENTY-FIVE

Mr. Bone Saw and the Real Estate Agent

"He's integral when there's the hope of credit, invisible when there's the certainty of blame."

—*NEW YORK TIMES* COLUMNIST FRANK BRUNI, ON JARED KUSHNER

Dwight Garner's review in *The New York Times* of Bob Woodward's book on the Trump administration's first year, *Fear,* noted that Woodward's sources generally regarded Jared Kushner and Ivanka Trump as "pointless," and cited Woodward's observation that "they were like a posse of second-guessers, hovering, watching." But that understates the damage Javanka have wrought. *Fear* almost certainly went to the printers before a report in *The Intercept* revealed that in the summer of 2017, Rex Tillerson had worked furiously to stop not just the blockade against Qatar, but also a full-blown war in the Persian Gulf. He had reportedly persuaded Saudi Crown Prince Mohammed bin Salman to back down from having Saudi troops circumvent the Al Udeid Air Base in Qatar and then seize Doha, the Qatari capital. A Qatari source told me they'd heard the plan was to "eliminate the Qatari leadership." So, instead of bringing peace to the Middle East, one might argue that Kushner almost started a new war there. Whatever the right word to describe his meddling in foreign affairs, "pointless" is almost certainly not it. "Potentially dangerous" is a phrase I heard used by a recently retired, very senior State Department official and a former senior Tillerson aide.

Fear was published in early September—a few weeks before *Washington Post* journalist Jamal Khashoggi, a Saudi-born critic of MBS's autocratic rule, walked into the Saudi consulate in Istanbul to get the papers he needed to remarry, and was reportedly killed by Saudi agents, members of a team of fifteen operatives who had flown to Istanbul, including several linked to MBS's security team. One of them, an autopsy expert, had come equipped with a bone saw, with which he reportedly dismembered the body. The deed was done in fifteen minutes. (The autopsy expert reportedly encouraged the assassination squad to calm themselves during the butchery by listening to music on their headphones.)

The Saudis at first maintained that Khashoggi had left the embassy alive, but the Turkish government disputed this and released surveillance footage that showed Khashoggi going in but never coming out. On October 10, the *Post* reported that despite Saudi claims, MBS had long had Khashoggi on a watch list and had been trying to lure him back to Saudi Arabia for months. Then, the Turks also released footage of a Khashoggi look-alike leaving the consulate, wearing the clothes Khashoggi had worn upon entering shortly before. The farce continued: before Turkish investigators were able to enter the consulate, the Associated Press reported that a cleaning crew, equipped with "mops, trash bags, and what appeared to be bottles of bleach," had entered the building.

The Saudi crown prince clumsily denied involvement in the murder, but the evidence was overwhelming, and MBS's new nickname, globally, was Mr. Bone Saw.

Kushner's friendship with the Saudi crown prince was now under widespread scrutiny for yet another reason. Rather than expressing moral outrage over the cold-blooded murder of an innocent man, Kushner did what he always does in a crisis: he went quiet. On October 16, the *Times*'s Frank Bruni blasted Kushner's "moral laryngitis," noting that he's "integral when there's the hope of credit, invisible when there's the certainty of blame."

In this crisis, MBS was also eager to avoid blame. He initially denied any knowledge of the killing, then allowed that it might have been a rogue operation, and *then* suggested it was an interrogation-and-capture operation gone wrong. The kingdom finally had eleven Saudis indicted for their alleged involvement in the killing of Khashoggi—five of whom may face the death penalty. But the buck would stop there—well short of MBS.

Kushner's next move was equally predictable. Khashoggi's murder, he reportedly argued, was just one more public relations dustup that would soon be forgotten; "a detail" in the bigger issue of the fight against Iran, which was essential to his peace plan.

He was, once again, wrong on an important issue; the murder stayed in the headlines for weeks as the Turkish government dribbled out damning details implicating MBS. Early on, Trump had tried to remain publicly agnostic about the Khashoggi murder for as long as he could. "I don't like hearing about it and hopefully that will sort itself out," he said. "Right now, nobody knows anything about it." (Many people knew a lot about it.) But as more and more of the grisly details seeped out, even Trump had to admit that the consequences for Saudi Arabia would "have to be very severe" if the murder was linked to the government.

Several days after Khashoggi was murdered, in what appeared to be yet another sign of the split between the White House and the State Department, someone inside State reached out to Khashoggi's family and offered them sanctuary if they could get to the U.S. consulate in Jeddah. The Saudis learned of this and warned the family not to try it. Instead, Khashoggi's eldest son, Salah, was given back his passport and told he could travel as he pleased—including to the U.S.

Ultimately, Trump sanctioned seventeen Saudis said to be directly involved, but still refused to speak ill of the crown prince. In a highly unusual gesture that smacked of rebellion, the *Post* obtained information on a CIA assessment that found MBS had likely authorized the murder. With that, Trump went on the counterattack. He defended MBS and the U.S. relationship with Saudi Arabia, and, as he had done many times as president, disputed U.S. intelligence to defend a brutal dictator. "It could very well be that the crown prince had knowledge of this tragic event— maybe he did and maybe he didn't," he said. "The United States intends to remain a steadfast partner of Saudi Arabia to ensure the interests of our country, Israel, and all other partners in the region."

Trump made no mention of Kushner, but he was covering for his son-in-law as much as he was covering for MBS. On October 16, Secretary of State Mike Pompeo was dispatched to Saudi Arabia on a fact-finding mission after Khashoggi's death. But Kushner had his own methods of fact-finding. News filtered out that Kushner and MBS had continued to speak privately as the days ticked by, as usual bypassing the State Department and its protocols.

Publicly, Kushner pressed on, focusing on what was important to him (and to another of his old-man mentors, Benjamin Netanyahu). In late October, he gave a rare interview with Van Jones at a CNN forum. He sidestepped questions about Khashoggi's murder—he said he told MBS to be "transparent"—and was hesitant to condemn what the prince was widely believed to have orchestrated: a political assassination of an American resident on foreign soil. "Saudi Arabia has been a very strong ally in terms of pushing back against Iran's aggression," he said. "The Middle East is a rough place. It's been a rough place for a very long time, and we have to be able to pursue our strategic objectives, but we also have to deal with what obviously seems to be a terrible situation."

It was a fraught situation for the White House as well. Trump finally got blowback for his defense of MBS (reminiscent of his "fine people on both sides" defense of the rioters in Charlottesville) from congressional Republicans, who had mostly sat by for two years as the president did as he damn well pleased at home, abroad, and on Twitter. The Republicans in Congress had shown little interest in finding out whether Vladimir Putin had a heavy hand in the 2016 presidential election, but they seemed eager to punch Trump in the nose for sucking up to MBS. In the first week of December, senators from both parties, among them prominent Republicans Bob Corker and Lindsey Graham, were briefed by CIA Director Gina Haspel about Khashoggi's killing. Coming out of the meeting, the lawmakers said they were firm in their belief that MBS had himself ordered Khashoggi to be killed.

Days later, *The New York Times* implicated Kushner further, reporting that since the killing, he had become "the prince's most important defender inside the White House" and that he and the prince had communicated more times than the White House had acknowledged. Following the report, a spokesman for Representative Eliot Engel, a Democrat soon to become chairman of the House Foreign Affairs Committee, said the panel planned to examine American policy on Saudi Arabia. A reporter asked if the committee would look into Kushner's relationship with MBS. The spokesman replied, "Everything is on the table."

The Selfie President

"When they are gone, I will tell you the real story about them."
—SENIOR WHITE HOUSE ADVISER, ON JARED KUSHNER
AND IVANKA TRUMP

Ivanka Trump has made no secret of the fact that she wants to be the most powerful woman in the world. Her father's reign in Washington, D.C., is, she believes, the beginning of a great American dynasty. "She thinks she's going to be president of the United States," Gary Cohn told people after leaving the White House. "She thinks this is like the Kennedys, the Bushes, and now the Trumps."

Ever since her father clinched the Republican nomination, Ivanka has been carefully positioning herself as his political heir. She was the Trump child chosen to introduce him at the Republican National Convention; she was the one making edits to his acceptance speech on Election Night; she marked out a suite of offices for herself in the East Wing (until First Lady Melania Trump slapped her hand away); her West Wing staff is remarkably large for an adviser without a portfolio; she has pushed her way into meetings with task forces and advisory councils, allowing her to network with captains of industry. Her eagerness to shape domestic policy earned her face time with politicians from both parties—many of whom she and Jared Kushner have hosted for policy dinners at their home in Washington. She has championed workplace initiatives and women pursuing careers in STEM fields. And she has been everywhere—from Seoul, South Korea, to Paintsville, Kentucky—touting her initiatives, her brand, herself. Her steady stream of social media posts has shown her flitting about the globe at such a dizzying pace, it's a wonder she has time to eat or have her hair styled (which she does almost every morning). Not long after her father plopped down behind his desk in the Oval Office, she had started her unofficial campaign to become the first Selfie President.

She has the ego and the ambition necessary for a presidential candidate, and she also has what her father calls "the look." The fact that she doesn't have any firm political ideology has not dissuaded her. She has tried to cast herself as a social liberal who wanted to reverse her father's travel ban, and who wanted to prevent her father's decision to pull out of the Paris climate accord. But, as has been pointed out in these pages, she failed on both those points. And none of those failures deter her. What really concerns her is her personal brand. Whenever that has seemed imperiled, whether because of the appearance of blatant self-dealing or the unsanctioned use of personal email, she kicked it into gear—or, more accurately, onto Fox News—and started spewing platitudes. I would argue her most memorable line was, "I try to stay out of politics." (That's the tell, the line that proves she intends to stay in politics.) Like her father, she is very talented at telling self-serving bald lies with a straight face, should the need arise.

Her husband has so far proven even more adept at thriving in Washington. He has, as of press date, dodged even more lethal bullets: investigations asking about his meetings with Russians, which he omitted from his security clearance forms; misuse of a personal email account; criminal questions about the firing of James Comey, in which he played a critical role; ethics questions about his limited divestiture; ethics questions about loans to Kushner Companies; questions about Kushner Companies' alleged misuse of the EB-5 visa program. His secretive bromance with the crown prince of Saudi Arabia played very poorly in the media after the CIA concluded in November 2018 that the crown prince had ordered the brutal murder of journalist Jamal Khashoggi. He is, clearly, his father's son in so many ways, including a disdain for rules, for ethics, for honesty. Charlie Kushner was comfortable hiring a prostitute in order to blackmail his sister and brother-in-law; Jared was apparently comfortable glossing over the political assassination of a U.S. resident who dared to criticize a ruthless autocrat.

Despite all that, the future looks bright for Javanka: In December 2018, Chief of Staff John Kelly, the only firewall between them and President Donald Trump, left the White House. With Kelly gone, their power will only increase.

But there is an equally plausible alternate scenario for the next two years (or more?) of the Trump administration, one in which Kushner and Ivanka finally face a reckoning.

First there is the Robert Mueller investigation. At the time of writing, there was speculation that dozens of sealed criminal indictments spotted on the docket for Washington, D.C., federal court could signal big charges to come. Even if Kushner survives that, he and Ivanka still face the very real possibility of being scrutinized by the Democrats who now hold power in the House of Representatives. Thanks to the blue wave of the 2018 midterms, they now have subpoena power. What had previously just been a public relations headache for Javanka became something far more serious. Incoming House Intelligence Committee chair Adam Schiff promised a "deep dive on Saudi Arabia," including examinations of whether Trump—and presumably Kushner—let conflicts of interest affect U.S. policy and relations with Riyadh.

(In the Senate, Lindsey Graham called for targeted sanctions reaching into the Saudi royal family, and Rand Paul demanded an end to arms sales to Riyadh. Outgoing Foreign Relations Committee chairman Bob Corker teamed up with Democratic colleagues to force the White House to look into Khashoggi's killing more closely.)

House Democrats are now entitled to ask for documentation on all the other thorny questions raised in these pages: Kushner's clearance forms omissions; his meetings with Russians and other government representatives while simultaneously conducting family business; any role Qatar may have played in paying off the loan on 666 Fifth Avenue; the facts as to whether Kushner had and maintained a profit-sharing arrangement with his brother Josh Kushner; who wanted the White House visitor logs made private and why? What did Jared know about Saudi Arabia's plans to attack Qatar?

How many times did Ivanka waste State Department resources trying to fly on a government plane? What was the link between her meetings with various heads of state and trademarks for her company?

If this is the direction the couple's story takes, then who knows how and where it ends? "One day, when Jared and Ivanka are gone, I will tell you the real story," one of my most important sources told me.

It didn't sound as though what he wanted to tell me was flattering.

Acknowledgments

This book would not have happened without the steadfast encouragement of Michael Flamini, my editor at St. Martin's, who understood as early as I did that the story of Javanka's rise and their corruption was essential reading for all those truly seeking insight into this bent administration and who fear for our country's future in their hands. Thanks also go to Dori Weintraub, Gwen Hawkes, David Lott, Steven Seighman, David Rotstein, and Lena Shekhter at St. Martin's. Thank you, as ever, to my agent Andy McNicol, at William Morris Endeavor, for her support and guidance. And to Sandi Mendelson and David Kass, whose publicity instincts are unrivaled. Jay Fielden and Michael Hainey, the two wise men atop *Esquire*, sparked the idea of writing about the Kushners back in 2016. And the inimitable Bobby Baird edited the magazine piece that was the genesis for this book. A book such as this is reported and written at great speed. I would be lost without Lee Smith, who provided editorial guidance and directed a crack team of researchers with patience, diligence, and his trademark painstaking eye for detail. I was lucky enough to find some remarkable young talent to work with me on this book, people who I know have glittering futures ahead of them, and I will miss the daily exchanges with them, as much as I am excited to follow their careers from the bleachers. Max Kutner is a stand-out reporter, writer, and editor who came from *Newsweek*. His leaving there was my gain. Delphine d'Amora, a former *Mother Jones* fellow and alum of the *Moscow Times*, has one of the most meticulous, sharp, and tenacious minds I have ever encountered. I was very fortunate to have *Newsweek*'s former deputy editor, Ross Schneiderman, on board for seventy percent of the project. He was invaluable. As the deadline got closer, Samuel Oakford and Jay Cassano, two industry veterans, worked all hours through the Thanksgiving weekend to help me cross the finish line, as did Connie Lin and Grace Phillips, who also helped with research and the book's end-notes. Much earlier in the process I was fortunate to have Eliza Carter and Leilani Zee summarize some of the numerous books out there on the Trump family. John Mintz and Philip Segal were invaluable in retrieving court documents and much else in the public record. Thank you, all.

I am also indebted to Erich Beckmann and his team at Beckmann Technologies, who made themselves available at any hour of any day to deal with numerous computer glitches. I'd like to thank Steven Brill, for giving me big-picture sage advice in ready supply. And I'd like to thank Rachel Morris and Greg Veis at *HuffPost Highline*, for sharpening my writing in the last couple of years and for introducing me to Delphine.

As ever, I must thank my "home peeps," for bearing up with me so patiently: Caroline von Reitzenstein and Adriana Pasarelu, my friends and executive assistants. Brigid Cotter. My sons, Lorcan and Orlando. And Richard Cohen, who is my greatest champion. I would have been lost without his patience and understanding during a period in which he barely saw me. Those of us who choose to be writers know that a solitary existence is par for the course, but I feel that gratitude is more rightly deserved by those closest to us who tolerate the loneliness without any expectation of reaping the reward.

January 2019

Notes

Much of the information presented in this book comes from interviews with sources who spoke on the condition of anonymity.

PROLOGUE

1   *received a rabbinical dispensation*: Joshua Davidovich, "Ivanka Trump, Jared Kushner Reportedly Get Green-Light to Drive to Balls on Shabbat," *Times of Israel*, January 20, 2017.

1   *Ivanka looked like Cinderella*: View Ivanka Trump's Instagram post, from January 21, 2017, at https://www.instagram.com/ivankatrump/p/BPjJVrClZm9/.

1   *After only a few minutes of*: View footage of the first dance, which took place on January 20, 2017, on *The New York Times* website at https://www.nytimes.com/video /us/politics/100000004879799/the-first-dance.html.

2   *And she'd attended an Ivy League*: "Ivanka Trump Weds Jared Kushner," *New York Times*, October 24, 2009.

2   *hadn't even been to college*: "Supermodel Karlie Kloss Talks Taylor Swift, Wearing Dior to Prom, and Life Off the Runway," *Glamour*, August 4, 2015.

2   *opening number from* Hamilton: View a White House performance of "Alexander Hamilton," which took place on March 14, 2016, at https://www.youtube.com/watch ?v=ZPrAKuOBWzw.

CHAPTER ONE

Some of the information in this chapter comes from Rae Kushner's 1982 interview with Sidney Langer, on the United States Holocaust Memorial Museum's website at https://collections.ushmm.org/search/catalog /irn504520.

4   *"A lot of these children who are"*: Interview with Alan Hammer, July 9, 2018.

4   *About half of her town*: Yehuda Bauer, "Nowogródek—The Story of a Shtetl," *Yad Vashem Studies*, Volume 35:2, 2007.

5   *His glasses had broken*: A series of video interviews with Rae Kushner are available on the Jewish Partisan Educational Foundation's website at http://www .jewishpartisans.org/partisans/rae-kushner.

7   *A 1980 series in* The Times *of Trenton*: John Mintz, "Refugee Builders: Two Stories in the Trenton Times," *Trenton Times*, June 1980, https://www.documentcloud.org /documents/5302092-Trenton-Times-Refugee-Builders.html.

7   *"The Kushners' experience was unusual"*: Interview with Michael Berenbaum, June 7, 2018.

8   *"rules are dangerous"*: Ibid.

8   *"Charlie had really no appreciation"*: Interview with Alan Hammer, July 9, 2018.

10   *"When I first met Charlie"*: Ibid.

10   *"He created the Orthodox community"*: Ibid.

11   *"Charlie probably acquired more"*: Ibid.

CHAPTER TWO

13   *where he was an average student*: Daniel Golden, *The Price of Admission* (New York: Broadway Books, 2007), p. 45.

13   *tens of thousands of so-called*: Lauren Elkies, "Charles Kushner," *The Real Deal*, November 5, 2007.

14   *His role as family patriarch meant*: Read the United States Court of Appeals for the Third Circuit's September 9, 2010, opinion on the U.S. Courts' website at http:// www2.ca3.uscourts.gov/opinarch/091575p.pdf.

14   *He was nicknamed "the Dapper Don"*: Craig Horowitz, "Jim McGreevey and His Main Man," *New York*, September 20, 2004.

14   *Kushner Companies still paid her annual bonuses*: Read the February 11, 2008, press release, "Former Accountant for Kushner Companies Admits Tax Fraud Conspiracy," on the Department of Justice's website at https://www.justice.gov/sites/default /files/usao-nj/legacy/2013/11/29/plot0211%20rel.pdf.

14   *was disguised to the IRS as a legal expense*: Read the United States Court of Appeals for the Third Circuit's September 9, 2010, opinion on the U.S. Courts' website at http://www2.ca3.uscourts.gov/opinarch/091575p.pdf.

14   *divided among Charlie and his three siblings*: Ibid.

14   *Charlie viewed his increasingly public profile*: Westminster Management's counterclaim against Robert Yontef is available at https://www.documentcloud.org /documents/5302033-Yontef-vs-Westminster-counterclaim.html.

14   *cost as much as one hundred thousand dollars*: Robert Yontef's complaint against Westminster Management is available at https://www.documentcloud.org/documents /5302031-Yontef-vs-Westminster.html.

14   *Rather than pay out of his own pocket*: Read the United States Court of Appeals for the Third Circuit's September 9, 2010, opinion on the U.S. Courts' website at http:// www2.ca3.uscourts.gov/opinarch/091575p.pdf.

15   *Those ranged from Charlie's home improvements*: Ibid.

15   *what was called a "Richard special"*: Ibid.

16   *Most of the senior members*: Ibid.

16   *Stadtmauer and Charlie's mantra was*: Ibid.

17   *"Richard was an abused child"*: Interview with Alan Hammer, July 9, 2018.

17   *"You had to do pretty much as you"*: Read the United States Court of Appeals for the Third Circuit's September 9, 2010, opinion on the U.S. Courts' website at http://www2.ca3.uscourts.gov/opinarch/091575p.pdf.

17   *But Charlie doggedly groomed his eldest son*: Gabriel Sherman, "The Legacy," *New York,* July 12, 2009.

18   *Around the time Jared was applying*: Daniel Golden, *The Price of Admission* (New York: Broadway Books, 2007), p. 45.

18   *and made additional promises to*: Ibid., p. 47.

18   *He also got New Jersey senator*: Ibid., p. 46.

18   *When Jared was accepted*: Ibid., p. 45.

18   *"His GPA did not warrant it"*: Ibid., p. 46.

19   *Murray Kushner grew increasingly suspicious*: Gabriel Sherman, "The Legacy," *New York,* July 12, 2009.

19   *Billy and Esther Schulder did attend that family Passover*: Ibid.

20   *rumored to be corruptible and in Charlie's pocket*: Craig Horowitz, "Jim McGreevey and His Main Man," *New York,* September 20, 2004.

20   *Charlie had been his top campaign donor*: Ronald Smothers, "Lurid Charges for Top Donor to McGreevey," *New York Times,* July 14, 2004.

20   *where McGreevey met a young Israeli*: James E. McGreevey, "The Making of a Gay American," *New York,* September 25, 2006.

20   *Charlie sponsored Cipel's visa*: Craig Horowitz, "Jim McGreevey and His Main Man," *New York,* September 20, 2004.

20   *on New York City's Upper West Side*: George James and David Kocieniewski, "A Governor Resigns: The Other Man; Details of a Past in Question Are Emerging One by One," *New York Times,* August 13, 2004.

20   *In 2002, he offered Charlie*: Craig Horowitz, "Jim McGreevey and His Main Man," *New York,* September 20, 2004.

21   *Charlie Kushner never got to properly accept*: Ibid.

21   *Yontef, who had been fired in November*: Robert Yontef's complaint against Westminster Management is available at https://www.documentcloud.org/documents/5302031-Yontef-vs-Westminster.html.

21   *"Murray directed the conspiracy"*: Westminster Management's counterclaim against Robert Yontef is available at https://www.documentcloud.org/documents/5302033-Yontef-vs-Westminster-counterclaim.html.

21   *The feds started to pressure*: Gabriel Sherman, "The Legacy," *New York,* July 12, 2009.

22   *He decided to coerce Esther into dropping*: Ibid.

22   *reportedly had his brother, a private investigator*: Ibid.

22   *O'Toole reportedly went to Charlie's home*: Ibid.

22 *In May 2004, right before her son Jacob's*: Ibid.

23 *"His siblings stole every piece of paper"*: Ibid.

CHAPTER THREE

24 *Charlie Kushner's friends figured he would fight*: Gabriel Sherman, "The Legacy," *New York*, July 12, 2009.

24 *"They were a very difficult group"*: Interview with Ted Moskowitz, June 12, 2018.

24 *"I think [the sting] put him"*: Interview with Alan Hammer, July 9, 2018.

25 *Because of Charlie's strong aversion to*: Lizzie Widdicombe, "Ivanka and Jared's Power Play," *New Yorker*, August 22, 2016.

25 *"The social stigma would be"*: Interview with Michael Berenbaum, June 7, 2018.

25 *"Whatever the rumors are"*: Interview with Alan Hammer, July 9, 2018.

26 *had tried to make a deal in which*: Ibid.

26 *Golan Cipel, the young Israeli with whom*: Gabriel Sherman, "The Legacy," *New York*, July 12, 2009.

26 *Cipel hadn't even passed a background*: George James and David Kocieniewski, "A Governor Resigns: The Other Man; Details of a Past in Question Are Emerging One by One," *New York Times*, August 13, 2004.

27 *Now Cipel was allegedly trying to extort McGreevey*: Laura Mansnerus, "A Governor Resigns: Overview; McGreevey Steps Down After Disclosing a Gay Affair," *New York Times*, August 13, 2004.

27 *reported that McGreevey's advisors*: David Kocieniewski and Joseph Berger, "Fallout From a Resignation: The Investigation; Inquiry Said to Be Focusing on Plan for Touro College," *New York Times*, August 17, 2004.

27 *quarreled with McGreevey on a conference call*: Craig Horowitz, "Jim McGreevey and His Main Man," *New York*, September 20, 2004.

27 *"My truth is that I am a gay American"*: Laura Mansnerus, "A Governor Resigns: Overview; McGreevey Steps Down After Disclosing a Gay Affair," *New York Times*, August 13, 2004.

27 *McGreevey's admission*: David Kocieniewski, "A Governor Unindicted, but Implicated," *New York Times*, July 9, 2004.

27 *pleaded guilty to eighteen counts*: Read the August 18, 2004, press release, "Political Contributor, Developer Charles Kushner Pleads Guilty to Tax Fraud, Witness Retaliation and Making False Statements to the Federal Election Commission," on the Department of Justice's website at https://www.justice.gov/archive/tax/usaopress/2004/txdv04kush0818_r.htm.

27 *"I want to be very clear about this"*: Craig Horowitz, "Jim McGreevey and His Main Man," *New York*, September 20, 2004.

27 *Every weekend, he was visited by Jared*: Gabriel Sherman, "The Legacy," *New York*, July 12, 2009.

27 *"He can be a very difficult man"*: Interview with Alan Hammer, July 9, 2018.

28 *"When I was there, we made"*: Ibid.

28 *"There's no raising your voice"*: Ibid.

28 *"He worked like a dog"*: Ibid.

.28 *In 2006, he was indicted*: "Briefs: Justice; Kushner Executive Indicted," *New York Times*, April 16, 2006.

28 *Plotkin and two other former senior*: Ted Sherman, "Former Kushner CFO Admits Guilt in Scheme," *NJ.com*, February 11, 2008, https://www.nj.com/news/index.ssf /2008/02/former_kushner_cfo_admits_guil.html.

28 *"I believe that Richard would sooner"*: Interview with Alan Hammer, July 9, 2018.

29 *Charlie had steered fifty thousand dollars*: Ted Sherman, "Newark Mayor Lags in Campaign Funds," *Star-Ledger*, April 20, 2002.

29 *"collaborating with Jews to take over"*: Seth Mnookin, "The New Natural," *New York*, April 22, 2002.

30 *"I don't understand. I certainly think"*: Interview with Alan Hammer, July 9, 2018.

30 *"They bought the* Observer": Ibid.

31 *Jonathan Goettlich, the son of someone*: David Kocieniewski and Caleb Melby, "Kushner's Felon Father Back at Helm of New York Empire with Two Fellow Inmates," *Bloomberg*, January 27, 2017.

CHAPTER FOUR

32 *"Perception is more important than reality"*: Ivanka Trump, *The Trump Card* (New York: Touchstone, 2009), p. 166.

33 *"Does it mean I'm not going to be"*: Marie Brenner, "After the Gold Rush," *Vanity Fair*, September 1990.

33 *she'd call him during the day*: Brian Rokus, "Ivanka Explains What It Was Like Growing Up Trump," CNN, July 21, 2016.

33 *"She was always Daddy's little girl"*: On-the-record interview with Nikki Haskell, May 14, 2018.

33 *"Donald was there when he was"*: Ibid.

33 *"He may be different to some"*: Interview with Ivanka Trump, April 11, 2013.

33 *"brought me and my brothers much closer"*: Ivanka Trump, *The Trump Card* (New York: Touchstone, 2009), p. 62.

33 *she was reportedly asked not to return to Chapin*: Courtney Weaver, "'I Will Not Be Distracted by the Noise,'" *Financial Times*, September 14, 2017.

34 *she spent less time on campus than many*: Ivana Trump, *Raising Trump* (New York: Gallery Books, 2017), p. 220.

34 *She would later say she was*: Lisa DePaulo, "Ivanka Trump's Plan for Total World Domination," *GQ*, April 12, 2007.

34 *that he was wary about her modeling*: Jennifer Steinhauer, "Her Cheekbones (High) or Her Name (Trump)?" *New York Times*, August 17, 1997.

35 *"I mean, I've even heard him say that"*: George Gurley, "Trump Power: Ivanka Trump," *Marie Claire*, January 29, 2007.

36 *"Donald likes that organized confusion"*: Interview with Nikki Haskell, May 14, 2018.

36 *"Once we went into the franchise business"*: Interview with Louise Sunshine, March 26, 2018.

37 *would later serve as an asset*: Read Loretta Lynch's February 9, 2015, response on the

National Review website at http://c6.nrostatic.com/sites/default/files/Lynch%20 response%20to%20Hatch%20(1).pdf.

37   *He got into a drunken bar brawl*: Charles V. Bagli, "Real Estate Executive with Hand in Trump Projects Rose From Tangled Past," *New York Times,* December 17, 2007.

37   *Sater lost his broker's license*: Read Felix Sater's December 2017 statement at https://www.documentcloud.org/documents/4406681-3851126-v1-Day-of-Revised-FS-StatementDOCX.html.

37   *He pleaded guilty in the racketeering*: Anthony Cormier and Jason Leopold, "How a Player in the Trump-Russia Scandal Led a Double Life as an American Spy," *BuzzFeed News,* March 12, 2018.

38   *Sater was secretly working for the FBI*: Bill Powell, "Donald Trump Associate Felix Sater Is Linked to the Mob and the CIA—What's His Role in the Russia Investigation?," *Newsweek,* June 7, 2018.

38   *Sater and his Bayrock colleagues took office space*: Andrew Rice, "The Original Russia Connection," *New York,* August 3, 2017.

38   *pleaded with a member of Vladimir Putin's*: Anthony Cormier and Jason Leopold, "Trump Moscow: The Definitive Story of How Trump's Team Worked the Russian Deal During the Campaign," *BuzzFeed News,* May 17, 2018.

38   *She told* The San Diego Union-Tribune: Roger Showley, "She's the Real Deal: Ivanka's Aggressive Style, Big-Business Savvy Proves She's Not Just Another Pretty Trump," *San Diego Union-Tribune,* March 4, 2007.

39   *One of her chief points of contact*: Ned Parker, Stephen Grey, Stefanie Eschenbacher, Roman Anin, Brad Brooks, and Christine Murray, "Ivanka and the Fugitive From Panama," *Reuters,* November 17, 2017.

39   *90 percent of the units had been snatched up*: Lloyd Grove, "Ivanka Trump," *Portfolio .com,* November 10, 2008, https://www.entrepreneur.com/article/198386.

39   *This was not the case*: Heather Vogell, Andrea Bernstein, Meg Cramer, and Peter Elkind, "Pump and Trump," *ProPublica* and WNYC, October 17, 2018.

39   *In Azerbaijan, it's been reported*: Adam Davidson, "Donald Trump's Worst Deal," *New Yorker,* March 13, 2017.

40   *The company's original partner for a project*: Robert Cribb, Marco Chown Oved, Jeremy Blackman, Sylvia Varnham O'Regan, Micah Maidenberg, and Susanne Rust, "How Every Investor Lost Money on Trump Tower Toronto (but Donald Trump Made Millions Anyway)," *The Star,* October 21, 2017.

40   *would be extradited to the U.S.*: Heidi Brown and Nathan Vardi, "Man of Steel," *Forbes,* March 28, 2005.

40   *who, it was reported, appeared to be using*: Tom Burgis, "Tower of Secrets: The Russian Money Behind a Donald Trump Skyscraper," *Financial Times,* July 11, 2018.

40   *By March 2018, the FBI was looking into*: Sara Murray, Shimon Prokupecz, and Kara Scannell, "FBI Counterintel Investigating Ivanka Trump Business Deal," CNN, March 2, 2018.

40   *in the former Soviet republic of Georgia*: Adam Davidson, "Trump's Business of Corruption," *New Yorker,* August 21, 2017.

40   *Ivanka participated in the interior design*: Dan Alexander, "Exclusive Investigation: Inside the Wild Plan to Create a Fake Trump Tower," *Forbes*, August 1, 2017.

40   *2016, a Brazilian*: Manuela Andreoni, "The Criminal Ties of Trump's Partners in Brazil in the Run-Up to the Olympics," Univision News, February 26, 2018.

40   *The project was largely financed by*: Blake Schmidt and Michael Smith, "Why the Trump Organization Was Cited in a Brazil Corruption Probe," *Bloomberg*, February 15, 2017.

40   *Ivanka had said in a video*: Michael Finnegan, "Trump's Failed Baja Condo Resort Left Buyers Feeling Betrayed and Angry," *Los Angeles Times*, June 27, 2016.

41   *In June 2008, Ivanka and Don Jr.*: Andrea Bernstein, Jesse Eisinger, Justin Elliott, and Ilya Marritz, "How Ivanka Trump and Donald Trump, Jr., Avoided a Criminal Indictment," *New Yorker* and WNYC, and "Ivanka and Donald Trump Jr. Were Close to Being Charged With Felony Fraud," *ProPublica*, October 4, 2017.

41   *Trump settled with the investors in 2011*: Mike McIntire, "Donald Trump Settled a Real Estate Lawsuit, and a Criminal Case Was Closed," *New York Times*, April 5, 2016.

41   *Sater's lurid past was exposed in* The New York Times: Charles V. Bagli, "Real Estate Executive with Hand in Trump Projects Rose From Tangled Past," *New York Times*, December 17, 2007.

CHAPTER FIVE

43   *"Charlie was always a big fish in the little pond"*: Interview with Robert Torricelli, May 7, 2018.

43   *returned home from prison in August 2006*: Inmate release dates are made public on the Federal Bureau of Prisons' website at https://www.bop.gov/inmateloc/.

43   *one of New York's trophy office towers*: Read Cushman & Wakefield's report, "666 Fifth Avenue," at http://www.jonleedesigns.com/PDFS/666_OM.pdf.

43   *Jared phoned Speyer to ask about 666 Fifth*: Adam Piore, "Behind the Record Deal for 666 Fifth Avenue," *The Real Deal*, October 22, 2007.

43   *"When you buy a trophy property"*: Interview with Alan Hammer, July 9, 2018.

44   *Debt was Charlie's friend*: Ibid.

44   *On paper, he'd made around two billion dollars*: Charles V. Bagli, "Kushners Sought to Oust Rent-Regulated Tenants, Suit Says," *New York Times*, July 16, 2018.

44   *the day after Thanksgiving, 2006*: David Kocieniewski and Caleb Melby, "Kushners' China Deal Flop Was Part of Much Bigger Hunt for Cash," *Bloomberg*, August 31, 2017.

44   *Documents show that the colossal amount*: Read Columbia University's Center for Urban Real Estate's May 2013 report, "666 Fifth Avenue New York, NY," on Crown Acquisitions' website at http://www.cacq.com/images/site_images/666%20Fifth%20Ave_Case%20Study.pdf.

44   *In February 2005, the Federal Reserve Board*: Read the February 10, 2005, press release, "Federal Reserve and FDIC Issue Enforcement Actions Against the Nor-Crown Trust and Charles Kushner," on the Federal Reserve Board's website at

https://www.federalreserve.gov/boarddocs/press/enforcement/2005/20050210/default.htm.

45 *got to announce the close of the 666 Fifth*: "666 Fifth Avenue Deal Closes," *New York Observer,* January 30, 2007.

45 *"The building shows very, very well"*: Adam Piore, "Behind the Record Deal for 666 Fifth Avenue," *Real Deal,* October 22, 2007.

45 *Although the Kushners had posted*: Read Columbia University's Center for Urban Real Estate's May 2013 report, "666 Fifth Avenue New York, NY," on Crown Acquisitions' website at http://www.cacq.com/images/site_images/666%20Fifth%20Ave_Case%20Study.pdf.

46 *it was announced that the Carlyle Group and Crown*: Read the July 1, 2008, press release on the Carlyle Group's website at https://www.carlyle.com/media-room/news-release-archive/carlyle-group-and-crown-acquisitions-acquire-controlling-interest.

46 *it was reported that a major tenant*: Steve Cuozzo, "Devil in Details for 666 Fifth," *New York Post,* October 14, 2008.

46 *As part of his desperate search for capital*: David Kocieniewski and Caleb Melby, "Kushners' China Deal Flop Was Part of Much Bigger Hunt for Cash," *Bloomberg,* August 31, 2017.

47 *pleaded guilty in February 2008*: Read the February 11, 2008, press release, "Former Accountant for Kushner Companies Admits Tax Fraud Conspiracy," on the Department of Justice's website at https://www.justice.gov/sites/default/files/usao-nj/legacy/2013/11/29/plot0211%20rel.pdf.

47 *who had turned state's evidence against Charlie*: Read the United States Court of Appeals for the Third Circuit's September 9, 2010, opinion on the U.S. Courts' website at http://www2.ca3.uscourts.gov/opinarch/091575p.pdf.

48 *"There was no role for him"*: Interview with Alan Hammer, July 9, 2018.

48 *Per his contract and a formula that had worked*: Kevin Swill's complaint against Westminster Management is available at https://www.documentcloud.org/documents/5301987-Westminster-vs-Swill.html.

48 *Charlie eventually agreed to pay him $750,000*: Ibid.

48 *Swill argued he was now entitled to a larger share*: Ibid.

48 *Charlie countersued, claiming a breach*: Westminster Management's complaint against Kevin Swill is available at https://www.documentcloud.org/documents/5301987-Westminster-vs-Swill.html.

49 *in addition to Richie Goettlich*: David Kocieniewski and Caleb Melby, "Kushner's Felon Father Back at Helm of New York Empire with Two Fellow Inmates," *Bloomberg,* January 27, 2017.

49 *a very close, old friend of*: Meryl Gordon, "Little Big Man," *New York,* January 12, 1998.

CHAPTER SIX

50 *"It put Jared on the map socially"*: Interview with Alan Hammer, July 9, 2018.

50 *It was Jared who handed the ten-million-dollar check*: Gabriel Sherman, "The Legacy," *New York,* July 12, 2009.

51 *He befriended media moguls like*: Ibid.

51   *creating the Power 100*: "The 100 Most Powerful People in New York Real Estate," *New York Observer*, May 13, 2008.

51   *and ultimately a separate real estate paper*: Richard Perez-Pena, "New York Observer Starts a Paper on Real Estate," *New York Times*, August 23, 2009.

51   *But at a networking lunch thrown by*: Yisroel Besser, "Polish Your Diamond," *Mishpacha*, April 5, 2017.

52   *"You're the closest people to your"*: Interview with Alan Hammer, July 9, 2018.

52   *on a boating holiday orchestrated by Rupert*: Lizzie Widdicombe, "Ivanka and Jared's Power Play," *New Yorker*, August 22, 2016.

52   *Soon after, Ivanka agreed to convert*: Gabriel Sherman, "The Legacy," *New York*, July 12, 2009.

52   *"This wasn't like, 'Talk to a rabbi'"*: Interview with Bob Sommer, July 12, 2016.

53   *Trump, a Presbyterian*: Hannah Seligson, "Is Ivanka for Real?," *Huffington Post Highline*, September 7, 2016.

53   *Women were given shawls*: "Details From Inside Ivanka & Jared's Wedding," *Page Six*, October 27, 2009.

53   *Ivanka's dress covered her shoulders*: Emily Jane Fox, *Born Trump* (New York: Harper Collins, 2018), p. 226.

53   *The sexes were asked to dance separately*: Ibid., p. 227.

54   *"reach consists of up to 20,000"*: Read the April 4, 2018 press release, "HFF Announces Sale of 360-Unit Multi-Housing Property in Hackensack, New Jersey," on Business Wire's website at https://www.businesswire.com/news/home/20180404006270/en/HFF-Announces-Sale-360-Unit-Multi-Housing-Property-Hackensack.

55   *there was not a book in sight*: Interview with Elizabeth Spiers, May 9, 2018.

55   *"Nobody knows who this Martin Amis guy"*: Ibid.

55   *Spiers and Jared clashed over a long*: Ibid.

55   *Jared seemed not to understand them*: Ibid.

55   *"He'd be condescending to them"*: Ibid.

56   *"When I first took the job, he wrote"*: Ibid.

56   *This meant running hit pieces*: Interview with Elizabeth Spiers, July 7, 2016.

56   *When new allegations surfaced in 2011*: Nick Davies and Amelia Hill, "Missing Milly Dowler's Voicemail Was Hacked by News of the World," *Guardian*, July 4, 2011.

56   *Charlie refused to shake her hand*: Interview with Elizabeth Spiers, May 9, 2018.

56   *Jared's temper occasionally bubbled*: Ibid.

57   *Her decision came after she and a colleague*: Ibid.

57   *She suggested at one point that she*: Ibid.

59   *I reported for* Esquire *that Jared did*: Vicky Ward, "Jared Kushner's Second Act," *Esquire*, August 18, 2016.

CHAPTER SEVEN

60   *In early 2010, LNR Partners*: Adam Pincus, "Kushner's 666 Fifth Goes to Special Servicer," *Real Deal*, March 4, 2010.

60   *By the summer of 2010*: Read the July 30, 2010 press release, "Vornado Announces

26.2% Equity Investment in LNR Property Corporation," on Vornado Realty Trust's website at https://www.vno.com/press-release/pc1uir3z3e/vornado-announces-26 -2-equity-investment-in-lnr-property-corporation.

60 *had more than twenty billion dollars in assets*: Vornado Realty Trust's 2010 Annual Report is made public at https://materials.proxyvote.com/Approved/929042 /20110330/AR_88400/HTML2/vornado_realty_trust-ar2010_0003.htm.

61 *Kushner Companies began selling off the rest*: Read Columbia University's Center for Urban Real Estate's May 2013 report, "666 Fifth Avenue New York, NY," on Crown Acquisitions's website at http://www.cacq.com/images/site_images/666%20 Fifth%20Ave_Case%20Study.pdf.

62 *Donald Trump put him in touch*: Michael Kranish and Jonathan O'Connell, "Kush-ner's White House Role 'Crushed' Efforts to Woo Investors for NYC Tower," *Washington Post,* September 13, 2017.

62 *Kushner Companies negotiated to sell*: Read Columbia University's Center for Urban Real Estate's May 2013 report, "666 Fifth Avenue New York, NY," on Crown Acquisitions's website at http://www.cacq.com/images/site_images/666%20Fifth%20 Ave_Case%20Study.pdf.

62 *Vornado announced it had bought 49.5 percent*: Read the December 16, 2011, press release, "Vornado and the Kushner Companies Announce the Recapitalization of 666 Fifth Avenue," on Vornado Realty Trust's website at https://www.vno.com/press -release/v1xqmhzsbc/vornado-and-the-kushner-companies-announce-the -recapitalization-of-666-fifth-avenue.

62 *And then, in 2012, it bought*: Read the December 6, 2012, press release, "Vornado Completes Acquisition of Retail at 666 Fifth Avenue, Expanding Its Best-in-Class Manhattan Street Retail Portfolio," on Vornado Realty Trust's website at https:// www.vno.com/press-release/2vefql84eu/vornado-completes-acquisition-of-retail-at -666-fifth-avenue-expanding-its-best-in-class-manhattan-street-retail-portfolio.

63 *was valued at $820 million*: Read Columbia University's Center for Urban Real Estate's May, 2013 report, "666 Fifth Avenue New York, NY," on Crown Acquisitions's website at http://www.cacq.com/images/site_images/666%20Fifth%20Ave _Case%20Study.pdf.

63 *deferred until February 2019*: Terry Pristin, "Surviving a Big Risk on Fifth Avenue," *New York Times,* January 17, 2012.

63 *They had partnered on the Monmouth Mall*: Read the October 11, 2002, press release, "Vornado Acquires 50% Interest in the Monmouth Mall in New Jersey," on Vornado Realty Trust's website at https://www.vno.com/press-release/pcf8xneu1m /vornado-acquires-50-interest-in-the-monmouth-mall-in-new-jersey.

63 *the* New York Post *revealed*: Lois Weiss, "Real Estate Heavyweights Mull Turning Fifth Ave. Tower Into Mall," *New York Post,* September 10, 2015.

63 *"It would be worth a lot more"*: David Kocieniewski and Caleb Melby, "Kushners' China Deal Flop Was Part of Much Bigger Hunt for Cash," *Bloomberg,* August 31, 2017.

64 *Kushner asked Spiers, the* Observer *editor*: View Elizabeth Spiers's blog post, "The

Big Dick Mack Story," from July 7, 2016, at https://www.elizabethspiers.com/the
-big-dick-mack-story/.

64   *She noticed he tried to kill stories*: Ibid.

64   *What she did not know was that*: Elizabeth Spiers, "No, Jared Kushner, It Was Not Okay to Delete My Journalists' Work," *Washington Post*, August 9, 2018.

65   *Two involved the New York City landlord Vantage Properties*: Steven Perlberg, "Jared Kushner Used to Personally Order the Deletion of Stories at His Newspaper," *BuzzFeed News*, August 6, 2018.

65   *"People who didn't want to be seen"*: Interview with Alan Hammer, July 9, 2018.

65   *"For a long time, Jared did a lot to"*: Interview with Andrew Silow-Carroll, July 4, 2018.

67   *As of October 2018*: View Thrive Capital's blog post, from October 23, 2018, at https://medium.com/@thrivecapital/thrive-vi-6862ece9f331.

67   *"This is big-boy-type stuff"*: Interview with Jon Winkelried, July 1, 2016.

67   *"I had heard when Josh"*: Interview with Alan Hammer, July 9, 2018.

68   *It would be called Oscar*: Steven Levy, "Oscar Is Disrupting Health Care in a Hurricane," *Wired*, January 5, 2017.

68   *Schlosser would later say*: "Oscar CEO Mario Schlosser on Data, Narrow Networks, and the Cleveland Clinic," *Bloomberg*, February 12, 2018.

68   *Jared and Josh talked every day*: Steven Bertoni, "Josh Kushner's Complex World: How Jared's Liberal Brother Runs a Billion Dollar Fund in Trump Era," *Forbes*, April 10, 2017.

CHAPTER EIGHT

71   *a Chinese group bought Trump*: Farah Stockman and Keith Bradsher, "Donald Trump Soured on a Deal, and Hong Kong Partners Became Litigants," *New York Times*, May 30, 2016.

71   *the Chinese used the proceeds*: Ibid.

71   *which is why Trump felt*: Shawn Tully, "How Donald Trump Lucked Into the Most Lucrative Deal of his Career," *Fortune*, April 27, 2016.

71   *taking control of the property in 2014*: Craig Karmin, "CIM Group to Take Control of New York's Trump SoHo Hotel-Condo," *Wall Street Journal*, November 20, 2014.

72   *a reported $1.2 billion*: Luisa Kroll and Kerry Dolan, "Meet the Members of the Three-Comma Club," *Forbes*, March 6, 2018.

72   *reportedly listened to a pitch*: David Kocieniewski and Caleb Melby, "Kushners' China Deal Flop Was Part of Much Bigger Hunt for Cash," *Bloomberg*, August 31, 2017.

72   *recently bought the Waldorf Astoria*: Michael Cole, "Chinese Insurer Buys Waldorf Astoria for a Record $1.95B," *Forbes*, October 6, 2014.

73   *It was unclear who owned*: Michael Forsythe, "Behind China's Anbang: Empty Offices and Obscure Names," *New York Times*, September 1, 2016.

73   *donated one hundred thousand dollars*: PAC donors are made public on OpenSecrets .org at https://www.opensecrets.org/pacs/pacgave2.php?cmte=C00580373&cycle =2016.

73   *He'd later say that a rally*: Steven Bertoni, "How Jared Kushner Won Trump the White House," *Forbes*, November 22, 2016.

73   *Trump turned to him for help*: Emily Flitter, "Behind Donald Trump, a Son-in-Law Who Is Also an Adviser," *Reuters*, April 4, 2016.

73   *March 2016 speech to the American Israel*: Sarah Begley, "Read Donald Trump's Speech to AIPAC," *Time*, March 21, 2016.

73   *Jared got help from Israeli Ambassador*: Emily Jane Fox, *Born Trump* (New York: HarperCollins, 2018), pp. 54–55.

73   *Ken Kurson, who did not disclose*: Michael Calderone, "New York Observer Editor Doesn't Regret Involvement with Donald Trump's AIPAC Speech," *Huffington Post*, April 4, 2016.

74   *Murdoch's* New York Post *endorsed Trump*: "The Post Endorses Trump for NY Primary," *New York Post*, April 14, 2016.

74   *relayed Ivanka's thoughts*: Katherine Clarke, "Kushner Conflicted," *Real Deal*, September 1, 2016.

74   *has allegedly used the*: Omarosa Manigault Newman, *Unhinged* (New York: Gallery Books, 2018), p. xiii.

75   *Lewandowski was seen on videotape*: Maggie Haberman and Michael M. Grynbaum, "Corey Lewandowski, Donald Trump's Campaign Manager, is Charged with Battery," *New York Times*, March 29, 2016.

75   *"my Corey"*: *New Day*, transcript, CNN, July 11, 2016, http://www.cnn.com/TRANSCRIPTS/1607/11/nday.06.html.

75   *numerous contacts in the Middle East*: Julie Creswell, "Contrarian Adding Bets in Mideast," *New York Times*, April 5, 2011.

75   *Barrack suggested to Kushner*: Glenn Thrush, "To Charm Trump, Paul Manafort Sold Himself as an Affordable Outsider," *New York Times*, April 8, 2017.

75   *he'd taken money from Ukrainian oligarchs*: Franklin Foer, "The Plot Against America," *Atlantic*, March 2018.

75   *he violated the Foreign Agents Registration Act*: Sharon LaFraniere, "Manafort Case Puts New Scrutiny on Foreign Lobbying Law's Shortcomings," *New York Times*, September 13, 2018.

76   *six-figure shopping sprees*: Read the United States District Court for the Eastern District of Virginia's February, 2018 indictment on the Department of Justice's website at https://www.justice.gov/file/1038391/download.

76   *in elections in Argentina, Kenya, Ghana*: Devjyot Ghoshal, "Mapped: The Breathtaking Global Reach of Cambridge Analytica's Parent Company," *Quartz*, March 28, 2018.

76   *to conduct propaganda analysis*: Sue Halpern, "How He Used Facebook to Win," *The New York Review of Books*, June 8, 2017.

77   *the majority stakeholders in* Breitbart: Gregory Zuckerman, Keach Hagey, Scott Patterson, and Rebecca Ballhaus, "Meet the Mercers: A Quiet Tycoon and His Daughter Become Power Brokers in Trump's Washington," *Wall Street Journal*, January 8, 2017.

CHAPTER NINE

80   *Nix claimed Cambridge Analytica was*: Matthew Rosenberg, Nicholas Confessore, and Carole Cadwalladr, "How Trump Consultants Exploited the Facebook Data of Millions," *New York Times*, March 17, 2018.

81   *"spanning tens of millions of Facebook"*: Harry Davies, "Ted Cruz Using Firm That Harvested Data on Millions of Unwitting Facebook Users," *Guardian*, December 11, 2015.

81   *"I would show up to a meeting"*: Interview with Brad Parscale, March 11, 2017.

82   *On June 23, a contract reportedly was signed*: Rebecca Ballhaus and Julie Bykowicz, "Data Firm's WikiLeaks Outreach Came as It Joined Trump Campaign," *Wall Street Journal*, November 10, 2017.

82   *on July 29, according to FEC records*: Disbursements are made public on the Federal Election Commission's website at https://www.fec.gov/data/disbursements/?two _year_transaction_period=2016&data_type=processed&committee_id=C0058 0100&recipient_name=cambridge+analytica&min_date=01%2F01%2F2015 &max_date=12%2F31%2F2016.

82   *"I made the decision"*: Interview with Brad Parscale, March 15, 2017.

82   *Nix reached out to WikiLeaks founder*: Rebecca Ballhaus and Julie Bykowicz, "Data Firm's WikiLeaks Outreach Came as It Joined Trump Campaign," *Wall Street Journal*, November 10, 2017.

82   *More than a year later,* The Wall Street Journal: Rebecca Ballhaus, "Trump Donor Asked Data Firm If It Could Better Organize Hacked Emails," *Wall Street Journal*, October 27, 2017.

82   *Kissinger introduced Jared to Cui Tiankai*: Adam Entous and Evan Osnos, "Jared Kushner Is China's Trump Card," *New Yorker*, January 29, 2018.

82   *Anbang was entering negotiations with*: Susanne Craig, Jo Becker, and Jesse Drucker, "Jared Kushner, a Trump In-Law and Adviser, Chases a Chinese Deal," *New York Times*, January 7, 2017.

82   *Barrack introduced Kushner to the United Arab Emirates*: David D. Kirkpatrick, "Who Is Behind Trump's Links to Arab Princes? A Billionaire Friend," *New York Times*, June 13, 2018.

83   *"You will love him, and he agrees"*: Ibid.

83   The Wall Street Journal *reported in 2017*: Bradley Hope and Tom Wright, "U.A.E.'s Ambassador to U.S. Linked to 1MDB Scandal," *Wall Street Journal*, June 30, 2017.

83   *"Any chance we can get an introduction"*: David Hearst, "How Trump Confidant Was Ready to Share Inside Information with UAE," *Middle East Eye*, June 28, 2018.

83   *"I would like to align in Donald's mind"*: David D. Kirkpatrick, "Who Is Behind Trump's Links to Arab Princes? A Billionaire Friend," *New York Times*, June 13, 2018.

84   *they reportedly believed Vladimir Putin*: Adam Entous, "Israeli, Saudi, and Emirati Officials Privately Pushed for Trump to Strike a 'Grand Bargain' with Putin," *New Yorker*, July 9, 2018.

84 *Trump's first major foreign policy speech*: View Donald Trump's speech, delivered on April 27, 2016, on C-SPAN's website at https://www.c-span.org/video/?408693-1 /donald-trump-speech-foreign-policy.

84 *he was introduced to Sergey Kislyak*: "Jared Kushner's Statement on Russia to Congressional Committees," CNN, July 24, 2017.

84 *forwarded to Kushner*: Read the March 22, 2018, report on the House Permanent Select Committee on Intelligence's website at https://intelligence.house.gov /uploadedfiles/final_russia_investigation_report.pdf.

84 *meeting in Trump Tower on June 9*: Senate Judiciary Committee interviews regarding the June 9, 2016, meeting in Trump Tower are available on the Committee on the Judiciary's website at https://www.judiciary.senate.gov/press/releases/materials -from-inquiry-into-circumstances-surrounding-trump-tower-meeting.

84 *The meeting had been organized by*: "Read the Emails on Donald Trump Jr.'s Russia Meeting," *New York Times,* July 11, 2017.

85 *Kushner in July 2017 released a statement*: "Jared Kushner's Statement on Russia to Congressional Committees," CNN, July 24, 2017.

85 *"blood coming out of her wherever"*: Holly Yan, "Donald Trump's 'Blood' Comment About Megyn Kelly Draws Outrage," CNN, August 8, 2015.

85 *the first Republican debate*: View the presidential debate, which took place on August 6, 2015, on the Fox News website at https://video.foxnews.com/v/4406746003001/.

85 *"His actions speak louder than the words"*: CNN, transcript, April 13, 2016, http:// edition.cnn.com/TRANSCRIPTS/1604/13/cnr.07.html.

85 *"He's not a groper"*: "Ivanka Trump Responds to 'Disturbing' Accusations About Her Father," CBS News, May 18, 2016.

86 *"empathy and generosity towards"*: View Ivanka Trump's introduction speech, delivered on July 21, 2016, at https://www.youtube.com/watch?v=mXENfQ JeQ gA.

86 *"Shop Ivanka's look from her #RNC speech"*: View Ivanka Trump's tweet, from July 22, 2016, at https://twitter.com/IvankaTrump/status/756492146484580352.

86 *Trump had tweeted an image*: Alan Rappeport, "Donald Trump Deletes Tweet Showing Hillary Clinton and Star of David Shape," *New York Times,* July 2, 2016.

87 *criticized Kushner in his own newspaper*: Dana Schwartz, "An Open Letter to Jared Kushner, From One of Your Jewish Employees," *New York Observer,* July 5, 2016.

87 *Kushner wrote a response*: Jared Kushner, "Jared Kushner: The Donald Trump I Know," *New York Observer,* July 6, 2016.

87 *Two of Kushner's cousins complained on Facebook*: Eli Stokols, "Trump's Son-in-Law Under Fire from Family," *Politico,* July 7, 2016.

CHAPTER TEN

89 *"They didn't build a ground organization"*: Interview with Rick Davis, July 18, 2017.

89 *was the headline in* The New York Times *on August*: Alexander Burns and Maggie Haberman, "Inside the Failing Mission to Tame Donald Trump's Tongue," *New York Times,* August 13, 2016.

89 *met with Bannon over lunch*: Bob Woodward, *Fear* (New York: Simon & Schuster, 2018), p. 12.

89   *Bannon headed immediately*: Ibid., p. 19.

90   *published an in-depth article showing*: Andrew E. Kramer, Mike McIntire, and Barry Meier, "Secret Ledger in Ukraine Lists Cash for Donald Trump's Campaign Chief," *New York Times*, August 15, 2016.

90   *It was now clear to Bannon*: Bob Woodward, *Fear* (New York: Simon & Schuster, 2018), pp. 20–22.

90   *Photographs of Ivanka posing with Wendi Deng*: Emily Jane Fox, "Ivanka Trump Is Vacationing with Wendi Deng," *Vanity Fair*, August 15, 2016.

92   *spent more than $175 million*: Jedd Rosche, "RNC Chief of Staff Describes the $175 Million Tool That Wins Elections (They Hope)," CNN, November 2, 2016.

92   *such as what kind of car*: Bob Woodward, *Fear* (New York: Simon & Schuster, 2018), p. 25.

93   *69 percent of all individual contributions*: Read the February 21, 2017, press release, "President Trump, with RNC Help, Raised More Small Donor Money Than President Obama; as Much as Clinton and Sanders Combined," on the Campaign Finance Institute's website at http://www.cfinst.org/Press/PReleases/17-02-21 /President_Trump_with_RNC_Help_Raised_More_Small_Donor_Money_than _President_Obama_As_Much_As_Clinton_and_Sanders_Combined.aspx.

94   *"They would go to small events"*: Interview with Sam Nunberg, April 16, 2017.

95   *sent the Mexican presidential helicopter*: Zeke J. Miller, "Mystery Surrounds Payment for Donald Trump's Mexican Helicopter Ride," CNN, September 28, 2016.

95   *Trump walked onto the platform with Peña Nieto*: View the press conference, which took place on August 31, 2016, on C-SPAN's website at https://www.c-span.org /video/?414590-1/donald-trump-mexican-president-deliver-joint-statement.

95   *two donors essential to his campaign*: Cynthia Gordy Giwa, "How to 'Follow the Money' When It Comes to Political Campaigns," *ProPublica*, October 19, 2018.

95   *Kushner had sought the support of*: Kenneth P. Vogel and Ben Schreckinger, "Trump Courted Megadonors He Now Scorns," *Politico*, November 4, 2015.

95   *"that was a bust"*: Interview with Sam Nunberg, April 26, 2017.

95   *in late July that he wouldn't support*: Leigh Ann Caldwell, "Charles Koch Explains To Donors Why He Won't Support Trump," NBC News, August 1, 2016.

97   *emails were released by WikiLeaks*: View WikiLeaks' tweet, from October 7, 2016, at https://twitter.com/wikileaks/status/784491543868665856.

97   The Washington Post *published a video from 2005*: David A. Fahrenthold, "Trump Recorded Having Extremely Lewd Conversation About Women in 2005," *Washington Post*, October 8, 2016.

98   *the response video was finally shot*: View Donald Trump's response video, posted on October 7, 2016, at https://www.facebook.com/DonaldTrump/videos/10157844642270725/.

98   *At 1 P.M., Trump's running mate*: Bob Woodward, *Fear* (New York: Simon & Schuster, 2018), p. 33.

99   *Kathy Shelton, who said*: Glenn Kessler, "The Facts About Hillary Clinton And The Kathy Shelton Rape Case," *Washington Post*, October 11, 2016.

99   *Trump was extremely irritated*: Bob Woodward, *Fear* (New York: Simon & Schuster, 2018), p. 41.

99   *had been paid more than twenty million*: Matea Gold and Anu Narayanswamy,

"Donald Trump's Campaign Spending More Than Doubled In September. Here's Where The Money Went," *Washington Post*, October 20, 2016.

99   *through which the campaign paid for advertising*: Disbursements are made public on the Federal Election Commission's website at https://www.fec.gov/data/disburse ments/?two_year_transaction_period=2016&data_type=processed&committee_id =C00580100&recipient_name=giles+parscale&min_date=01%2F01%2F2015 &max_date=12%2F31%2F2016.

100   *At 2:29 A.M., the Associated Press*: Lauren Easton, "Calling the Presidential Race State by State," *Associated Press*, November 9, 2016.

100   *"Now it's time for Americans to bind"*: "Transcript: Donald Trump's Victory Speech," *New York Times*, November 9, 2016.

CHAPTER ELEVEN

102   *four thousand jobs to fill*: Bonnie Berkowitz and Kevin Uhrmacher, "It's Not Just the Cabinet: Trump's Transition Team May Need to Find About 4,100 Appointees," *Washington Post*, December 5, 2016.

103   *"lock her up"*: Bob Woodward, *Fear* (New York: Simon & Schuster, 2018), p. 60.

103   *Trump and Kushner visited the White House*: Julie Hirschfeld Davis, "Trump and Obama Hold Cordial 90-Minute Meeting in Oval Office," *New York Times*, November 10, 2016.

103   *Obama gave Trump*: Kristen Welker, Peter Alexander, Dafna Linzer, and Ken Dilanian, "Obama Warned Trump Against Hiring Mike Flynn, Say Officials," NBC News, May 8, 2017.

104   *The next morning, that 11 A.M. meeting*: Jane Mayer, "The Danger of President Pence," *New Yorker*, October 23, 2017.

104   *"his amazing loyalty"*: Ibid.

104   *"It was like Princess Ivanka"*: Ibid.

105   *amid allegations of spousal abuse*: Patrick O'Connor, "Sweeney's Wife Claims Abuse," *Politico*, July 23, 2007.

105   *convicted multiple times*: Emily Donohue, "Former Rep. John Sweeney Officially Sentenced for Second DWI," *Saratogian*, April 23, 2010.

106   *he had had an affair with Christie's*: Read the March 26, 2014, publication "Report of Gibson, Dunn & Crutcher LLP Concerning Its Investigation on Behalf of the Office of the Governor of New Jersey Into Allegations Regarding the George Washington Bridge Lane Realignment and Superstorm Sandy Aid to the City of Hoboken," on the *Wall Street Journal* website at https://online.wsj.com/public /resources/documents/nybridge0327.PDF.

106   *exploded in public around Christmas*: Marc Caputo, Josh Dawsey, and Alex Isenstadt, "Trump Pick Backs Out of White House Job After Affair Allegations," *Politico*, December 25, 2016.

106   *In October, he'd begun*: McKay Coppins, "From Trump Aide to Single Mom," *Atlantic*, August 15, 2017.

107   *Kushner had introduced Cohn*: Nick Timiraos, Michael C. Bender, and Damian

Paletta, "Gary Cohn Has Emerged as an Economic-Policy Powerhouse in Trump Administration," *Wall Street Journal,* February 11, 2017.

107 *it was immediately leaked that Kushner*: Julianna Goldman, "Trump Team Seeks Top-Secret Security Clearances for Trump's Children," CBS News. November 15, 2016.

107 *"I am not trying to get 'top-level security'"*: View Donald Trump's tweet, from November 16, 2016, at https://twitter.com/realDonaldTrump/status/798850338384023552.

108 *Kushner spokesman told* The New Yorker: Adam Entous and Evan Osnos, "Jared Kushner Is China's Trump Card," *New Yorker,* January 29, 2018.

108 *wrote a letter to Pence asking whether Kushner*: Read the November 16, 2016, letter on the House Committee on Oversight and Government Reform's website at https://democrats-oversight.house.gov/sites/democrats.oversight.house.gov/files/documents/2016-11-16.EEC%20to%20Pence_0.pdf.

108 *"The idea is, we're supposed to"*: Interview with Antony Blinken, April 20, 2018.

108 *emailed out a "style alert"*: Vanessa Friedman, "Ivanka Trump Blurs the Line Between Professional and Political," *New York Times,* November 15, 2016.

108 *hosted by the chairman of the Chinese insurance giant*: Susanne Craig, Jo Becker, and Jesse Drucker, "Jared Kushner, a Trump In-Law and Adviser, Chases a Chinese Deal," *New York Times,* January 7, 2017.

109 *"Chinese delicacies and $2,100 bottles"*: Ibid.

109 *reportedly popped into Trump Tower*: Carol E. Lee, Julia Ainsley, and Robert Windrem, "Mueller Team Asking If Kushner Foreign Business Ties Influenced Trump Policy," NBC News, March 2, 2018.

109 *Ethical questions were raised*: Eric Lipton, "Ivanka Trump's Presence at Meeting With Japan's Leader Raises Questions," *New York Times,* November 18, 2016.

109 *Ivanka's brand was closing in on*: Matt Flegenheimer, Rachel Abrams, Barry Meier, and Hiroko Tabuchi, "Business Since Birth: Trump's Children and the Tangle That Awaits," *New York Times,* December 4, 2016.

109 *Those cavils were dismissed in the* Times: Eric Lipton, "Ivanka Trump's Presence at Meeting with Japan's Leader Raises Questions," *New York Times,* November 18, 2016.

110 *it was reported that the three eldest*: Aram Roston and Daniel Wagner, "Trump Gave His Kids a Big Stake in Huge Government Deal, Document Shows," *BuzzFeed News,* August 2, 2016.

110 *"She wasn't sacrificing any large investments"*: Interview with Leonard Stern, November 14, 2018.

110 *According to a statement later delivered*: Read the July 24, 2017 statement on the Committee on the Judiciary's website at https://www.judiciary.senate.gov/imo/media/doc/2017-07-24%20Kushner%20to%20CEG%20DF%20(Kushner%20Statement).pdf.

110 *"grand bargain" that was being negotiated between*: Adam Entous, "Israeli, Saudi, and Emirati Officials Privately Pushed for Trump to Strike a 'Grand Bargain' with Putin," *New Yorker,* July 9, 2018.

110 *"The Iranians regard Syria as"*: Interview with Bruce Riedel, August 8, 2018.

111 *"Obama set out to bring Jews and Arabs closer"*: Adam Entous, "Donald Trump's New World Order," *New Yorker,* June 18, 2018.

111 *Almost two weeks later*: Read the July 24, 2017, statement on the Committee on the Judiciary's website at https://www.judiciary.senate.gov/imo/media/doc/2017-07 -24%20Kushner%20to%20CEG%20DF%20(Kushner%20Statement).pdf.

111 *Kushner would later testify before Congress*: Ibid.

111 *"with a number of representatives of "*: "Russian Bank VEB Says Executives Had Talks with Trump Son-in-Law," *Reuters,* March 27, 2017.

112 *John McCain had been openly concerned*: Ryan Lizza, "John McCain Has a Few Things to Say About Donald Trump," *New Yorker,* July 16, 2015.

112 *McCain had issued a strong statement*: Read the November 15, 2016, press release on John McCain's website at https://www.mccain.senate.gov/public/index.cfm/2016 /11/statement-by-sasc-chairman-john-mccain-on-u-s-russia-relations.

112 *a stance since termed "One China"*: Max Fisher, "Trump, Taiwan and China: The Controversy, Explained," *New York Times,* December 3, 2016.

113 *"The President of Taiwan CALLED ME"*: View Donald Trump's tweet, from December 2, 2016, at https://twitter.com/realDonaldTrump/status/804848711599882240.

113 *He later gave an interview*: Caren Bohan and David Brunnstrom, "Trump Says U.S. Not Necessarily Bound by 'One China' Policy," *Reuters,* December 11, 2016.

113 *The meeting with Yang and the Chinese ambassador*: Adam Entous and Evan Osnos, "Jared Kushner Is China's Trump Card," *New Yorker,* January 29, 2018.

113 *where Beijing has built up a military presence*: Frances Mangosing, "New Photos Show China Is Nearly Done with Its Militarization of South China Sea," *Philippine Daily Inquirer,* February 5, 2018.

114 *Trump would eventually change his mind on Taiwan*: Read the February 9, 2017, statement, "Readout of the President's Call with President Xi Jinping of China," on the White House's website at https://www.whitehouse.gov/briefings-statements/readout -presidents-call-president-xi-jinping-china/.

114 *published on January 7 by* The New York Times: Susanne Craig, Jo Becker, and Jesse Drucker, "Jared Kushner, a Trump In-Law and Adviser, Chases a Chinese Deal," *New York Times,* January 7, 2017.

114 Forbes *published the online version*: Steven Bertoni, "How Jared Kushner Won Trump the White House," *Forbes,* November 22, 2016.

115 *Tom Barrack, who'd been busy attempting to broker*: David D. Kirkpatrick, "Who Is Behind Trump's Links to Arab Princes? A Billionaire Friend," *New York Times,* June 13, 2018.

115 *nearly 20 percent stake in Rosneft*: Read the December 7, 2016, press release, "Russian Government Announcement Regarding Privatisation of Shares in Rosnef [*sic*]," on Glencore's website at http://www.glencore.com/media-and-insights/news/russian -government-announcement-regarding-privatisation-of-shares-in-rosnef.

115 *would be involved in the transfer*: Read Intesa Sanpaolo's 2016 report at https://www .group.intesasanpaolo.com/scriptIsir0/si09/contentData/view/content-ref?id =CNT-05-00000004D7191.

116 *British prime minister, who, it had been reported*: Edward Malnick, Claire Newell,

Robert Mendick, and Luke Heighton, "Revealed: The True Scale of Tony Blair's Global Business Empire," *Telegraph,* June 11, 2015.

116 *between Blackwater founder Erik Prince*: Read Erik Prince's November 30, 2017, testimony at https://docs.house.gov/meetings/IG/IG00/20171130/106661/HHRG-115-IG00-Transcript-20171130.pdf.

116 *MBZ arrived in the U.S. without bothering to*: Adam Entous, "Donald Trump's New World Order," *New Yorker,* June 18, 2018.

117 *having consulted with Netanyahu*: Ibid.

117 *"[The Obama people] had their turn"*: Ibid.

117 *The idea was that these people*: Read the United States District Court for the District of Columbia's December 1, 2017, statement on the Department of Justice's website at https://www.justice.gov/file/1015126/download.

117 *with fourteen votes for it*: Kate O'Keeffe and Farnaz Fassihi, "Inside the Trump Team's Push on Israel Vote That Mike Flynn Lied About," *Wall Street Journal,* January 5, 2018.

117 *Trump hosted a roundtable of technology*: Nikhil Sonnad, "The Seating Chart at Trump's Table of Tech Giants," *Quartz,* December 14, 2016.

118 *Kushner went to the offices*: Andrew Rice, "The Young Trump," *New York,* January 9, 2017.

118 *he'd given more interview access to Sinclair*: Josh Dawsey and Hadas Gold, "Kushner: We Struck Deal with Sinclair for Straighter Coverage," *Politico,* December 16, 2016.

119 *"Nobody is apparently telling you this"*: Michael Wolff, *Fire and Fury* (New York: Henry Holt & Co., 2018), p. 29.

120 New York Times *report on the Anbang dinner*: Susanne Craig, Jo Becker, and Jesse Drucker, "Jared Kushner, a Trump In-Law and Adviser, Chases a Chinese Deal," *New York Times,* January 7, 2017.

121 *this one of a report by the U.S. intelligence*: Read the January 6, 2017, report, "Background to 'Assessing Russian Activities and Intentions in Recent US Elections': The Analytic Process and Cyber Incident Attribution," on the Director of National Intelligence's website at https://www.dni.gov/files/documents/ICA_2017_01.pdf.

121 *said Jared would be resigning from*: Susanne Craig, Jo Becker, and Jesse Drucker, "Jared Kushner, a Trump In-Law and Adviser, Chases a Chinese Deal," *New York Times,* January 7, 2017.

121 *According to* The Washington Post, *he still owned*: Darla Cameron, Amy Brittain, and Jonathan O'Connell, "What Jared Kushner Still Owns," *Washington Post,* May 21, 2017.

CHAPTER TWELVE

122 *She deplaned from New York*: View Ivanka Trump's Instagram post, from January 19, 2017, at https://www.instagram.com/ivankatrump/p/BPdL8UeAK67/.

122 *She posted herself on Instagram*: View Ivanka Trump's Instagram post, from January 19, 2017, at https://www.instagram.com/ivankatrump/p/BPd8H_5gEyl/.

122 *She wore an asymmetrical*: View Ivanka Trump's Instagram post, from January 20, 2017, at https://www.instagram.com/ivankatrump/p/BPf-sqRAWFe/.

122 *speculation about their marital problems*: Emily Heil, "How Are Donald and Melania

Doing? Why America Cares About the Presidential Marriage," *Washington Post*, March 22, 2018.

123 *Ivanka, it would later be reported*: Emily Jane Fox, *Born Trump* (New York: Harper-Collins, 2018), p. 10.

123 *fifteen thousand dollars a month*: Mark Maremont and James V. Grimaldi, "Ivanka Trump and Jared Kushner's Rent in Washington: $15,000 a Month," *Wall Street Journal*, April 3, 2017.

123 *Ivanka had said she was*: View Ivanka Trump's Facebook post, from January 11, 2017, at https://www.facebook.com/IvankaTrump/posts/10154998180397682.

123 *However, she did not*: Emily Jane Fox, "Ivanka Trump and Jared Kushner Will Resign From Their Jobs, Sell Assets," *Vanity Fair*, January 9, 2017.

123 *She claimed to be selling*: Ibid.

123 *It was an arrangement that ethics experts*: Joanna Walters, "Brand Ivanka: Inside the Tangled Empire of the President's Closest Ally," *Guardian*, May 1, 2017.

123 *"I think of it as shorthand for"*: Benjamin Freed, "Javanka Is the Perfect Celebrity Nickname for Our Strange Era," *Washingtonian*, March 7, 2017.

124 *and was photographed walking*: "Photos: Scenes From the Women's March on Washington," *Washingtonian*, January 21, 2017.

124 *Cecile Richards's memoir*: Cecile Richards, *Make Trouble* (New York: Touchstone, 2018), pp. 246–249.

124 *campaign promises on a whiteboard*: Jim Acosta, et al., "Inside Donald Trump's Tumultuous First 100 Days," CNN, April 2017.

124 *who had given twenty million dollars*: Justin Elliott, "Trump's Patron-in-Chief," *ProPublica*, October 10, 2018.

125 *his children presented licensing deals*: Peter Robison and Michael Smith, "How the Boys Run Trump Inc.: With Other People's Money and Some Dubious Partners," *Bloomberg Businessweek*, August 22, 2017.

125 *unofficial title as "Secretary of Everything"*: Kevin Liptak, "Trump's Secretary of Everything: Jared Kushner," CNN, April 4, 2017.

126 *Peña Nieto said publicly*: View Enrique Peña Nieto's tweet, from January 25, 2017, at https://twitter.com/EPN/status/824447050066468865.

126 *"If Mexico is unwilling to pay"*: View Donald Trump's tweet, from January 26, 2017, https://twitter.com/realDonaldTrump/status/824616644370714627.

126 *according to* Vanity Fair: Emily Jane Fox, "Can Jared and Ivanka Outrun Donald Trump's Scandals?," *Vanity Fair*, January 30, 2017.

126 *Oscar's valuation around the time*: Steven Bertoni, "Oscar Health Gets $400 Million And A $2.7 Billion Valuation from Fidelity" *Forbes*, February 22, 2016.

127 *higher than that of 666 Fifth*: Charles V. Bagli, "At Kushners' Flagship Building, Mounting Debt and a Foundered Deal," *New York Times*, April 3, 2017.

127 *"We publicly opposed the Administration's"*: Email from Joel Klein, November 16, 2018.

127 *The first Friday of the Trump*: Kaileen Gaul, "The Kushners Break Bread with Team Trump: Jared and Ivanka Welcome Several Members of the President's Cabinet

for the First Big Shabbat Meal at Their New DC Home," DailyMail.com, January 27, 2017, https://www.dailymail.co.uk/news/article-4166088/The-Kushners -break-bread-Team-Trump.html.

127 *the White House announced*: Read the January 27, 2017, executive order on the White House's website at https://www.whitehouse.gov/presidential-actions/executive-order -protecting-nation-foreign-terrorist-entry-united-states/.

128 *The night after the travel ban*: View Ivanka Trump's Instagram post, from January 29, 2017, at https://www.instagram.com/p/BP1fuJsAeiK/.

128 *A pairing of this picture with one*: "Ivanka Trump Called 'Tone Deaf' for Donning $5,000 Worth of Aluminum Foil Amid Immigration Chaos," *National Post*, January 30, 2017.

129 *appeared on the February 13*: View Time's February 13, 2017, cover at http://time .com/magazine/us/4657637/february-13th-2017-vol-189-no-5-u-s/.

130 *to a Lunar New Year party*: Emily Heil, "Ivanka Trump Is Surprise Attendee at the Chinese Embassy's New Year's Party," *Washington Post*, February 1, 2017.

130 *"My daughter Ivanka has been"*: View Donald Trump's tweet, from February 8, 2017, at https://twitter.com/realdonaldtrump/status/829356871848951809.

130 *"Go buy Ivanka's stuff"*: "Kellyanne Conway on Ivanka Trump's Fashion Line: 'Go Buy It Today!,'" Fox News, February 9, 2017.

130 *broke an ethics rule*: Use of Public Office for Private Gain, 5 C.F.R. 2635.702 at https:// www.gpo.gov/fdsys/granule/CFR-2012-title5-vol3/CFR-2012-title5-vol3 -sec2635-702.

131 *Ivanka attended a roundtable of a dozen*: Sabrina Siddiqui, "Ivanka Trump Talks Women in Business at White House as Her Own Brand Falters," *Guardian*, February 13, 2017.

131 *"essentially elevated a family member"*: Annie Karni, "Ivanka Trump Faces Skeptical Audience in Berlin," *Politico*, April 24, 2017.

131 *the couple was skiing in Aspen*: Emily Jane Fox, "Jared and Ivanka's West Wing Vanishing Act," *Vanity Fair*, March 24, 2017.

132 *The "foreign contacts" section*: Kara Scannell, "Background Check Chief Has 'Never Seen' Mistakes and Omissions at Level of Jared Kushner Forms," CNN, February 13, 2018.

132 *broke the stories of Kushner's meetings*: Michael S. Schmidt, Matthew Rosenberg, and Matt Apuzzo, "Kushner and Flynn Met with Russian Envoy in December, White House Says," *New York Times*, March 2, 2017.

132 *and Gorkov*: Jo Becker, Matthew Rosenberg, and Maggie Haberman, "Senate Committee to Question Jared Kushner Over Meetings with Russians," *New York Times*, March 27, 2017.

132 *"Flynn, Sessions, Kushner"*: William Saletan, "Jared Knew," *Slate*, March 3, 2017.

133 *warned Kushner that he was*: Adam Entous and Evan Osnos, "Jared Kushner Is China's Trump Card," *New Yorker*, January 29, 2018.

133 *"chatter" about how it was possible to*: Adam Entous, "Donald Trump's New World Order," *New Yorker*, June 18, 2018.

133   *MBS, was welcomed at the White House*: Julie Hirschfeld Davis, "Trump Meets Saudi Prince as U.S. and Kingdom Seek Warmer Relations," *New York Times*, March 14, 2017.

133   *list the shares of Aramco*: FT Reporters, "Saudi Aramco poised for complex call on IPO venue," *Financial Times*, March 9, 2017.

133   *her assets were put in a trust*: Rachel Abrams, "Despite a Trust, Ivanka Trump Still Wields Power Over Her Brand," *New York Times*, March 20, 2017.

133   *one of her companies also applied*: Eva Dou, "Ivanka Trump's Company Applied for Chinese Trademarks Day Before Her White House Appointment," *Wall Street Journal*, June 2, 2017.

133   *the same day Trump hosted*: Benjamin Haas, "Ivanka Trump Brand Secures China Trademarks on Day US President Met Xi Jinping," *Guardian*, April 19, 2017.

136   *Justice Department sued to block*: Brian Fung, "The Justice Department Is Suing AT&T To Block Its $85 billion Bid For Time Warner," *Wall Street Journal*, November 20, 2017.

136   *In late March, Kushner had*: Read the March 27, 2017, statement, "President Donald J. Trump Announces the White House Office of American Innovation (OAI)," on the White House's website at https://www.whitehouse.gov/briefings-statements/president-donald-j-trump-announces-white-house-office-american-innovation-oai/.

136   *"the government should be run"*: Ashley Parker and Philip Rucker, "Trump Taps Kushner to Lead a SWAT Team to Fix Government with Business Ideas," *Washington Post*, March 26, 2017.

136   *draw the scrutiny of ethics watchdogs*: Read the July 6, 2017, press release, "CREW Files Ethics Complaint Against Jared Kushner," on Citizens for Responsibility and Ethics in Washington's website at https://www.citizensforethics.org/press-release/crew-files-ethics-complaint-jared-kushner/.

136   *On April 14*: Zeke J. Miller, "The White House Will Keep Its Visitor Logs Secret," *Time*, April 14, 2017.

137   *Ivanka appeared on* CBS: "Ivanka Trump: 'I'll Weigh In with My Father on the Issues I Feel Strongly About,'" CBS News, April 5, 2017.

137   *recent episode of* Saturday Night: View Saturday Night Live's sketch, aired March 11, 2017, at https://www.youtube.com/watch?v=F7o4oMKbStE.

137   *It had been reported just the day before*: Jill Disis, "Ivanka Trump's Stake in D.C. Hotel Renews Ethics Questions," CNN Money, April 4, 2017.

CHAPTER THIRTEEN

140   *Jared and Josh posed together*: View Josh Kushner's Instagram post, from January 22, 2017, at https://www.instagram.com/p/BPlQuThjYwz/.

140   *"He was incredibly proud of"*: Interview with Alan Hammer, July 9, 2018.

140   *Since Jared had undertaken only a limited*: Susanne Craig and Maggie Haberman, "Jared Kushner Will Sell Many of His Assets, but Ethics Lawyers Worry," *New York Times*, January 9, 2017.

140   *Kushner's visitors at the White House*: Jesse Drucker, Kate Kelly, and Ben Protess,

"Kushner's Family Business Received Loans After White House Meetings," *New York Times,* February 28, 2018.

141   *whom Jared had wanted to hire*: Stephanie Kirchgaessner, "Wall St Star Approached to Be Trump Budget Chief a Year Before Loan to Kushner Firm," *Guardian,* April 9, 2018.

142   *Kushners' deal with the Chinese insurer Anbang*: David Kocieniewski and Caleb Melby, "Kushners May Get $400 Million From Chinese on Tower," *Bloomberg,* March 13, 2017.

142   *five members of Congress*: Read the March 24, 2017, letter on Elizabeth Warren's website at https://www.warren.senate.gov/files/documents/2017-3-24_Letter _Mnuchin_CFIUS-Anbang-Kushner.pdf.

142   *666 Fifth was down to 70 percent*: Charles V. Bagli, "At Kushners' Flagship Building, Mounting Debt and a Foundered Deal," *New York Times,* April 3, 2017.

142   *$1.95 billion*: Chelsey Dulaney, "Waldorf Astoria Hotel Sale Completed," *Wall Street Journal,* February 11, 2015.

142   *Wu Xiaohui, who had married*: Keith Bradsher and Sui-Lee Wee, "Why Did China Detain Anbang's Chairman? He Tested a Lot of Limits," *New York Times,* June 14, 2017.

143   *two subsequent potential acquisitions*: Xie Yu, "As Anbang's Hotel Takeover Gets Blocked, Expect More Government Interventions as Chinese Firms Continue to Snap Up US Assets," *South China Morning Post,* October 24, 2016.

143   *In 2018, Wu was convicted*: Maggie Zhang, Xie Yu and Jun Mai, "Anbang's Ex-Chief Wu Xiaohui Sentenced to 18 Years Behind Bars for US$12 Billion Fraud, Embezzlement," *South China Morning Post,* May 10, 2018.

143   *By the end of March*: Lois Weiss, "Chinese Investor Backs Out of Kushner Companies Project," *New York Post,* March 28, 2017.

143   *"We are well on our way"*: Charles V. Bagli, "At Kushners' Flagship Building, Mounting Debt and a Foundered Deal," *New York Times,* April 3, 2017.

CHAPTER FOURTEEN

144   *he was questioned in great detail*: Read the January 11, 2017, transcript, "Nomination of Rex Tillerson to be Secretary of State," on the Senate Foreign Relations Committee's website at https://www.foreign.senate.gov/download/transcript -nomination-011117&download=1.

144   *The vote had the most opposition*: "How Senators Voted on Rex Tillerson," *New York Times,* February 1, 2017.

144   *more than $350 billion*: Kenneth Kiesnoski, "The Top 10 US Companies by Market Capitalization," CNBC, March 8, 2017.

145   *The U.S. issued a statement*: Read the February 2, 2017, statement on the White House's website at https://www.whitehouse.gov/briefings-statements/statement -press-secretary/.

145   *started calling him Saint Rex*: Robert F. Worth, "Can Jim Mattis Hold the Line in Trump's 'War Cabinet'?," *New York Times,* April 1, 2018.

146 *referring to an effort to isolate*: Read Scott A. Snyder's October 2, 2018, story, "China's Shifting Roles on the Korean Peninsula: Unintended Consequences of the Singapore Summit," on the Council on Foreign Relations's website at https://www .cfr.org/blog/chinas-shifting-roles-korean-peninsula-unintended-consequences -singapore-summit.

146 *China comprises more than 90 percent*: Read Eleanor Albert's March 28, 2018, story, "The China–North Korea Relationship," on the Council on Foreign Relations' website at https://www.cfr.org/backgrounder/china-north-korea-relationship.

146 *Tillerson was "wasting his time"*: View Donald Trump's tweet, from October 1, 2017, at https://twitter.com/realDonaldTrump/status/914497877543735296.

146 *Even the decision in April*: View Donald Trump's speech, delivered on April 6, 2017, on the *New York Times* website at https://www.nytimes.com/2017/04/06/world /middleeast/transcript-video-trump-airstrikes-syria.html.

146 *years earlier had criticized Obama*: View Donald Trump's tweet, from August 29, 2013, at https://twitter.com/realDonaldTrump/status/373146637184401408.

147 *increasingly lean State Department*: Jack Corrigan, "The Hollowing Out of the State Department Continues," *Atlantic*, February 11, 2018.

147 *2016 execution in Saudi Arabia*: Merrit Kennedy, "Who Was the Shiite Sheikh Executed by Saudi Arabia?," NPR, January 4, 2016.

147 *As defense minister, the prince*: Dexter Filkins, "A Saudi Prince's Quest to Remake the Middle East," *New Yorker*, April 9, 2018.

147 *"the world's worst humanitarian crisis"*: Read the April 3, 2018, statement, "Secretary-General's Remarks to the Pledging Conference on Yemen [As Delivered]," on the United Nations's website at https://www.un.org/sg/en/content/sg/statement/2018-04 -03/secretary-generals-remarks-pledging-conference-yemen-delivered.

147 *"Vision 2030"*: Read the details of the plan on the Kingdom of Saudi Arabia's website at https://vision2030.gov.sa/en.

147 *Kushner had MBS to his home*: Annie Karni, "How Trump's Aides Pulled Off Middle East Tour," *Politico*, May 23, 2017.

147 *prince and "prince" were still communicating*: Alex Emmons, Ryan Grim, and Clayton Swisher, "Saudi Crown Prince Boasted That Jared Kushner Was 'In His Pocket,'" *Intercept*, March 21, 2018.

148 *he had visited King Salman in Riyadh*: President Barack Obama's travels are made public on the Office of the Historian's website at https://history.state.gov /departmenthistory/travels/president/obama-barack.

148 *needed to figure out a "cold peace"*: Jeffrey Goldberg, "The Obama Doctrine," *Atlantic*, April 2016.

148 *"Our plan was to annihilate the physical"*: Dexter Filkins, "A Saudi Prince's Quest to Remake the Middle East," *New Yorker*, April 9, 2018.

149 *high unemployment rate*: Read the press release, "The Labour Force Survey Results Fourth Quarter (January–March 2018) Round," on the Palestinian Central Bureau of Statistics's website at http://www.pcbs.gov.ps/post.aspx?lang=en&ItemID=3135.

149 *named deputy RNC finance chairman*: Read the April 3, 2017, press release, "RNC Announces Additions to RNC Finance Leadership Team," on the Republican Na-

tional Committee's website at https://gop.com/rnc-announces-additions-to-rnc
-finance-leadership-team/.

149   *a convicted child molester*: Bradley Klapper and Karel Janicek, "Mueller's Witness is
Convicted Pedophile with Shadowy Past," *Associated Press*, March 15, 2018.

149   *a pay-to-play scheme in 2009*: Karen Freifeld, "LA Money Manager Gets No Jail
Time in NY Corruption Case," *Reuters*, November 26, 2012.

149   *discussed lobbying American support*: Desmond Butler and Tom LoBianco,
"The Princes, the President, and the Fortune Seekers," *Associated Press*, May 21,
2018.

150   *population 2.8 million*: Qatar's population is made public on the Ministry of Development Planning and Statistics's website at https://www.mdps.gov.qa/en/statistics1
/pages/default.aspx.

150   *It has one of the highest*: GNI per capita data is made public on the World Bank's
website at https://data.worldbank.org/indicator/NY.GNP.PCAP.CD?year_high
_desc=true.

150   *the second-highest*: GDP per capita data is made public on the Central Intelligence
Agency's website at https://www.cia.gov/library/publications/the-world-factbook
/rankorder/2004rank.html.

150   *who had considered financing*: Will Parker and Konrad Putzier, "Kushner, Unfiltered," *Real Deal,* June 1, 2018.

151   *he had been photographed*: View the photograph, taken April 4, 2017, at https://www
.gettyimages.com/detail/news-photo/in-this-handout-provided-by-the-department
-of-defense-jared-news-photo/665429294.

151   *on an inspection of the troops*: Read the April 4, 2017, press release, "Dunford, Kushner Visit U.S., Iraqi Forces Near Mosul," on the Department of Defense's website
at https://dod.defense.gov/News/Article/Article/1140772/dunford-kushner-visit-us
-iraqi-forces-near-mosul/.

151   *lampooned the absurd outfit*: View *Saturday Night Live*'s sketch, aired April 15, 2017,
at https://www.youtube.com/watch?v=CgNgkwTusM4.

151   *Kushner met with a Saudi delegation*: Mark Landler, Eric Schmitt, and Matt Apuzzo,
"$110 Billion Weapons Sale to Saudis Has Jared Kushner's Personal Touch," *New
York Times,* May 18, 2017.

152   *wrote for Brookings*: Bruce Riedel, "The $110 Billion Arms Deal to Saudi Arabia Is
Fake News," The Brookings Institution, June 5, 2017.

152   *Trump made his first overseas trip as president*: Read the December 19, 2017, statement, "President Donald J. Trump's First Year of Foreign Policy Accomplishments,"
on the White House's website at https://www.whitehouse.gov/briefings-statements
/president-donald-j-trumps-first-year-of-foreign-policy-accomplishments/.

152   *reportedly planned to spend nearly sixty-eight million*: "Saudi Arabia Spending $68
Million to Host Donald Trump," *Alwaght News & Analysis*, May 8, 2017.

152   *would write in* Fire and Fury: Michael Wolff, *Fire and Fury* (New York: Henry
Holt & Co., 2018), p. 230.

152   *outlined in a May 21 speech*: Read the May 21, 2017, statement, "President Trump's
Speech to the Arab Islamic American Summit," on the White House's website at

https://www.whitehouse.gov/briefings-statements/president-trumps-speech-arab-islamic-american-summit/.

152   *Trump and King Salman signed*: Julie Pace and Jonathan LeMire, "Saudis Welcome Trump with Gold Medal, Receive Arms Package," *Associated Press*, May 20, 2017.

153   *announced a twenty-billion-dollar bid investment*: Caleb Melby and Hui-yong Yu, "Kushners' Blackstone Connection Put on Display in Saudi Arabia," *Bloomberg*, May 25, 2017.

153   *gathered around a huge*: "What Was That Glowing Orb Trump Touched in Saudi Arabia?," *New York Times*, May 22, 2017.

153   *had dinner with MBS*: Annie Karni, "How Trump's Aides Pulled Off Middle East Tour," *Politico*, May 23, 2017.

153   *in his speech that day*: Read the May 21, 2017, statement, "President Trump's Speech to the Arab Islamic American Summit," on the White House's website at https://www.whitehouse.gov/briefings-statements/president-trumps-speech-arab-islamic-american-summit/.

153   *On June 5*: Read the August 7, 2018, report, "Integrated Country Strategy: Qatar," on the Department of State's website at https://www.state.gov/documents/organization/285245.pdf.

153   *U.S. intelligence would determine*: Karen DeYoung and Ellen Nakashima, "UAE Orchestrated Hacking of Qatari Government Sites, Sparking Regional Upheaval, According to U.S. Intelligence Officials," *Washington Post*, July 16, 2017.

153   *does not always read his briefings*: Carol D. Leonnig, Shane Harris, and Greg Jaffe, "Breaking with Tradition, Trump Skips President's Written Intelligence Report and Relies on Oral Briefings," *Washington Post*, February 9, 2018.

153   *tweeted his support for the blockade*: View Donald Trump's tweet, from June 6, 2017, at https://twitter.com/realDonaldTrump/status/872062159789985792.

154   *reportedly failed to persuade the administration*: Caleb Melby, "Tom Barrack Got Trump Right, Then Things Went Wrong," *Bloomberg*, October 26, 2018.

155   *reportedly intervened to stop*: Alex Emmons, "Saudi Arabia Planned to Invade Qatar Last Summer. Rex Tillerson's Efforts to Stop It May Have Cost Him His Job," *Intercept*, August 1, 2018.

156   *Kushner's family had been courting*: Clayton Swisher and Ryan Grim, "Jared Kushner's Real-Estate Firm Sought Money Directly from Qatar Government Weeks Before Blockade," *Intercept*, March 2, 2018.

CHAPTER FIFTEEN

157   *In April 2017, Qatari Finance Minister*: Dexter Filkins, "A Saudi Prince's Quest to Remake the Middle East," *New Yorker*, April 9, 2018.

157   *told The New Yorker's Dexter Filkins*: Ibid.

158   *That same week*: Clayton Swisher and Ryan Grim, "Joshua Kushner Met with Government of Qatar to Discuss Financing in the Same Week Father Charles Kushner Did," *Intercept*, March 23, 2018.

158   *On March 13, Bloomberg reported*: David Kocieniewski and Caleb Melby, "Kushners May Get $400 Million from Chinese on Tower," *Bloomberg*, March 13, 2017.

158   *That was also the view of three Democratic U.S. Senators*: Read the April 21, 2017, letter on Dianne Feinstein's website at https://www.feinstein.senate.gov/public/_cache/files/1/0/10889aab-e46f-403d-af1d-dd06a86c7972/AAA786DCFADE F931C1F698128C3329AE.2017.04.21-df-et-al.-to-mcgahn-re-trump-kushner -eb-5.pdf.

159   *to pitch more than one hundred Chinese investors*: Javier C. Hernández, Cao Li, and Jesse Drucker, "Jared Kushner's Sister Highlights Family Ties in Pitch to Chinese Investors," *New York Times,* May 6, 2017.

159   *told* The New York Times *that the sales*: Ibid.

159   *"In the course of discussing"*: "Jared Kushner's Family Apologizes for Name Drop in Pitch to Chinese Investors," *Guardian,* May 8, 2017.

160   *That May, Kushner Companies was subpoenaed*: Erica Orden, Aruna Viswanatha and Byron Tau," U.S. Attorney Subpoenas Kushner Cos. Over Investment-For-Visa Program," *Wall Street Journal,* August 3, 2017.

160   *That same month, the U.S. Securities and Exchange*: Erica Orden, "SEC Looks Into Kushner Cos. Over Use of EB-5 Program for Immigrant Investors," *Wall Street Journal,* January 6, 2017.

160   *On April 26,* The New York Times: Jesse Drucker, "Bribe Cases, a Jared Kushner Partner and Potential Conflicts," *New York Times,* April 26, 2017.

160   *In May, it emerged*: Jean Eaglesham, Juliet Chung, and Lisa Schwartz, "Trump Adviser Kushner's Undisclosed Partners Include Goldman and Soros," *Wall Street Journal,* May 3, 2017.

160   *jointly published a deep dive*: Alec MacGillis, "Jared Kushner's Other Real Estate Empire," *New York Times,* and "The Beleaguered Tenants of 'Kushnerville,'" *ProPublica,* May 23, 2017.

161   *A recent financial disclosure*: Courtney Weaver, Sam Fleming, and Shawn Donnan, "White House reveals Ivanka Trump and Jared Kushner wealth," *Financial Times,* April 1, 2017.

161   *An April 19 public opinion poll*: Read the April 19, 2017, press release on Quinnipiac University's website at https://poll.qu.edu/images/polling/us/us04192017 _Uwpg863m.pdf/.

161   *Ivanka shared a stage in Berlin*: Annie Karnie, "Ivanka Trump Gets Booed, Hissed at During Berlin Event," *Politico,* April 25, 2017.

161   *"a tremendous champion of"*: Ibid.

161   *There was a report the next day*: Drew Harwell, "Workers Endured Long Hours, Low Pay at Chinese Factory Used by Ivanka Trump's Clothing-Maker," *Washington Post,* April 25, 2017.

CHAPTER SIXTEEN

162   *On April 6,* The New York Times: Jo Becker and Matthew Rosenberg, "Kushner Omitted Meeting with Russians on Security Clearance Forms," *New York Times,* April 6, 2017.

162   *Kushner's lawyer, Jamie Gorelick*: Ibid.

162   *by both the House and Senate intelligence committees*: Devlin Barrett, Philip Rucker,

and Karoun Demirjian, "Kushner questioned by Senate investigators on Russia," *Washington Post,* July 24, 2017.

162   *and the Department of Justice*: Marshall Cohen, "Mueller's investigators questioned Kushner about potential Russian collusion, obstruction." CNN, May 24, 2018.

162   *In March, FBI Director James Comey had confirmed to Congress*: Stuart A. Thompson, Alicia Parlapiano, and Wilson Andrew, "The Events That Led to Comey's Firing, and How the White House's Story Changed," *New York Times,* June 7, 2017.

163   *blamed him for her election loss*: Read the November 10, 2016, Hillary Clinton campaign memo on the *New York Times* website at https://www.nytimes.com/interactive /2016/11/12/us/politics/document-Clinton-Senior-Staff-Memo-Why-We-Lost .html.

163   *he had announced there was new*: Read James Comey's October 28, 2016, letter to Congress on the *New York Times* website at https://www.nytimes.com/interactive /2016/10/28/us/politics/fbi-letter.html.

164   *Obama expelled thirty-five suspected Russian*: Read the December 29, 2016, press release, "Statement by the President on Actions in Response to Russian Malicious Cyber Activity and Harassment," on the White House Office of the Press Secretary's website at https://obamawhitehouse.archives.gov/the-press-office/2016/12/29 /statement-president-actions-response-russian-malicious-cyber-activity.

164   *the thirty-five-page dossier*: Ken Bensinger, Miriam Elder, and Mark Schoofs, "These Reports Allege Trump Has Deep Ties To Russia," *BuzzFeed News,* Jan 10, 2017.

165   *"patronage relationship"*: Read James B. Comey's June 8, 2017, statement for the Record Senate Select Committee on Intelligence on their website at https://www .intelligence.senate.gov/sites/default/files/documents/os-jcomey-060817.pdf.

166   *"It is an abuse of power"*: Washington Post Staff, "Comey Firing: Reaction from Members of Congress on FBI Director's Dismissal," *Washington Post,* May 9, 2017.

166   *"When I decided to just do it"*: View Trump's interview with Lester Holt on May 12, 2017, at the NBC News website https://www.nbcnews.com/nightly-news/video/pres -trump-s-extended-exclusive-interview-with-lester-holt-at-the-white-house -941854787582?v=railb&.

167   *reported that Trump accepted*: Rebecca R. Ruiz and Mark Landler, "Robert Mueller, Former F.B.I. Director, Is Named Special Counsel for Russia Investigation," *New York Times,* May 17, 2017.

167   *reported that Kushner was a focus of*: Matt Zapotosky, Sari Horwitz, Devlin Barrett, and Adam Entous, "Jared Kushner Now a Focus in Russia Investigation," *Washington Post,* May 25, 2017.

167   *business dealings were also being investigated*: Matt Zapotosky, Sari Horwitz, and Adam Entous, "Special Counsel Is Investigating Jared Kushner's Business Dealings," *Washington Post,* June 15, 2017.

167   *the U.S. attorney's office in Brooklyn would*: Michael Kranish, "Federal Prosecutors in N.Y. Requested Kushner Cos. Records on Deutsche Bank Loan," *Washington Post,* December 27, 2017.

167   *requested more information about Kushner's*: Read the June 22, 2017, letter on the Committee on the Judiciary's website at https://www.judiciary.senate.gov/imo

/media/doc/2017-06-22%20CG%20DF%20LG%20SW%20to%20White%20 House%20FBI%20(Kushner%20Clearance).pdf.

168   *Kushner's advice to Trump*: Peter Nicholas, Aruna Viswanatha, and Rebecca Ballhaus, "Special Counsel Mueller Probes Jared Kushner's Contacts with Foreign Leaders," *Wall Street Journal*, November 21, 2017.

168   *would pull out of the Paris Agreement*: Read the June 1, 2017, press release "Statement by President Trump on the Paris Climate Accord," on the White House's website at https://www.whitehouse.gov/briefings-statements/statement-president-trump -paris-climate-accord/.

168   *This had been Ivanka's battle*: Annie Karni, "After Climate Loss, Ivanka Moves On," *Politico*, June 1, 2017.

168   *"It's no secret that Ivanka"*: Cristiano Lima, "Gore Praises Ivanka Trump on Climate Policy After Meeting," *Politico*, December 5, 2016.

169   *"a reckless and indefensible"*: View Al Gore's comment, "Statement by Former Vice President Al Gore on Today's Decision by the Trump Administration to Withdraw from the Paris Agreement," posted on June 1, 2017, on his website at https:// algore.com/news/statement-by-former-vice-president-al-gore-on-today-s-decision -by-the-trump-administration-to-withdraw-from-the-paris-agreement.

170   *"trade thoughts from morning until"*: Jodi Kantor, Rachel Abrams, and Maggie Haberman, "Ivanka Trump Has the President's Ear. Here's Her Agenda," *New York Times*, May 2, 2017.

170   *"Where I disagree with my father"*: View Ivanka Trump's interview, April 5, 2017, on the CBS News website at https://www.cbsnews.com/news/ivanka-trump-interview -full-transcript/.

170   *"a level of viciousness that I was not"*: Betsy Klein, "Ivanka Trump: 'There Is a Level of Viciousness That I was Not Expecting,'" CNN, June 12, 2017.

CHAPTER SEVENTEEN

172   *"Dear Mr. President"*: View Mark Corallo's tweet, from May 7, 2017, at https://twitter .com/MarkCorallo1/status/861179547471015936.

172   *Corallo took a screenshot*: Interview with Mark Corallo, October 30, 2018. The information presented in this chapter comes mainly from an on-the-record interview with Corallo.

174   Forbes *cover article*: Steven Bertoni, "How Jared Kushner Won Trump the White House," *Forbes*, December 20, 2016.

177   *On June 19*, The New York Times: Julie Hirschfeld Davis and Maggie Haberman, "A Top Presidential Public Defender was Also a Twitter Critic," *New York Times*, June 19, 2017.

178   *published an article about the meeting*: Jo Becker, Matt Apuzzo, and Adam Goldman, "Trump Team Met with Lawyer Linked to Kremlin During Campaign," *New York Times*, July 8, 2017.

178   *reported that it had been dictated*: Ashley Parker, Carol D. Leonnig, Philip Rucker, and Tom Hamburger, "Trump Dictated Son's Misleading Statement on Meeting with Russian Lawyer," *Washington Post*, July 31, 2017.

179   *The* Times *published the emails*: "Read the Emails on Donald Trump Jr.'s Russia Meeting," *New York Times,* July 11, 2017.

179   *"business people who were supporters"*: Read Sept. 7, 2017, testimony for Senate Judiciary Committee on the Committee on the Judiciary's website at https://www .judiciary.senate.gov/imo/media/doc/Trump%20Jr%20Transcript_redacted.pdf.

180   *On July 11,* ProPublica *published*: Justin Elliott and Jesse Eisinger, "Trump's Russia Lawyer Isn't Seeking Security Clearance, and May Have Trouble Getting One," *ProPublica,* July 11, 2017.

180   *"I'm on you now. You are"*: Justin Elliott, "Trump Lawyer Marc Kasowitz Threatens Stranger in Emails: 'Watch Your Back, Bitch,'" *ProPublica,* July 12, 2017.

CHAPTER EIGHTEEN

181   *A Palestinian official told*: Jack Khoury, Barak Ravid, and Amir Tibon, "After Kushner-Abbas Meeting, Issue of Payments to Palestinian Terrorists' Families Remains Unresolved," *Haaretz,* June 22, 2017.

181   *Palestinian diplomat Saeb Erekat told*: Adam Entous, "Donald Trump's New World Order," *New Yorker,* June 18, 2018.

181   *In one of their conversations*: Ibid.

182   *Ivanka Trump broke protocol*: Abby Phillip, "Ivanka Trump Takes Father's Seat at G-20 Leaders' Table in Break from Diplomatic Protocol," *Washington Post,* July 8, 2017.

182   *"I'm a better person than this"*: Interview with Mark Corallo, May 23, 2018.

182   The Washington Post *published "Ivanka Inc."*: Matea Gold, Drew Harwell, Maher Sattar, and Simon Denyer, "Ivanka, Inc.," *Washington Post,* July 14, 2017.

182   *Ivanka dropped in on her father*: "Excerpts from The Times's Interview with Trump," *New York Times,* July 19, 2017.

182   *She did the same thing*: Josh Dawsey and Hadas Gold, "Full Transcript: Trump's *Wall Street Journal* Interview," *Politico,* August 1, 2017.

182   *A report in the paper two days later*: Rachel Abrams and Jesse Drucker, "Ivanka Trump Received at Least $12.6 Million Since 2016, Disclosure Shows," *New York Times,* July 21, 2017.

184   *Trump tried to get Spicer to stay on*: Glenn Thrush and Maggie Haberman, "Sean Spicer Resigns as White House Press Secretary," *New York Times,* July 21, 2017.

184   *assets worth up to eighty-five million*: Lorraine Woellert, "Scaramucci Still Stands to Profit from SkyBridge from the White House," *Politico,* July 26, 2017.

184   *"In light of the leak"*: Cristiano Lima, "Scaramucci Claims 'Felony' Over Report of Public Disclosures," *Politico,* July 27, 2017.

184   *He and Trump had discussed*: Bob Woodward, *Fear* (New York: Simon & Schuster, 2018), p. 234.

184   *tweeted that his secretary of homeland security*: View Donald Trump's tweet, from July 28, 2017, at https://twitter.com/realDonaldTrump/status/891038014314598400.

185   *Kushner testified before the Senate Intelligence*: Read "Jared Kushner's Prepared Remarks to Congressional Investigators," given on July 24, 2017, on the *New York Times* website at https://www.nytimes.com/interactive/2017/07/24/us/politics/document -Read-Jared-Kushner-s-Statement-to-Congressional.html.

185 *as had been reported*: Ned Parker and Jonathan Landay, "Trump Son-in-Law Had Undisclosed Contacts with Russian Envoy—Sources," *Reuters*, May 27, 2017.

186 *That same day, Kushner*: View Jared Kushner's statement, delivered on July 24, 2017, on the *Washington Post* website at https://www.washingtonpost.com/news/post-politics/wp/2017/07/24/kushner-let-me-be-very-clear-i-did-not-collude-with-russia-nor-do-i-know-of-anyone-else-in-the-campaign-who-did-so/.

187 *concerning a "sealed real estate deal"*: Wendy Dent, Ed Pilkington, and Shaun Walker, "Jared Kushner Sealed Real Estate Deal with Oligarch's Firm Cited in Money-laundering Case," *Guardian*, July 24, 2017.

187 *published on July 27*: Ryan Lizza, "Anthony Scaramucci Called Me to Unload About White House Leakers, Reince Priebus, and Steve Bannon," *New Yorker*, July 27, 2017.

188 *"I am proud to support"*: View Ivanka Trump's tweet, from June 2, 2017, at https://twitter.com/IvankaTrump/status/870450538235785217.

188 *a move that apparently took her by surprise*: Annie Karni and Eliana Johnson, "Ivanka and Jared Find Their Limits In Trump's White House," *Politico*, July 20, 2017.

188 *tweeted his support of*: View Donald Trump's tweet, from August 9, 2017, at https://twitter.com/realDonaldTrump/status/895091395379245056.

189 *I reported on this at the time*: Vicky Ward, "Kushner Again: How He Helped Push Trump Into a Ditch in Alabama," *Huffington Post*, September 28, 2017.

189 *facing ugly allegations that he had*: Stephanie McCrummen, Beth Reinhard, and Alice Crites, "Woman Says Roy Moore Initiated Sexual Encounter When She Was 14, He Was 32," *Washington Post*, November 9, 2017.

189 *reportedly had been banned*: Charles Bethea, "Locals Were Troubled by Roy Moore's Interactions with Teen Girls at the Gadsden Mall," *New Yorker*, November 13, 2017.

190 *Trump condemned "hatred"*: Ben Jacobs and Warren Murray, "Donald Trump Under Fire After Failing to Denounce Virginia White Supremacists," *Guardian*, August 13, 2017.

190 *"There should be no place in society"*: View Ivanka Trump's tweet, from August 13, 2017, at https://twitter.com/IvankaTrump/status/896705195228381187.

190 *statement, which he put out on Monday*: Read the August 14, 2017, statement on the White House's website at https://www.whitehouse.gov/briefings-statements/statement-president-trump/.

190 *"very fine people on both sides"*: View Donald Trump's August 15, 2017, press conference on C-SPAN's website at https://www.c-span.org/video/?432633-1/president-trump-there-blame-sides-violence-charlottesville.

191 *Instead, Trump whipped out*: Bob Woodward, *Fear* (New York: Simon & Schuster, 2018), p. 245.

CHAPTER NINETEEN

192 *"reassessing the financing structure"*: Herbert Lash, "Kushners Seek New Plan for Flagship NY Office After Failed Qatar Deal," *Reuters*, July 11, 2017.

192 *"We have been internally debating"*: Herbert Lash, "No Plan Yet on Kushner's Flagship Manhattan Tower—Vornado CEO," *Reuters*, August 1, 2017.

192 *"the Jenga puzzle piece that could"*: David Kocieniewski and Caleb Melby, "Kushner's

China Deal Flop Was Part of Much Bigger Hunt for Cash," *Bloomberg*, August 31, 2017.

193 *"just about completely chilled"*: Michael Kranish and Jonathan O'Connell, "Kushner's White House Role 'Crushed' Efforts to Woo Investors for NYC Tower," *Washington Post*, September 13, 2017.

193 *"the newspaper industry"*: Interview with Alan Hammer, July 9, 2018.

193 *Jesse Drucker reported*: Jesse Drucker, "Tenants Sue Kushner Companies Claiming Rent Rule Violations," *New York Times*, August, 15, 2017.

193 *Next, the* Post *reported*: Amy Brittain, "Days After Sister's Visa Pitch, Kushner Divested Asset Related to Jersey City Project," *Washington Post*, August 31, 2017.

193 *following reports about issues*: Alec MacGillis, "Jared Kushner's Other Real Estate Empire," *New York Times*, and "The Beleaguered Tenants of 'Kushnerville,'" *ProPublica*, May 23, 2017.

193 *"I try not to focus in my life"*: Michael Kranish, "Jared Kushner's Father on Probe into Family Company: 'We Are Not At All Concerned,'" *Washington Post*, January 22, 2018.

193 *"It's likely that those are not feasible"*: Caleb Melby and David M. Levitt, "Kushner Partner Says Teardown of Fifth Avenue Tower Unlikely," *Bloomberg*, October 31, 2017.

194 *In December 2017, it was reported*: Ben Protess, Jessica Silver-Greenberg, and David Enrich, "Prosecutors Said to Seek Kushner Records from Deutsche Bank," *New York Times*, December 22, 2017.

194 *seventy-four million dollars*: Michael Kranish, "Kushner Firm's $285 Million Deutsche Bank Loan Came Just Before Election Day," *Washington Post*, June 25, 2017.

194 *"I've seen him in very high-level"*: Interview with Alan Hammer, July 9, 2018.

CHAPTER TWENTY

196 *Articles in* Politico: Josh Dawsey, "Kushner Used Private Email to Conduct White House Business," *Politico*, September 24, 2017.

196 *and* Newsweek: Max Kutner and Nina Burleigh, "Ivanka Trump Used a Personal Email Account for Government Work," *Newsweek*, September 25, 2017.

196 The Washington Post *would report*: Carol D. Leonnig and Josh Dawsey, "Ivanka Trump Used a Personal Email Account to Send Hundreds of Emails About Government Business Last Year," *Washington Post*, November 19, 2018.

196 *"Exiles on Pennsylvania Avenue"*: Sarah Ellison, "Exiles on Pennsylvania Avenue: How Jared and Ivanka Were Repelled by Washington's Elite," *Vanity Fair*, October, 2017.

196 *previous interview with* Forbes: Steven Bertoni, "How Jared Kushner Won Trump the White House," *Forbes*, November 22, 2016.

197 *including paid family leave*: Maggie Haberman, "Ivanka Trump Swayed the President on Family Leave. Congress Is a Tougher Sell," *New York Times*, May 21, 2017.

197 *and childcare tax credits*: Jim Tankersley, "Trump Wanted a Bigger Tax Cut for the Rich, Ivanka Went Elsewhere," *New York Times*, November 29, 2017.

197 *modernizing the government*: Ashley Parker and Philip Rucker, "Trump Taps Kushner

to Lead a SWAT Team to Fix Government with Business Ideas," *Washington Post,* March 26, 2017.

197 *prison reform*: Elana Schor and Heather Caygle, "Kushner-Backed Prisons Bill Surges Ahead," *Politico,* May 9, 2018.

197 *peace in the Middle East*: Mark Landler, "Trump Vows to Release Mideast Peace Plan Within 4 Months," *New York Times,* September 26, 2018.

197 *NAFTA*: Josh Wingrove, Jennifer Jacobs, and Eric Martin, "How the U.S. and Canada Ended Their Feud and Clinched a Nafta Deal," *Bloomberg,* October 2, 2018.

198 *had issued a list*: Patrick Wintour, "Qatar Given 10 Days to Meet 13 Sweeping Demands by Saudi Arabia," *Guardian,* June 23, 2017.

198 *Kushner made his third trip*: Annie Karni, "Kushner Took Unannounced Trip to Saudi Arabia," *Politico,* October 29, 2017.

198 *"stayed up until nearly 4 A.M."*: David Ignatius, "The Saudi Crown Prince Just Made a Very Risky Power Play," *Washington Post,* November 5, 2017.

198 *MBS had around two hundred*: David D. Kirkpatrick, "Saudi Arabia Arrests 11 Princes, Including Billionaire Alwaleed bin Talal," *New York Times,* November 4, 2017.

199 *seventeen of the captives reportedly*: Ben Hubbard, David D. Kirkpatrick, Kate Kelly, and Mark Mazzetti, "Saudis Said to Use Coercion and Abuse to Seize Billions," *New York Times,* March 11, 2018.

199 *Dexter Filkins reported*: Dexter Filkins, "A Saudi Prince's Quest to Remake the Middle East," *New Yorker,* April 9, 2018.

199 *In March 2018,* The Intercept: Alex Emmons, Ryan Grim, and Clayton Swisher, "Saudi Crown Prince Boasted That Jared Kushner Was 'In His Pocket,'" *Intercept,* March 21, 2018.

199 *"It's an interesting form of dictatorship"*: Robin Wright, "The Saudi Royal Purge—With Trump's Consent," *New Yorker,* November 6, 2017.

199 *"The Saudis have spent"*: Interview with Bruce Riedel, August 6, 2018.

200 *Trump tweeted that Saudi Arabia*: View Donald Trump's tweet, from November 4, 2017, at https://twitter.com/realDonaldTrump/status/926793510723796993.

200 *he tweeted his support of*: View Donald Trump's tweet, from November 6, 2017, at https://twitter.com/realdonaldtrump/status/927672843504177152.

200 *A painting,* Salvator Mundi: Denise Blostein, Robert Libetti, and Kelly Crow, "How a $450 Million da Vinci Was Lost in America—And Later Found," *Wall Street Journal,* September 19, 2018.

200 *it fetched $450.3 million*: Robin Pogrebin and Scott Reyburn, "Leonardo da Vinci Painting Sells for $450.3 Million, Shattering Auction Highs," *New York Times,* November 15, 2017.

200 *had paid $127.5 million*: Hugo Miller and Stephanie Baker, "Russian Billionaire's Record da Vinci Sale Could Complicate a Different Legal Battle," *Bloomberg,* November 16, 2017.

200 *It was reported in December*: Shane Harris, Kelly Crow, and Summer Said, "Saudi Arabia's Crown Prince Identified as Buyer of Record-Breaking da Vinci," *Wall Street Journal,* December 7, 2017.

200 *the Saudis denied it*: Yara Bayoumy, "Abu Dhabi to Acquire Leonardo da Vinci's 'Salvator Mundi': Christie's," *Reuters*, December 8, 2017.

200 *MBS had thought he was bidding*: Ryan Parry and Josh Boswell, "The World's Most Expensive Painting Cost $450 Million Because Two Arab Princes Bid Against Each Other by Mistake and Wouldn't Back Down (but Settled by Swapping It for a Yacht)," *DailyMail.com*, March 28, 2018, https://www.dailymail.co.uk/news/article -5554969/Two-Arab-princes-cost-450MILLION-bidding-war-Da-Vincis -Salvator-Mundi.html.

201 *On December 6*: Read the December 6, 2017, statement on the White House's web-site at https://www.whitehouse.gov/briefings-statements/statement-president-trump -jerusalem/.

201 *take place in Jerusalem in May*: Julie Hirschfield Davis, "Jerusalem Embassy Is a Victory for Trump, and a Complication for Middle East Peace," *New York Times*, May 14, 2018.

201 *Mahmoud Abbas, was not able to tell*: Adam Entous, "Donald Trump's New World Order," *New Yorker*, June 18, 2018.

201 *"Things will be much better"*: Roger Cohen, "The Prince Who Would Remake the World," *New York Times*, June 21, 2018.

202 *on December 20*: Thomas Kaplan, "House Gives Final Approval to Sweeping Tax Overhaul," *New York Times*, December 20, 2017.

202 *got basic facts about the tax reform bill*: Aaron Blake, "Ivanka Trump's Fox News Interview was Full of Weird Claims," *Washington Post*, December 21, 2017.

202 *"very senior member"*: Read the United States District Court for the District of Co-lumbia's December 1, 2017, statement on the Department of Justice's website at https://www.justice.gov/file/1015126/download.

202 *scrutiny of Kushner was "deserved"*: View Chris Christie's interview, which took place on December 19, 2017, on the MSNBC website at https://www.msnbc.com/deadline-white -house/watch/chris-christie-jared-kushner-deserves-scrutiny-1120092227648.

202 *DailyMail.com ran a story*: Martin Gould, "White House Romance! Trump's Comms Director Hope Hicks Is Seen Canoodling with President's High Level Staff Sec-retary Rob Porter," *DailyMail.com*, February 1, 2018, https://www.dailymail.co.uk /news/article-5325941/White-House-Comms-director-Hope-Hicks-dating-Rob -Porter.html.

203 *the site published another*: Louise Boyle, "'He Pulled Me, Naked and Dripping From the Shower to Yell at Me.' Ex-Wife of Trump Aide Rob Porter Who's Dating Hope Hicks, Tells How He Called Her a 'F***ing B***h' on Their Honeymoon and She Filed a Protective Order Against Him," *DailyMail.com*, February 6, 2018, https:// www.dailymail.co.uk/news/article-5359731/Ex-wife-Rob-Porter-Trumps -secretary-tells-marriage.html.

203 *"verbally, emotionally, and physically"*: Ibid.

203 *"I have worked directly with"*: Ibid.

203 *tweeted several photographs*: View Ryan Grim's tweet, from February 6, 2018, at https://twitter.com/ryangrim/status/961130828804902913.

203 *claimed was given to her*: Ryan Grim and Alleen Brown, "Former Wives of Top

White House Aide Rob Porter Both Told FBI He Abused Them," *Intercept*, February 7, 2018.

203 *"every individual deserves the right"*: Andrew Restuccia and Eliana Johnson, "In New Statement, Kelly Says He Was 'Shocked' by Porter Allegations and Condemns Abuse," *Politico*, February 7, 2018.

204 *On February 16, Kelly issued*: Read John Kelly's February 16, 2018, memo on the *Washington Post* website at https://apps.washingtonpost.com/g/documents/politics /read-kellys-memo-of-proposed-changes-to-white-house-security-clearance -process/2777/.

204 *"significant information requiring"*: Carol D. Leonnig, Robert Costa, and Josh Dawsey, "Top Justice Dept. Official Alerted White House 2 Weeks Ago to Ongoing Issues in Kushner's Security Clearance," *Washington Post*, February 23, 2018.

204 *"The new policy announced"*: Michael D. Shear, "Chief of Staff Orders an Overhaul for Security Clearances," *New York Times*, February 16, 2018.

204 *reported that Kushner saw what Kelly*: Julie Hirschfeld Davis and Maggie Haberman, "Kushner Resists Losing Access as Kelly Tackles Security Clearance Issues," *New York Times*, February 20, 2018.

204 *On February 27,* The Washington Post: Shane Harris, Carol D. Leonnig, Greg Jaffe, and Josh Dawsey, "Kushner's Overseas Contacts Raise Concerns as Foreign Officials Seek Leverage," *Washington Post*, February 27, 2018.

205 *"may have been a quid pro"*: Jed Handelsman Shugerman, "L'Affaire Kushner," *Slate*, March 2, 2018.

205 *NBC News reported that Qatari*: Julia Ainsley, Carol E. Lee, Robert Windrem, and Andrew W. Lehren, "Qataris Opted Not to Give Info on Kushner, Secret Meetings to Mueller," NBC News, March 12, 2018.

206 *April 2017 opinion piece*: Charles Wald and Michael Makovsky, "The Two Faces of Qatar, a Dubious Mideast Ally," *Wall Street Journal*, April 24, 2017.

206 *May 2017 conference hosted by*: Desmond Butler and Tom LoBianco, "The Princes, the President, and the Fortune Seekers," *Associated Press*, May 21, 2018.

206 *to support legislation to sanction Qatar*: Desmond Butler, Tom LoBianco, and Bradley Klapper, "A Top Trump Fundraiser Took $2.5 million from Dubai Before Pushing an anti-Qatar Agenda in Congress," *Associated Press*, May 26, 2018.

206 *Nader had been at a January 2017 meeting*: Bradley Klapper and Karel Janicek, "Mueller Witness Is Convicted Pedophile With Shadowy Past," *Associated Press*, March 15, 2018.

206 *"You have to hear in private"*: Desmond Butler and Tom LoBianco, "The Princes, the President, and the Fortune Seekers," *Associated Press*, May 21, 2018.

CHAPTER TWENTY-ONE

207 *On March 18, the Associated Press*: Bernard Condon, "Kushner Cos. Filed False NYC Housing Paperwork," *Associated Press*, March 18, 2018.

207 *the Department of Buildings confirmed*: Bernard Condon, "NYC Agency Investigating More Than a Dozen Kushner Buildings," *Associated Press*, March 21, 2018.

207 *Around that same time*: Erica Orden, "Kushner Cos. Subpoenaed for Information Related to Housing Filings," *Wall Street Journal*, April 19, 2018.

207 *it was reported that officials*: Stephen Braun, "White House Probing Huge Loans to Kushner's Family Firm," *Associated Press*, March 26, 2018.

208 *the White House denied that*: Stephen Braun, "White House Denies Probe Into Loans to Kushner Company," *Associated Press*, March 27, 2018.

208 *reported that some investors were now*: Sharon LaFraniere and Katie Benner, "The Kushners Saw Redemption in the White House. It Was a Mirage," *New York Times*, April 1, 2018.

208 *"I believe we now have a handshake"*: David M. Levitt, David Kocieniewski, and Caleb Melby, "Vornado Says It Has 'Handshake' for Kushners to Buy It Out of 666 Fifth Ave.," *Bloomberg*, April 6, 2018.

209 *"Go knock yourselves out"*: Sharon LaFraniere and Katie Benner, "The Kushners Saw Redemption in the White House. It Was a Mirage," *New York Times*, April 1, 2018.

209 *"We survived Donald Trump"*: Ibid.

209 *between twenty-five and fifty million*: Jared Kushner 2018 OGE Financial Disclosure, available at https://www.documentcloud.org/documents/5302021-Jared-Kushner-2018-OGE-financial-disclosure.html.

209 *backed by the governments of*: Arash Massoudi, Kana Inagaki, and Leslie Hook, "SoftBank's Son Uses Rare Structure for $93bn Tech Fund," *Financial Times*, June 12, 2017.

209 *When initial reports of SoftBank's*: David Kocieniewski and Stephanie Baker, "Kushner's Cadre in Talks with Saudi-Backed SoftBank Fund," *Bloomberg*, May 22, 2018.

209 *"For the avoidance of conflict"*: Interview with Mike Fascitelli, December 10, 2018.

CHAPTER TWENTY-TWO

210 *"We've become very good friends"*: Read the March 20, 2018, statement, "Remarks by President Trump and Crown Prince Mohammed Bin Salman of the Kingdom of Saudi Arabia Before Bilateral Meeting," on the White House's website at https://www.whitehouse.gov/briefings-statements/remarks-president-trump-crown-prince-mohammed-bin-salman-kingdom-saudi-arabia-bilateral-meeting/.

210 *120,000 American jobs*: Read the March 21, 2018, statement, "Readout of President Donald J. Trump's Meeting with Crown Prince Mohammed Bin Salman of Saudi Arabia," on the White House's website at https://www.whitehouse.gov/briefings-statements/readout-president-donald-j-trumps-meeting-crown-prince-mohammed-bin-salman-saudi-arabia/.

210 *Trump tweeted the news*: View Donald Trump's tweet, from March 13, 2018, at https://twitter.com/realDonaldTrump/status/973540316656623616.

210 *and before he told Tillerson*: Ali Vitali, Andrea Mitchell, and Monica Alba, "Trump Fires Rex Tillerson, Selects Mike Pompeo as New Secretary of State," NBC News, March 13, 2018.

210 *the same amount he had reportedly*: Paul Sonne and Karen DeYoung, "Trump Wants to Get the U.S. Out of Syria's War, So He Asked the Saudi King for $4 Billion," *Washington Post*, March 16, 2018.

210 *MBS looked visibly offended*: View footage of the March 20, 2018, meeting between Mohammad bin Salman and Donald Trump at https://www.youtube.com/watch?v=ykJXkcepiIQ.

211 *Al Thani of Qatar met with Trump*: Read the April 10, 2018, statement, "Readout of President Donald J. Trump's Meeting with Amir Tamim Bin Hamad Al Thani," on the White House's website at https://www.whitehouse.gov/briefings-statements/readout-president-donald-j-trumps-meeting-amir-tamim-bin-hamad-al-thani/.

211 *"a friend of mine"*: Read the April 10, 2018, statement, "Remarks by President Trump and Amir Tamim Bin Hamad Al Thani of the State of Qatar Before Bilateral Meeting," on the White House's website at https://www.whitehouse.gov/briefings-statements/remarks-president-trump-amir-tamim-bin-hamad-al-thani-state-qatar-bilateral-meeting/.

212 *to discuss the impending repeal*: Read the April 29, 2018, transcript, "Remarks with Saudi Foreign Minister Adel al-Jubeir," on the Department of State's website at https://www.state.gov/secretary/remarks/2018/281292.htm.

212 *reportedly warned him to stop*: Gardiner Harris, "Pompeo's Message to Saudis? Enough Is Enough: Stop Qatar Blockade," *New York Times,* April 28, 2018.

212 *had visited Qatar in January*: Julie Bykowicz, "The New Lobbying: Qatar Targeted 250 Trump 'Influencers' to Change U.S. Policy," *Wall Street Journal,* August 29, 2018.

212 *"I spent two days with Jared"*: Interview with Alan Dershowitz, August 17, 2018.

213 *Qatari money rebuilt much of*: "Emir of Qatar Tours South Lebanon," Al Jazeera, July 31, 2010.

213 *"Nobody's happy right now"*: Interview with Rick Davis, July 18, 2018.

213 *"recent reports suggest that"*: Read the April 25, 2018, letter on Catherine Cortez Masto's website at https://www.cortezmasto.senate.gov/imo/media/doc/WH%20OAI%20Letter%20Final.pdf.

214 *not reported until the following month*: Marshall Cohen, "Mueller's Investigators Questioned Kushner About Potential Russian Collusion, Obstruction," CNN, May 23, 2018.

214 *Later that same month*: Arthur Allen, "Kushner-Backed Health Care Project Gets 'Devastating' Review," *Politico,* May 11, 2018.

214 *Two software providers had wanted*: Ashley Feinberg, "Full Audio of Jared Kushner's Remarks to Congressional Interns," *Wired,* August 1, 2017.

214 *Shulkin published an op-ed*: David J. Shulkin, "Privatizing the V.A. Will Hurt Veterans," *New York Times,* March 28, 2018.

214 *he said it would be his top priority*: Jessica Davis, "Cerner EHR Project Would Be Top Priority, VA Secretary Nominee Wilkie Says," *Healthcare IT News,* June 28, 2018.

215 *comments he made in December*: Read the December 3, 2017, transcript, "'America First' and the Middle East: A Keynote Conversation with Jared Kushner," on the Brookings Institution's website at https://www.brookings.edu/wp-content/uploads/2017/11/fp_20171205_keynote_kushner.pdf.

215 *"Iran's aggression threatens the many"*: Steve Holland, "Kushner: Peace Deal to Benefit Both Sides in Mideast Conflict," *Reuters,* May 14, 2018.

215 *More than twenty-seven hundred*: David M. Halbfinger, Isabel Kershner, and

Declan Walsh, "Israel Kills Dozens at Gaza Border as U.S. Embassy Opens in Jerusalem," *New York Times*, May 14, 2018.

215 *sixty-two were killed*: Ian Lee and Salma Abdelaziz, "Hamas Claims 50 of Its Members Died in Monday's Clashes in Gaza," CNN, May 16, 2018.

215 *"provoking violence are part of"*: Alana Abramson, "Jared Kushner Says Palestinian Protestors Are 'Part of the Problem,'" *Time*, May 14, 2018.

215 *"We believe that Hamas is responsible"*: Alex Ward, "White House Absolves Israel of All Responsibility in Gaza Deaths," *Vox*, May 15, 2018.

215 *thanked him personally*: Adam Entous, "Donald Trump's New World Order," *New Yorker*, June 18, 2018.

215 *Saeb Erekat, wrote an op-ed*: Saeb Erekat, "Partners in Occupation: Trump Provides the Anti-Palestinian Incitement, Israel the Bullets," *Haaretz*, May 17, 2018.

215 *in his own* Haaretz *op-ed*: Jason Greenblatt, "Trump Mideast Envoy: The Palestinians Deserve So Much More Than Saeb Erekat," *Haaretz*, June 10, 2018.

216 *has given hundreds of thousands*: Judy Maltz, "Kushner Foundation Donated to West Bank Settlement Projects," *Haaretz*, December 6, 2016.

216 *Israel carried out air strikes*: Oliver Holmes, "Israeli Airstrikes Target Militant Sites in Gaza," *Guardian*, May 17, 2018.

216 *It even paid for the Washington*: Faiz Siddiqui, "Metro Late-Night Service Back On for Caps Game After Qatar Agrees to Provide Funding Through Business Group," *Washington Post*, May 17, 2018.

216 *"It was very nice"*: Interview with Bruce Riedel, August 6, 2018.

216 *reported that Kushner was shocked*: Aruna Viswanatha and Rebecca Ballhaus, "GOP Fundraiser Sues Qatar Over Stolen Emails," *Wall Street Journal*, March 26, 2018.

CHAPTER TWENTY-THREE

217 *On May 17, 2018,* The New York Times: Charles V. Bagli and Jesse Drucker, "Kushners Near Deal with Qatar-Linked Company for Troubled Tower," *New York Times*, May 17, 2018.

217 *told attendees at a real estate conference*: Konrad Putzier and Will Parker, "Brookfield's Ric Clark Talks 666 Fifth Plan," *Real Deal*, May 18, 2018.

217 *it had agreed to sell its 49.5 percent stake*: Peter Grant, "Kushner Cos. Signs Deal to Buy Remaining Stake in 666 Fifth Ave.," *Wall Street Journal*, June 1, 2018.

218 The Real Deal *published an interview*: Will Parker and Konrad Putzier, "Kushner, Unfiltered," *Real Deal*, June 1, 2018.

218 *claiming the value of the real estate*: Scott Deveau, "Kushners Unload 666 Fifth Ave. to Brookfield in 99-Year Lease," *Bloomberg*, August 3, 2018.

219 *On August 3,* The Wall Street Journal: Peter Grant, "Kushner Family Closes Deal to Unload 666 Fifth Avenue," *Wall Street Journal*, August 3, 2018.

219 *reportedly negotiated a reduction*: Charles V. Bagli and Kate Kelly, "Deal Gives Kushners Cash Infusion on 666 Fifth Avenue," *New York Times*, August 3, 2018.

219 The New York Times *noted that the Kushners*: Ibid.

219 *including updating the lobby*: Peter Grant, "Kushner Family Closes Deal to Unload 666 Fifth Avenue," *Wall Street Journal*, August 3, 2018.

220   *announced their engagement*: View Karlie Kloss's Instagram post, from July 24, 2018, at https://www.instagram.com/p/BlnwAWIH5Y6/.

220   *"We are very excited about"*: Email from Charlie Kushner, July 24, 2018.

220   *Alan Hammer told me in July 2018*: Interview with Alan Hammer, July 9, 2018.

220   *"It has troubled him deeply"*: Ibid.

221   *To marry Josh*: Lindsay Kimble and Colleen Kratofil, "Karlie Kloss Is Married! Supermodel Weds Joshua Kushner in Custom Dior Gown," *People*, October 18, 2018.

221   *a small Jewish ceremony*: Ibid.

221   *what would become a nationwide program*: Sarah Buhr, "Supermodel Karlie Kloss Chats With Us About the Launch of Kode With Klossy, a Coding Camp for Girls," *TechCrunch*, April 1, 2016.

221   *It now offers one thousand*: Abrar Al-Heeti, "Supermodel Karlie Kloss' Coding Camp for Girls Is Expanding," *CNET*, March 16, 2018.

221   *In May, her YouTube channel*: View Karlie Kloss's video, posted on May 15, 2018, at https://www.youtube.com/watch?v=GoH5WNTH6Ak.

221   *made the* Time *100 list*: Diane von Furstenberg, "Karlie Kloss," *Time*, April 21, 2016.

221   *"Karlie isn't who most people picture"*: Chioma Nnadi, "Karlie Kloss Gets Candid About Politics, Her Relationship, and Women in Tech," *Vogue*, September 11, 2018.

222   *She attended the pro-gun-regulation*: View Josh Kushner's Instagram post, from March 25, 2018, at https://www.instagram.com/p/BgwJK7snznQ/.

222   *spoke out against family separations*: View Karlie Kloss's Instagram post, from June 20, 2018, at https://www.instagram.com/p/BkPVubkhrWL/.

222   *"96 Americans are killed by guns"*: View Karlie Kloss's Instagram post, from November 5, 2018, at https://www.instagram.com/p/Bpzb5v-lhBF/.

CHAPTER TWENTY-FOUR

223   *as* The New York Times *would soon report*: Glenn Thrush and Danielle Ivory, "Turf War Between Kushner and Sessions Drove Federal Prisons Director to Quit," *New York Times*, May 24, 2018.

223   *"I think he saw through his father"*: Interview with Mark Inch, July 20, 2018.

224   *"was attentive in trying to learn"*: Ibid.

224   *December 18*: View the December 18, 2018 session on C-SPAN's website at https://www.c-span.org/video/?456093-1/us-senate-debates-criminal-justice-reform-bill.

224   *"So proud of my husband!"*: View Ivanka Trump's Instagram post, from December 18, 2018, at https://www.instagram.com/p/BrjQrP7hLr4/.

224   *In April, it was reported that*: Caitlin Dickerson, "Hundreds of Immigrant Children Have Been Taken From Parents at U.S. Border," *New York Times*, April 20, 2018.

224   *Ivanka posted on Instagram a photograph of*: View Ivanka Trump's Instagram post, from May 27, 2018, at https://www.instagram.com/p/BjSXlG1lTuj/.

225   *"When you have babies being taken"*: View an episode clip of *Morning Joe*, aired June 15, 2018, on the MSNBC website at https://www.msnbc.com/morning-joe/watch/mika-again-ivanka-trump-misses-the-mark-1256438339637.

225   *"hates to see children separated"*: Kate Bennett, "Melania Trump 'Hates to See' Children Separated From Their Families at Borders," *CNN*, June 18, 2018.

225 *executive order that apparently ended the*: Read the June 20, 2018, executive order, "Affording Congress an Opportunity to Address Family Separation," on the White House's website at https://www.whitehouse.gov/presidential-actions/affording -congress-opportunity-address-family-separation/.

225 *she tweeted her gratitude*: View Ivanka Trump's tweet, from June 20, 2018, at https:// twitter.com/IvankaTrump/status/1009518490401812481.

225 *On August 6*, BuzzFeed News: Steven Perlberg, "Jared Kushner Used to Person-ally Order the Deletion of Stories at His Newspaper," *BuzzFeed News*, August 6, 2018.

226 *"Jared doesn't care about ethics"*: Erin B. Logan, "Jared Kushner's Newspaper Scrubbed Stories Unfavorable to His Friends, Ex-Worker Claims," *Washington Post*, August 7, 2018.

226 *It was later pointed out in* The Washington Post: Carol D. Leonnig, Josh Dawsey, and Ashley Parker, "Jared Kushner Lacks Security Clearance Level to Review Some of the Nation's Most Sensitive Intelligence in White House Role," *Washington Post*, July 12, 2018.

226 *testified in a hearing at the British*: Ellen Barry, "Cambridge Analytica Whistle-Blower Contends Data-Mining Swung Brexit Vote," *New York Times*, March 27, 2018.

226 *undercover Channel 4 News investigation*: View Channel 4's investigative report, aired on March 19, 2018, at https://www.youtube.com/watch?v=mpbeOCKZFfQ.

226 *came under the scrutiny of*: Sara Murray, Shimon Prokupecz, and Kara Scannell, "Exclusive: FBI Counterintel Investigating Ivanka Trump Business Deal," CNN, March 2, 2018.

227 *"the whole country would turn"*: View Rudy Giuliani's interview with Sean Hannity, which took place on May 2, 2018, on the Fox News website at https://video.foxnews .com/v/5779706421001/.

227 *working with Chinese President Xi Jinping*: View Donald Trump's tweet, from May 13, 2018, https://twitter.com/realDonaldTrump/status/995680316458262533.

227 *approval for five new trademarks*: Caroline Zhang, "Ivanka Trump's Business Wins Approval for More China Trademarks," Citizens for Responsibility and Ethics in Washington, May 25, 2018.

227 *She would receive two more*: Sui-Lee Wee, "Ivanka Trump Wins China Trademarks, Then Her Father Vows to Save ZTE," *New York Times*, May 28, 2018.

227 *When she was asked to comment*: Maggie Haberman, "Ivanka Trump Abruptly Leaves Call After Question About China Trademarks," *New York Times*, May 30, 2018.

227 *"After 17 months in Washington"*: Ben Popken, "Ivanka Trump is Closing Down Her Fashion Business to Focus on Her White House Role," NBC News, July 24, 2018.

227 *According to Rakuten Intelligence*: Rebecca Ballhaus and Suzanne Kapner, "Ivanka Trump Closing Her Namesake Fashion Brand," *Wall Street Journal*, July 24, 2018.

227 *YouGov consumer perception survey*: Read the October 31, 2017, survey results on YouGov BrandIndex's website at http://www.brandindex.com/article/democrats-and -independents-slowly-gravitating-toward-ivanka-trump-brand.

227   *for sixteen new Chinese trademarks*: Caroline Zhang, "Ivanka Trump's Business Wins Approval for 16 New Chinese Trademarks Despite Shutting Down," Citizens for Responsibility and Ethics in Washington, November 5, 2018.

227   *pocketed eighty-two million dollars*: Amy Brittain, Ashley Parker, and Anu Narayanswamy, "Jared Kushner and Ivanka Trump Made at Least $82 Million in Outside Income Last Year While Serving in the White House, Filings Show," *Washington Post*, June 11, 2018.

228   *a net worth of $324 million*: Jesse Drucker and Emily Flitter, "Jared Kushner Paid No Federal Income Tax for Years, Documents Suggest," *New York Times*, October 13, 2018.

228   *killing the story*: Read the August 21, 2018, press release, "Michael Cohen Pleads Guilty in Manhattan Federal Court to Eight Counts, Including Criminal Tax Evasion and Campaign Finance Violations," on the Department of Justice's website at https://www.justice.gov/usao-sdny/pr/michael-cohen-pleads-guilty-manhattan-federal-court-eight-counts-including-criminal-tax.

228   *many favors Pecker did for Trump*: Jeffrey Toobin, "The National Enquirer's Fervor for Trump," *New Yorker*, July 3, 2017.

228   *quash stories about him*: Joe Palazzolo, Michael Rothfeld, and Lukas I. Alpert, "National Enquirer Shielded Donald Trump From Playboy Model's Affair Allegation," *Wall Street Journal*, November 4, 2016.

228   *$130,000 to stay quiet:* Michael Rothfeld and Joe Palazzolo, "Trump Lawyer Arranged $130,000 Payment for Adult-Film Star's Silence," *Wall Street Journal*, January 12, 2018.

228   *Cohen declared that he'd take a bullet*: Emily Jane Fox, "Michael Cohen Would Take a Bullet for Donald Trump," *Vanity Fair*, September 6, 2017.

228   *Pecker and*: Rebecca Davis O'Brien, Nicole Hong, and Joe Palazzolo, "Why Michael Cohen Agreed to Plead Guilty—and Implicate the President," *Wall Street Journal*, August 22, 2018.

228   *another executive close to*: Gabriel Sherman, "'Holy Shit, I Thought Pecker Would Be the Last One to Turn': Trump's National Enquirer Allies Are the Latest to Defect," *Vanity Fair*, August 23, 2018.

228   *On August 21*: Read the August 21, 2018, filing on the *New York Times* website at https://int.nyt.com/data/documenthelper/182-cohen-plea-deal/9bc6cd47e7c48e9f9469/optimized/full.pdf.

229   *intent to buy the rights to McDougal's*: Rebecca Ballhaus, Michael Rothfeld, and Joe Palazzolo, "Trump's Former Lawyer Michael Cohen Recorded Conversation About Stormy Daniels Payment With News Anchor," *Wall Street Journal*, July 25, 2018.

229   *On August 29*: View Donald Trump's tweet, from August 29, 2018, at https://twitter.com/realDonaldTrump/status/1034810550025433090.

229   The New York Times *reported he was pushed*: Julie Hirschfeld Davis, Michael S. Schmidt, and Maggie Haberman, "Don McGahn to Leave White House Counsel Job This Fall, Trump Says," *New York Times*, August 29, 2018.

230 *a* Washington Post *report said Trump*: Philip Rucker, Carol D. Leonnig, Josh Dawsey, and Ashley Parker, "'Winter Is Coming': Allies Fear Trump Isn't Prepared for Gathering Legal Storm," *Washington Post*, August 29, 2018.

230 *the U.S. announced a reworked*: Read the October 1, 2018, statement, "Remarks by President Trump on the United States-Mexico-Canada Agreement," on the White House's website at https://www.whitehouse.gov/briefings-statements/remarks -president-trump-united-states-mexico-canada-agreement/.

230 *"The deal fell apart more than once"*: David Ljunggren and Steve Holland, "How Trump's Son-in-Law Helped Salvage the North American Trade Zone," *Reuters*, October 1, 2018.

CHAPTER TWENTY-FIVE

231 *"He's integral when there's the hope"*: Frank Bruni, "Jared Kushner's Moral Laryngitis," *New York Times*, October 16, 2018.

231 *Dwight Garner's review*: Dwight Garner, "In 'Fear,' Bob Woodward Pulls Back the Curtain on President Trump's 'Crazytown,'" *New York Times*, September 5, 2018.

231 *"they were like a posse of second-guessers"*: Bob Woodward, *Fear* (New York: Simon & Schuster, 2018), p. 190.

231 *report in* The Intercept: Alex Emmons, "Saudi Arabia Planned to Invade Qatar Last Summer. Rex Tillerson's Efforts to Stop It May Have Cost Him His Job," *Intercept*, August 1, 2018.

232 *and was reportedly killed by*: David Gauthier-Villars, Jessica Donati, and Summer Said, "Turkey Details Alleged Killing of Saudi Journalist," *Wall Street Journal*, October 16, 2018.

232 *members of a team of fifteen*: David D. Kirkpatrick, Malachy Browne, Ben Hubbard, and David Botti, "The Jamal Khashoggi Case: Suspects Had Ties to Saudi Crown Prince," *New York Times*, October 16, 2018.

232 *One of them, an autopsy expert*: "Jamal Khashoggi: Who's Who in Alleged Saudi 'Hit Squad,'" BBC, October 19, 2018.

232 *reportedly encouraged*: David D. Kirkpatrick and Carlotta Gall, "Audio Offers Gruesome Details of Jamal Khashoggi Killing, Turkish Official Says," *New York Times*, October 17, 2018.

232 *The Saudis at first maintained*: David D. Kirkpatrick and Carlotta Gall, "Turkish Officials Say Khashoggi Was Killed on Order of Saudi Leadership," *New York Times*, October 9, 2018.

232 *On October 10, the* Post: Shane Harris, "Crown Prince Sought to Lure Khashoggi Back to Saudi Arabia and Detain Him, U.S. Intercepts Show," *Washington Post*, October 10, 2018.

232 *Turks also released footage of*: Gul Tuysuz, Salma Abdelaziz, Ghazi Balkiz, Ingrid Formanek, and Clarissa Ward, "Surveillance Footage Shows Saudi 'Body Double' in Khashoggi's Clothes After He Was Killed, Turkish Source Says," CNN, October 23, 2018.

232 *before Turkish investigators were able*: Jill Colvin, Matthew Pennington, and Fay

Abuelgasim, "Trump Suggests 'Rogue Killers' Murdered Saudi Journalist," *Associated Press*, October 15, 2018.

232 *suggested it was an interrogation*: Ben Hubbard, "Saudi Arabia Says Jamal Khashoggi Was Killed in Consulate Fight," *New York Times*, October 19, 2018.

232 *The kingdom finally had eleven*: Kareem Fahim and Zakaria Zakaria, "Saudi Arabia Distances Crown Prince From Killing of Journalist Jamal Khashoggi," *Washington Post*, November 15, 2018.

233 *Khashoggi's murder, he reportedly argued*: David D. Kirkpatrick and Ben Hubbard, "Saudis May Blame Intelligence Official for Killing Jamal Khashoggi," *New York Times*, October 18, 2018.

233 *"I don't like hearing about it"*: Zachary Cohen and Elise Labott, "Jamal Khashoggi: Trump 'Concerned' About Missing Journalist; Saudis Deny Involvement," CNN, October 9, 2018.

233 *Trump sanctioned seventeen Saudis*: Patricia Zengerle, "U.S. Sanctions 17 Saudis Over Killing of Journalist Khashoggi," *Reuters*, November 15, 2018.

233 *obtained information on a CIA assessment*: Shane Harris, Greg Miller, and Josh Dawsey, "CIA Concludes Saudi Crown Prince Ordered Jamal Khashoggi's Assassination," *Washington Post*, November 16, 2018.

233 *"It could very well be that the crown prince"*: Read the November 20, 2018, statement on the White House's website at https://www.whitehouse.gov/briefings-statements/statement-president-donald-j-trump-standing-saudi-arabia/.

234 *Pompeo was dispatched to Saudi Arabia*: Julian E. Barnes, Matthew Rosenberg, and Gardiner Harris, "U.S. Spy Agencies Are Increasingly Convinced of Saudi Prince's Ties to Journalist's Disappearance," *New York Times*, October, 17, 2018.

234 *Kushner and MBS had continued to speak*: David D. Kirkpatrick, Ben Hubbard, Mark Landler, and Mark Mazzetti, "The Wooing of Jared Kushner: How the Saudis Got a Friend in the White House," *New York Times*, December 8, 2018.

234 *gave a rare interview with Van Jones*: View Jared Kushner's interview with Van Jones on CNN, which took place on October 22, 2018, at https://www.youtube.com/watch?v=td9qhhOJp2U.

EPILOGUE

235 *policy dinners at their home in Washington*: Maggie Haberman and Katie Rogers, "Still Standing, Jared Kushner and Ivanka Trump Step Back in the Spotlight," *New York Times*, July 28, 2018.

235 *She has championed workplace initiatives*: Ivanka Trump, "Training for the Jobs of Tomorrow," *Wall Street Journal*, July 17, 2018.

235 *women pursuing careers in STEM*: Read the September 25, 2017, press release, "President Trump Signs Presidential Memo to Increase Access to STEM and Computer Science Education," on the White House's website at https://www.whitehouse.gov/articles/president-trump-signs-presidential-memo-increase-access-stem-computer-science-education/.

236 *from Seoul, South Korea*: View Ivanka Trump's Instagram post, from February 23, 2018, at https://www.instagram.com/p/BfitbDCl-A4/.

236   *to Paintsville, Kentucky*: View Ivanka Trump's Instagram post, from October 26, 2018, at https://www.instagram.com/p/BpZrYeuB9l9/.

236   *unsanctioned use of personal email*: Max Kutner and Nina Burleigh, "Ivanka Trump Used a Personal Email Account for Government Work: Exclusive," *Newsweek,* September 25, 2017.

236   *memorable line was "I try to stay out of politics"*: Cody Derespina, "Ivanka Trump: 'I Try to Stay Out of Politics,'" Fox News, June 26, 2017.

236   *misuse of a personal email account*: Josh Dawsey, "Kushner Used Private Email to Conduct White House Business," *Politico,* September 24, 2017.

236   *misuse of the EB-5 visa program*: Jesse Drucker and Adam Goldman, "Kushner Companies Said to Be Under Investigation Over Visa Program," *New York Times,* August 3, 2017.

237   *speculation that dozens of sealed*: Matthew Mosk and Allison Pecorin, "There Are Dozens of Sealed Criminal Indictments on the DC Docket. Are They From Mueller?," *ABC News*, November 16, 2018.

237   *"deep dive on Saudi Arabia"*: Greg Sargent, "Democrats Must Hold Trump Accountable on Saudi Arabia. Adam Schiff Explains How," *Washington Post,* November 23, 2018.

237   *called for targeted sanctions*: View Lindsey Graham's interview, which took place on October 16, 2018, at https://www.youtube.com/watch?v=ptxP9GSg44s.

237   *facts as to whether Kushner*: Jean Eaglesham, Juliet Chung, and Lisa Schwartz, "Trump Adviser Kushner's Undisclosed Partners Include Goldman and Soros," *Wall Street Journal,* May 3, 2017.

Index